INTRODUCTION TO HINDI GRAMMAR

INTRODUCTION TO HINDI GRAMMAR

Usha R. Jain

Centers for South and Southeast Asia Studies
University of California at Berkeley

Library of Congress Cataloging-in-Publication Data

Jain, Usha R.
Introduction to Hindi grammar / Usha R. Jain.
p. cm.
ISBN 0-944613-25-X (pbk. : alk. paper)
1. Hindi language—Grammar. I. Title.
PK1933.J34 1995
491'.4382421—dc20 95-30451
CIP

To Amita, Sharad,
and their generation

संस्कृति से भाषा का उद्गम,
भाषा संस्कृति का चिर-दर्पण ।
पूर्वजों की पुण्य धरोहर यह,
सस्नेह तुम्हें करती अर्पण ॥

TABLE OF CONTENTS

PREFACE

The idea for this book grew out of my experience teaching elementary Hindi-Urdu with a variety of textbooks. Most textbooks explain the grammatical constructions of the language as they appear in the readings and conversations. Hence, while students learn individual constructions, they find it difficult to comprehend the broad structure of the language. I felt that there was a need to supplement the existing textbooks with a book that would present a comprehensive introduction to Hindi language and grammar. I believe that the present book fulfills this need. It presents all the major grammatical constructions of the language in logical sequence, and each construction is reinforced by means of simple drills, using only the most elementary vocabulary. This format enables students to understand the basic structure of the language and gives them sufficient practice to master individual constructions. I have tested these drills in the classroom over the past several years and have found that the students' command of Hindi-Urdu grammar has dramatically improved by the use of such exercises.

The format of *Introduction to Hindi Grammar* provides language instructors and students with the core linguistic skills needed for an effective competency-based program of instruction. The book is designed to be as versatile as possible, so that it can complement courses of instruction that might use different approaches. Whether instructors wish to place more emphasis on oral abilities or on reading and writing skills, they will find this textbook equally useful in the classroom. Even innovative multimedia approaches to language acquisition cannot dispense with a systematic and accessible introduction to grammar.

The book is divided into forty-two sections. The first section provides a detailed explanation of the Hindi phonetic and writing system (the Devanagari script) and is followed by pronunciation drills and writing exercises. The remaining forty-one sections cover all the grammatical structures of Hindi-Urdu generally taught in first-year college programs in the United States. In keeping with the practical focus of this book, all explanations are written in nontechnical language suitable for students who have no linguistic background; yet they are detailed enough to allow for clarity and comprehension. An alphabetical glossary that groups words by grammatical categories is provided in an appendix.

A set of audiotapes has been prepared to accompany the *Introduction to Hindi Grammar*. These tapes can be obtained by contacting:

The Language Laboratory
Department of Tape Duplication
33 Dwinelle Hall
University of California, Berkeley
Berkeley, CA 94720
Telephone (510) 642-4067

I would like to thank all those who helped with this project for their unfailing cooperation and support. Professor John J. Gumperz's pioneering drills in his *Conversational Hindi-Urdu* have been an inspiration to me in writing this book; many of his principles and ideas have been incorporated into my work. I would also like to express my gratitude to my colleague Professor Bruce Pray for making available his expertise in linguistics and for his insightful comments on the manuscript, and to Dr. Karine Schomer, Dildar Gartenburg, Dr. Linda Hess, and Simona Sawhney for their comments and suggestions. I am particularly thankful to Kristi Wiley for her help and advice throughout the project. Her comments were especially useful since they reflected both an editor's and a student's perspective. Sandeep Pandey deserves special thanks for entering the entire manuscript on computer and Alka Hingorani for patiently incorporating changes in the course of several revisions. Last but not least, I thank my husband, Santosh, and my children, Amita and Sharad, for their constant understanding, support, and encouragement.

Part of the project received support from the Committee on Teaching at the University of California, Berkeley, in the form of two mini-grants. I am grateful for this assistance and for an instructional improvement grant from the Office of Educational Development at the University of California, Berkeley.

Usha R. Jain
Berkeley
March 1995

1. THE DEVANAGARI SCRIPT

Hindi is written in the Devanagari script (देवनागरी लिपि), which is also used for Sanskrit, Nepali, and Marathi and is closely related to many other writing systems of India (e.g., Bengali, Gujarati, Punjabi, etc.). The Devanagari script is relatively easy to learn because it represents the sounds of Hindi with remarkable consistency, enabling the student to accurately pronounce most Hindi words written in it.

There are thirty-three consonants and eleven vowels in the Devanagari script, which is written from left to right. Each letter consists of a basic form topped by a horizontal line. Since the study of phonetics was very advanced in ancient India, the Devanagari alphabet is systematically arranged on a scientific basis. The vowels come first, and the consonants are arranged according to their place and manner of articulation in the mouth.

Vowels

There are eleven vowels in Hindi, ten of which have two distinct forms: an independent form and a dependent (*maatraa*) form. The independent form represents the vowel when it occurs alone, at the beginning of words, or after other vowel symbols. The dependent (*maatraa*) form represents the vowel following consonants.

Vowels in their independent forms:

अ आ इ ई उ ऊ ऋ ए ऐ ओ औ

The following English words give the approximate equivalent of the vowel sounds, although the best method for learning correct pronunciation is to learn from a teacher or from a native speaker.

Pronunciation of the vowels:

अ as in English "cup," "again," "but."
आ as in English "father," "palm," "far."
इ as in English "in," "kin," "hit."
ई as in English "meat," "cheap," "seat."
उ as in English "put," "pull."
ऊ as in English "shoot," "cool."
ऋ as in English "rip," "grip," "ripple." (Occurs only in words that are directly borrowed from Sanskrit.)
ए as in English "pay," "late."
ऐ as in English "bat," "sat," "rat." (But speakers of Eastern Hindi dialect pronounce it as in English "kite," "dive.")
ओ as in English "go," "coat."
औ as in English "caught," "saw," "bought." (But speakers of Eastern Hindi dialect pronounce it as in English "house," "mouse," "cow.")

Vowels in their dependent (*maatraa*) forms: When a vowel occurs after a consonant, then it is written in its *maatraa* form, which is added to that consonant. *Maatraa* forms occur only when vowels follow consonants and are never used at the beginning of a word or after another vowel symbol.

The first vowel, अ, has no special *maatraa* form but is part of every consonant sound and is assumed present unless the consonant is followed by the *maatraa* form of a vowel other than an अ.

In Hindi (unlike Sanskrit) the vowel अ is not pronounced at the end of a word unless the word is a single-letter word.

In the following chart vowels are given in their independent and *maatraa* forms. The consonant स (*sa*) is used to demonstrate the *maatraa* forms when added to a consonant.

Independent Form	***Maatraa* form**	**With the consonant स**
अ	none	स
आ	ा	सा

इ	ि	सि
ई	ी	सी
उ	ु	सु
ऊ	ू	सू
ऋ	ृ	सृ
ए	े	से
ऐ	ै	सै
ओ	ो	सो
औ	ौ	सौ

<u>Nasalization of vowels:</u> With the exception of ऋ, all vowels in Hindi may be nasalized. The nasalization of vowels is indicated by placing either “ ँ ” or “ ं ” above the vowel symbol. The symbol “ ँ ” is called चंद्रबिंदु (*candrabindu* - “moon and dot”) and is used when no part of the vowel symbol extends above the top horizontal line. The symbol “ ं ” is called बिंदु (*bindu* - “dot”) and is used when part or all of the vowel symbol appears above the top horizontal line, e.g.,

अँ आँ इँ ईं उँ ऊँ एँ ऐं ओं औं

सँ साँ सिं सीं सुँ सूँ सें सैं सों सौं

The modern tendency is to use the *bindu*, i.e., the plain dot, in all situations, especially in printed materials. Some typewriters have only the plain dot.

Consonants

As mentioned before, most of the consonants in the Devanagari script are arranged in a systematic pattern according to their place and manner of articulation. Out of thirty-three consonants, twenty-five are arranged in the following five series, based on their place of articulation in the mouth. Each of these series contains five consonants.

1. Velar: Velar consonants are pronounced with the back of the tongue touching the velum (i.e., soft palate).

2. Palatal: Palatal consonants are pronounced with the tongue touching the hard palate.

3. Retroflex: Retroflex consonants are pronounced with the tongue straight up, the tip of the tongue curling slightly backwards and touching the front portion of the hard palate.

4. Dental: Dental consonants are pronounced with the tip of the tongue touching the back of the upper front teeth.

5. Labial: Labial consonants are pronounced with the lips.

Based on the manner of their articulation, the consonants in the above five series can be further classified as unvoiced or voiced, unaspirated or aspirated, and nasal.

Unvoiced: Unvoiced consonants are pronounced without vibration of the vocal cords, as in "pass," "fan," "Sue," "pack."

Voiced: Voiced consonants are pronounced with vibration of the vocal cords, as in "zoo," "dig," "good."

Unaspirated: Unaspirated consonants are pronounced without any breath of air following the consonant. In English the only position in which stops (i.e., those consonants formed by completely blocking the breath at one of the points of articulation) are pronounced without aspiration is after "s" in words such as "spin," "stop," and "sketch." Compare your pronunciation of these words with "pin," "top," and "catch" to see if you can recognize the presence or absence of aspiration. This is an absolutely critical distinction in Hindi. You must be able to recognize and control aspiration after stop consonants since many words are distinguished only by the presence or absence of aspiration.

Aspirated: Aspirated consonants are pronounced with a strong breath of air following the consonant. In English all stop consonants, such as p, t, and k, are aspirated before a stressed vowel and in final position, as in "pat," "two," "cake."

Nasal: Nasal consonants are pronounced with some of the air coming through the nose.

Among the remaining eight consonants, there are four semivowels, three sibilants, and one glottal sound, which is similar to the English "h" sound.

All the consonants are given below with their approximate English equivalents in pronunciation. Keep in mind that all the consonants are pronounced with the अ sound.

Velar Consonants:

क is pronounced as in English "scold," "skin."
ख is pronounced as क but with strong aspiration.
ग is pronounced as in English "gate," "good," "beg."
घ is pronounced as ग but with strong aspiration.
ङ is pronounced as in English "swing," "sing," "junk."

Palatal Consonants:

च is pronounced as in English "check," "cheek."
छ is pronounced as च but with strong aspiration.
ज is pronounced as in English "joy," "judge."
झ is pronounced as ज but with strong aspiration.
ञ is pronounced as in English "punch."

Retroflex Consonants:

ट is similar to English "t" but is pronounced with the tongue in retroflex position.

ठ is pronounced as ट but with strong aspiration.

ड is similar to English "d" but is pronounced with the tongue in retroflex position.

ढ is pronounced as ड but with strong aspiration.

ण is similar to English "n" but is pronounced with the tongue in retroflex position.

Hindi also uses two tongue-flap sounds that are not found in Sanskrit:

ड़ is pronounced by flapping the tongue from the retroflex position (without touching the top of the mouth) forward up to the tooth ridge.

ढ़ is similar to ड़ but is pronounced with aspiration.

Dental Consonants:

त is similar to English "t" but is pronounced with the tongue in dental position.

थ is pronounced as त but with strong aspiration.

द is similar to English "d" but is pronounced with the tongue in dental position.

ध is pronounced as द but with strong aspiration.

न is pronounced as in English "name" but with the tongue in dental position.

Labial Consonants:

प is pronounced as in English "spoon," "spot."

फ is pronounced as प but with strong aspiration.

ब is pronounced as in English "ball," "bin."

भ is pronounced as ब but with strong aspiration.

म is pronounced as in English "mother," "mail."

Semivowels:

य is pronounced as in English "yell," "yam."

र is pronounced as in English "thrill," "three," "drain."
ल is pronounced as in English "leave," "leaf," "lip."
व is pronounced as in English "voice," "win." व is an intermediate sound between English "v" and "w."

Sibilants:
श is pronounced as in English "cash," "shame."
ष is pronounced as श but with tongue in retroflex position.
स is pronounced as in English "song," "sum."

Glottal:
ह is pronounced as in English "head," "house" but with vibration of the vocal cords.

Note:

(1) The two nasal consonants ङ and ञ never appear independently but occur only as part of a conjunct consonant (ङ before a velar consonant and ञ before a palatal consonant).

(2) The Devanagari script has no equivalent of English "t" and "d," which are pronounced with the tip of the tongue on the alveolar ridge behind the top teeth. Although this place of articulation is between Devanagari retroflex and dental "t" and "d," Hindi speakers use the retroflex "t" and "d" for these sounds when they occur in English loan words.

It is extremely important to practice making the distinction between dental stops, त, थ, द, ध, and the corresponding retroflex stops, ट, ठ, ड, ढ. Since the English "t" and "d" sounds are much nearer the Hindi retroflex series, using the English pronunciation will sound to Hindi speakers like their retroflex stops. It is therefore essential for the students of Hindi to concentrate on learning to make and hear the Hindi dental stops, त, थ, द, ध, by placing the tip of the tongue far forward on the upper front teeth.

(3) Hindi speakers do not make a distinction between English "v" and "w" sounds. Thus "व" is sometimes pronounced as English "v" and sometimes as "w."

(4) In modern Hindi श and ष are pronounced in the same manner. The use of ष is limited to words borrowed from Sanskrit.

(5) The symbol " : " is called विसर्ग (*visarga*) and is pronounced in a manner similar to ह्. It occurs in the final and medial positions of a few words borrowed from Sanskrit.

(6) The vowels उ and ऊ take special forms when used as *maatraa* with the consonant "र": र + उ = रु and र + ऊ = रू.

(7) Devanagari has no capital letters.

Borrowed Sounds

There are five sounds used in modern Hindi that had no symbols in the Devanagari script. These sounds were incorporated by placing a dot under the symbols used for the phonetically related sounds. These symbols are used in Hindi to reproduce Persian, Arabic, or English sounds.

क़ is similar to क but is produced further back in the mouth.
ख़ is a velar fricative sound similar to German "Bach."
ग़ is also a fricative sound similar to ख़ but pronounced with vibration of the vocal cords.
ज़ is identical to "z" in English as in "zeal."
फ़ is identical to "f" in English as in "fail," "fall."

Note:

(1) Many Hindi speakers find क़ and ग़ difficult to pronounce and substitute क and ग respectively for them.

(2) The special vowel sound in English loan words, e.g., ऑफ़िस (*office*), कॉलेज (*college*), is often transcribed into Hindi with ऑ. The modern tendency is, however, to drop "ॅ," e.g., आफ़िस.

Hindi Consonants

	Stops				Nasals
	Unvoiced		Voiced		
	unaspirated	aspirated	unaspirated	aspirated	
Velar	क	ख	ग	घ	ङ
Palatal	च	छ	ज	झ / झ	ञ
Retroflex	ट	ठ	ड ड़	ढ ढ़	ण / ण
Dental	त	थ	द	ध	न
Labial	प	फ	ब	भ	म
Semivowels	य	र	ल	व	
Sibilants	श	ष	स		
Glottal	ह				
Borrowed sounds	क़	ख़	ग़	ज़	फ़

Conjunct Consonants

Since a basic consonant symbol represents that consonant plus the vowel अ, Devanagari script uses the following two methods to suppress the अ vowel inherent in a basic consonant symbol:

1. The sign “ ् ” -- called a हलन्त (*halant*) -- may be written under a consonant to indicate that the vowel अ is not present, e.g., स्, ट्, म्.

2. The more commonly used method to show the absence of the vowel अ after a consonant, however, is to join it to the following consonant. Such combinations are called conjunct consonants. In a conjunct consonant the two consonants may be joined either horizontally or vertically.

Horizontal conjuncts: Horizontal conjuncts are used when the first member of a conjunct (i.e., the vowel-less consonant) ends in a vertical line (e.g., च, ज, स, etc.). This vertical line is removed and the rest of the symbol is joined to the second member, e.g.,

च् + छ = च्छ अच्छा न् + द = न्द हिन्दी
स् + त = स्त नमस्ते त् + य = त्य त्याग
म् + ब = म्ब बम्बई ल् + ल = ल्ल दिल्ली

Note that क, फ and झ do not end in a vertical line but the curve on the right is shortened, e.g.,

क् + य = क्य क्या फ़् + त = फ़्त मुफ़्त

Vertical conjuncts: Consonants that do not end in a vertical line often join the following consonant vertically. In a vertical conjunct it is the first member (i.e., the vowel-less consonant) that is written on top of the second consonant, e.g.,

ट् + ठ = ट्ठ चिट्ठी (चिट्ठी) ट् + ट = ट्ट पट्टा (पट्टा)

Because of typographical difficulties, vertical conjuncts are often replaced by a हलन्त (*halant*) in modern Hindi, as seen above.

Special conjuncts: The following conjuncts need special attention:

1. Conjuncts with nasal consonants:

Nasal consonants as the first member of the conjunct may be written either as regular conjuncts or as an अनुस्वार (i.e., a dot written above the horizontal line at the right side of the preceding consonant or vowel), e.g.,

ङ् + ग = ङ्ग   अङ्ग / अंग
ञ् + ज = ञ्ज   पञ्जा / पंजा
ण् + ड = ण्ड   अण्डा / अंडा
न् + त = न्त   सन्तरा / संतरा
म् + ब = म्ब   अम्बर / अंबर

Note that nasal consonants as the first member in a conjunct are followed by the consonants of the same series (e.g., velar, palatal, retroflex, dental, or labial).

2. Conjuncts with र:

(a) The consonant र as the first member of a conjunct has the shape of a small hook, which is written above and to the right of the following consonant. This hook should not be confused with the top part of the independent vowel symbol ई. If the following consonant is followed by a vowel symbol (i.e., *maatraa*), then the र is written above and to the right of that vowel symbol, e.g.,

र् + म = र्म   धर्म   र् + द = र्द   उर्दू
र् + ट + ई = र्टी   पार्टी   र् + म + आ = र्मा   शर्मा

(b) The consonant र as the second member of the conjunct is indicated by a slanted line "◌्र" placed on the vertical line of the preceding consonant near the bottom, e.g.,

ग् + र = ग्र   ग्राम   क् + र = क्र   शुक्रिया
प् + र = प्र   प्रेम   म् + र = म्र   उम्र

The four consonants ट, ठ, ड, ढ, which do not have a vertical line, indicate the following र by the symbol "‸" written under the preceding consonant, e.g.,

ट् + र = ट्र   राष्ट्र   ड् + र = ड्र   ड्रामा

3. Other conjunct consonants that occur mostly in words borrowed from Sanskrit are:

क् + त = क्त /	भक्त / भक्त
क् + ष = क्ष	कक्षा
ज् + ञ = ज्ञ	ज्ञान
त् + त = त्त	उत्तर / उत्तर
त् + र = त्र	छात्र
द् + द = द्द	गद्दी
द् + ध = द्ध	बुद्धि
द् + य = द्य	विद्या
द् + व = द्व	विद्वान
श् + र = श्र	श्रीमती
ह् + म = ह्म	ब्राह्मण

Note:

(1) ज्ञ is pronounced in Hindi as ग्य (*gya*).

(2) When a consonant is doubled in a conjunct (as in पत्ता, कच्चा, लज्जा, etc.), the consonant sound is held longer.

(3) Conjunct consonants are treated as a unit in terms of the placement of the vowel *maatraa*, e.g., शक्ति.

<u>Punctuation</u>

The only Devanagari punctuation sign is the विराम (*viraam*), which represents a full stop. A *viraam* is written as a straight vertical line at the end of a sentence. Other punctuation marks, such as a question mark, comma, colon, etc., are the same as in English. In Hindi a question mark is required when a sentence is a question but there is no specific question word in it. When there is a question word in a sentence, then either a *viraam* or a question mark can be used.

Devanagari numerals: The numerals used in Hindi are:

० १ २ ३ ४ ५ ६ ७ ८ ९

Dictionary order of the Devanagari alphabet: The alphabetical order of words in a dictionary is determined by these rules:

1. The vowels precede the consonants, starting with अ and ending with औ.

2. A nasalized vowel occurs before its oral (non-nasalized) counterpart, e.g., अँ, अ, आँ, आ, इँ, इ, and so on.

3. Consonants follow the vowels, starting with क and proceeding across each row, ending with ह.

4. Subscript dots are ignored for the purpose of alphabetization, and therefore क and क़, ख and ख़, ग and ग़, ज and ज़, ड and ड़, ढ and ढ़, फ and फ़ are treated as the same.

5. Non-conjunct forms of a consonant come before its conjunct forms.

The Complete Devanagari Alphabet

अ आ   इ ई   उ ऊ   ऋ   ए ऐ   ओ औ

क (क़)	ख (ख़)	ग (ग़)	घ	ङ
च	छ	ज (ज़)	झ	ञ
ट	ठ	ड (ड़)	ढ (ढ़)	ण
त	थ	द	ध	न
प	फ (फ़)	ब	भ	म
य	र	ल	व	
श	ष	स		
ह				

Exercises

Vowels

1. Read aloud

1. ओ 2. उ 3. आ 4. ई 5. अ 6. औ
7. ऋ 8. ए 9. ऊ 10. इ 11. ऐ

2. Read aloud

1. सा 2. सौ 3. सि 4. सृ 5. सु 6. स
7. से 8. सी 9. सो 10. सू 11. सै

3. Read aloud

1. आस 2. ओस 3. सोओ 4. ऐसा
5. सासू 6. ईसा 7. सिसी 8. ऋसि
9. उसी 10. सोई 11. सुआ 12. सिए
13. ऐसे 14. ईसाई 15. सौ 16. आसू

4. Rewrite the following vowels in the correct order

ई, आ, ए, उ, अ, ओ, ऐ, इ, औ, ऋ, ऊ

Nasalized vowels

5. Read aloud

1. साँस 2. आँसू 3. ईंस 4. औंस 5. सीं
6. सैं 7. अँस 8. सूँआ 9. सौं 10. सिंओ

Consonants (velar and palatal)

6. Read aloud

1. कासी	2. गाओ	3. कुछ	4. जागो
5. सूझ	6. सोचो	7. खास	8. कँघा
9. घुस	10. गूँगा	11. घास	12. चूँच
13. जूस	14. झाग	15. छुओ	16. सखी

7. Read aloud in pairs

1. गज	गाज	2. चेख	चैख	3. गास	घास
4. चौंक	छौंक	5. चिक	चीक	6. चोक	चौक
7. चक	छक	8. चुक	चूक	9. काक	खाक
10. जाग	झाग				

8. Write

1. च + ई + ख =	2. क + ओ + ई =	3. ग + ऐ + स =
4. छ + उ + ओ =	5. च + आ + च + ई =	6. ज + आ + ग + ओ =
7. ख + आ + ओ =	8. घ + इ + स =	9. ज + ओ + ग + ई =
10. झ + ऊ + क =		

All consonants

9. Read aloud

1. काठ	2. तुम	3. बाण	4. फटा
5. यहाँ	6. धूप	7. साथी	8. वकील
9. गाना	10. ढाल	11. हाथी	12. रात
13. बाजा	14. डोम	15. दूर	16. भागो
17. थाली	18. ऋषि	19. टूटा	20. पीला
21. शाम	22. मौसी	23. नौकर	24. भाषा

10. Write all the Devanagari alphabet

11. Write

1. म + इ + ठ + आ + ई =	2. त + ओ + त + आ =
3. ब + आ + र + इ + श =	4. ह् + व + आ + ई =
5. प + र +द + ए+ स + ई =	6. य + द + इ =
7. ध + न + उ + ष =	8. व + इ + द + ए+ श + ई =
9. ट + ऊ + ट + आ =	10. ढ + ओ + र =
11. ड + ल + इ +य + आ =	12. ग + ण + इ+ त =
13. त + ऐ + य + आ + र =	14. भ + आ + र + ई =

Additional sounds

12. Read aloud

1. ख़रीदना	2. ग़म	3. पेड़	4. ख़राब
5. क़ीमत	6. ज़ोर	7. फ़ालसा	8. बाज़ार
9. साड़ी	10. दाढ़ी	11. क़ौम	12. बूढ़ा
13. मेज़	14. साफ़	15. ग़ज़ब	16. ख़ुशी

13. Read aloud in pairs

1. कान	खान	2. चाम	छाम	3. ताल	थाल
4. टाक	ठाक	5. पास	फास	6. गाग	घाग
7. जाल	झाल	8. दूम	धूम	9. डोल	ढोल
10. बात	भात	11. काम	गाम	12. चाम	जाम
13. टोल	डोल	14. तार	दार	15. पास	बास
16. खुल	घुल	17. छक	झक	18. ठोस	ढोस
19. थागा	धागा	20. फार	भार	21. पीन	तीन
22. बाद	दाद	23. माता	नाता	24. फल	थल
25. तम	टम	26. थप	ठप	27. दाग	डाग
28. धक	ढक	29. बान	बाण	30. तौस	चौस
31. देल	जेल	32. थैप	छैप	33. धूम	झूम
34. टाल	चाल	35. डाग	जाग	36. ठन	छन

37. ढोल झोल　38. चल कल　39. जल गल
40. लाना राना　41. लाज राज　42. लात रात
43. याद लाद　44. यम थम

Conjuncts (horizontal)

14. Read aloud

1. प्यार　2. ध्यान　3. सत्य　4. शब्द
5. क्यारी　6. मुफ़्त　7. सस्ता　8. सन्तोष
9. अच्छा　10. हिन्दी　11. श्लोक　12. व्याख्यान
13. व्यापार　14. उष्मा　15. उल्लास　16. अभ्यास

Conjuncts (vertical and nasal)

15. Read aloud

1. चिट्ठी / चिट्ठी　2. पंकज / पङ्कज　3. खट्टा / खट्टा
4. अंजीर / अञ्जीर　5. आनंद / आनन्द　6. मुट्ठी / मुट्ठी
7. अंदर / अन्दर　8. कट्टर / कट्टर　9. लड्डू / लड्डू
10. ठंडा / ठण्डा　11. हड्डी / हड्डी　12. अंबा / अम्बा

Conjuncts with र

16. Read aloud

1. क्रिया　2. चन्द्रा　3. ख़र्चा　4. शर्मीला
5. मूर्ति　6. प्रेमिका　7. राष्ट्रीय　8. ड्रीम
9. ट्राली　10. पर्दा　11. ग्राम　12. निर्मल

Special conjuncts

17. Read aloud

1. छात्र	2. वक़्त	3. गद्य	4. पत्रिका
5. मोक्ष	6. शुद्ध	7. श्रमिक	8. कुत्ता
9. ब्राह्मण	10. शिक्षक	11. ज्ञानी	12. द्वारिका

2. NOUNS

Hindi nouns can be divided into two categories based on their gender: masculine and feminine. As in French or Spanish, there is no neuter gender in Hindi. Students should pay special attention to the gender of all nouns they learn. The grammatical gender of nouns (masculine vs. feminine) referring to animate beings is generally the same as the sex (male vs. female) of those beings. But for inanimate objects there are only a few rough guidelines. In most cases it is necessary to memorize the grammatical gender of each noun as it is encountered.

A. MASCULINE NOUNS

Masculine nouns can be divided into two categories. Nouns of the first type are called marked masculine nouns and the second type unmarked masculine nouns.

<u>Marked masculine nouns:</u> Marked masculine nouns end in the vowel आ, e.g., कमरा *room*, लड़का *boy*, तोता *parrot*, केला *banana*, जूता *shoe*, बेटा *son*.

To form the plural of marked masculine nouns, the ending आ is changed to ए. Examples:

एक लड़का	*one boy*	->	दो लड़के	*two boys*
एक बेटा	*one son*	->	दो बेटे	*two sons*
एक कमरा	*one room*	->	दो कमरे	*two rooms*

<u>Unmarked masculine nouns:</u> All masculine nouns that end in a consonant or a vowel other than आ are in this category, e.g., घर *home*, कागज़ *paper*, फल *fruit*, शहर *city*, जानवर *animal*, आदमी *man*.

Unmarked masculine nouns have the same form in singular and plural. Examples:

एक शहर	*one city*	->	तीन शहर	*three cities*
एक घर	*one home*	->	तीन घर	*three homes*
एक आदमी	*one man*	->	तीन आदमी	*three men*

Note:

(1) A small number of masculine nouns that end in the vowel आ do not change to ए in the plural, that is, the singular and plural forms are identical, e.g., राजा *king*, देवता *god*, पिता *father*, चाचा *paternal uncle*, दादा *grandfather*, मामा *maternal uncle*. These are mostly kinship terms or nouns of relationship. Examples:

एक पिता	*one father*	->	तीन पिता	*three fathers*
एक चाचा	*one uncle*	->	तीन चाचा	*three uncles*

(2) A very few masculine nouns that end in the nasalized vowel आँ carry the nasalization over to the plural form, changing to एँ. Example:

एक कुआँ	*one well*	->	चार कुएँ	*four wells*

Exercises

1. Transformation drill

room	rooms
कमरा	कमरे
पैसा	
जूता	
केला	
संतरा	
पपीता	
रुपया	
लड़का	
दरवाज़ा	
कपड़ा	
मोज़ा	

2. <u>Transformation drill</u>

There is a boy.	There are two boys.
एक लड़का है ।	दो लड़के हैं ।
एक पैसा है ।	
एक जूता है ।	
एक केला है ।	
एक संतरा है ।	
एक पपीता है ।	
एक रुपया है ।	
एक कमरा है ।	
एक दरवाज़ा है ।	

3. <u>Substitution drill</u>

Please give one banana.
एक केला दीजिये ।
one rupee
two shoes
an orange
three papayas
four bananas
two (pieces of) clothing
four socks

4. <u>Transformation drill</u>

There is a pen.	There are four pens.
एक कलम है ।	चार कलम हैं ।
एक स्कूल है ।	
एक घर है ।	
एक छात्र है ।	
एक शिक्षक है ।	
एक कागज़ है ।	
एक विदेशी है ।	

एक सेब है ।
एक बाज़ार है ।
एक फल है ।
एक बेर है ।
एक आम है ।
एक शहर है ।

5. Substitution drill

There are some boys here.
यहाँ कुछ लड़के हैं ।

papers
papayas
students
shoes
apples
customers
bananas
mangoes
oranges
fruits

6. Translation exercise

1. Please give two bananas.
2. There are some men here.
3. Please take three oranges.
4. There are five students.
5. Please take four fruits.
6. Please give some clothes.
7. There are two teachers.
8. There are four rupees.
9. Please give three papers.
10. There is a market.

B. FEMININE NOUNS

Like masculine nouns, feminine nouns can also be divided into two categories: marked and unmarked.

Marked feminine nouns: Marked feminine nouns end in the vowel ई, e.g., कुरसी *chair*, लड़की *girl*, गाड़ी *vehicle, car, train*, साड़ी *sari*, मिठाई *sweet.*

To make a marked feminine noun plural, the ending ई is changed to इयाँ. Examples:

एक मिठाई	*one sweet*	->	पाँच मिठाइयाँ	*five sweets*
एक लड़की	*one girl*	->	बहुत लड़कियाँ	*many girls*
एक साड़ी	*one sari*	->	कुछ साड़ियाँ	*some saris*

Note the spellings: If the noun ends in the vowel ई in independent form, then it is shortened to इ and याँ is added. If the noun ends in a consonant with ई *maatraa*, then the *maatraa* is shortened before adding the याँ ending.

Unmarked feminine nouns: All feminine nouns that end in a consonant or a vowel other than ई are in this category, e.g., किताब *book*, मेज़ *table*, औरत *woman*, भाषा *language*, माता *mother*.

To form the plural, एँ is added to unmarked feminine nouns. Examples:

एक किताब	*one book*	->	चार किताबें	*four books*
एक औरत	*one woman*	->	कुछ औरतें	*some women*
एक भाषा	*one language*	->	तीन भाषाएँ	*three languages*
एक माता	*one mother*	->	तीन माताएँ	*three mothers*

Note the spellings: If the noun ends in the *maatraa* form of a vowel, then एँ is added in independent form. If the noun ends in a consonant, then एँ takes its *maatraa* form.

Note:

(1) A small number of feminine nouns ending in इ and इया instead of ई have plural forms similar to marked feminine nouns. Examples:

चिड़िया	*bird*	->	चिड़ियाँ	*birds*
शक्ति	*power*	->	शक्तियाँ	*powers*
बुढ़िया	*old woman*	->	बुढ़ियाँ	*old women*

(2) If a feminine noun ends in ऊ, ऊ is shortened to उ before adding the suffix एँ to make it plural. Examples:

झाड़ू	*broom*	->	झाड़ुएँ	*brooms*
तराज़ू	*(weighing) balance*	->	तराज़ुएँ	*balances*
बहू	*bride*	->	बहुएँ	*brides*

SUMMARY

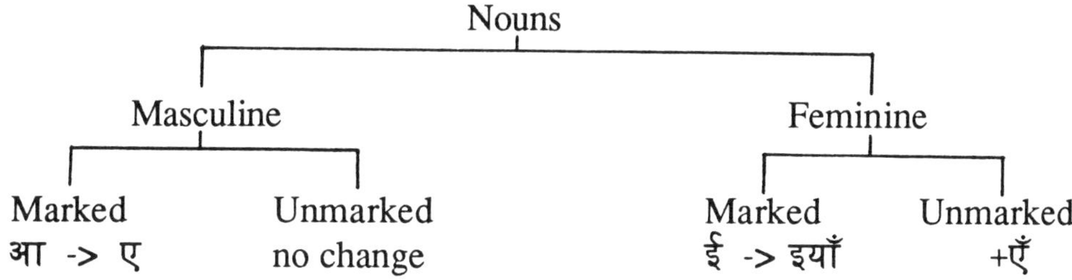

Note:

(1) If the same noun can be used for both males and females, it is declined as a masculine noun in the plural. For example, गाहक *customer*, विदेशी *foreigner*, छात्र *student*, शिक्षक *teacher* can be used for a male or female. In their plural forms they are declined as masculine nouns. Examples:

एक विदेशी	*one foreigner*	->	सब विदेशी	*all foreigners*
एक गाहक	*one customer*	->	कुछ गाहक	*some customers*

एक शिक्षक	*one teacher*	->	चार शिक्षक	*four teachers*
एक छात्र	*one student*	->	सब छात्र	*all students*

(2) There are only a few guidelines for determining the gender of inanimate objects in Hindi. For example, although nouns ending in आ are generally masculine nouns, there are feminine nouns ending in the vowel आ, e.g., भाषा *language*, सभ्यता *civilization*, परीक्षा *examination*.

Similarly, although nouns ending in ई are very often feminine nouns, there are some examples of masculine nouns ending in ई, e.g., आदमी *man*, धोबी *washerman*, पानी *water*.

(3) There are no definite or indefinite articles in Hindi like the English "a," "an," or "the." Thus the noun विदेशी may mean *a foreigner* or *the foreigner* depending on the context.

Exercises

1. Transformation drill

girl	girls
लड़की	लड़कियाँ
कुरसी	
मिठाई	
रोटी	
बेटी	
कहानी	
साड़ी	
टोपी	

2. Transformation drill

There is a sari.	There are some saris.
एक साड़ी है ।	कुछ साड़ियाँ हैं ।
एक संतरा है ।	
एक रोटी है ।	
एक कहानी है ।	
एक केला है ।	
एक साड़ी है ।	
एक पपीता है ।	
एक फल है ।	
एक कुरसी है ।	
एक जूता है ।	
एक मिठाई है ।	
एक टोपी है ।	
एक सेब है ।	
एक लड़की है ।	

3. Substitution drill

Please take these breads.
ये रोटियाँ लीजिये ।

oranges
sweets
apples
bananas
chairs
mangoes
papayas
papers
fruits
saris

4. Transformation drill

woman	women
औरत	औरतें
किताब	
दुकान	
पेंसिल	
मेज़	
चीज़	
कमीज़	
बहन	
बात	
माता	
चप्पल	

5. Substitution drill

There are many chairs here.
यहाँ बहुत कुरसियाँ हैं।

- women
- sweets
- shops
- papers
- pencils
- girls
- breads
- apples
- tables
- saris
- fruits
- books

6. Translation exercise

1. There are some boys and girls here.
2. There are five pencils.
3. Please give two notebooks and four pens.
4. Please take these chairs.
5. There are two tables here.
6. Please give some sweets.
7. Please eat these fruits.
8. Please give those books.
9. There are some shops here.
10. Please give two shirts and four socks.

3. ADJECTIVES

In Hindi adjectives, like nouns, can be divided into two categories: marked and unmarked.

Marked adjectives: Marked adjectives have an आ ending in their masculine singular form, e.g., अच्छा *good*, छोटा *small*, बुरा *bad*, लम्बा *tall*, मीठा *sweet*, सस्ता *cheap*, बड़ा *big*. Marked adjectives agree in number and gender with the nouns they modify and have three forms, depending on their agreement. They have an आ ending when modifying a masculine singular noun, an ए ending when modifying a masculine plural noun, and an ई ending when modifying a feminine noun — singular or plural. Examples:

अच्छा लड़का	*good boy*
अच्छे लड़के	*good boys*
अच्छी लड़की	*good girl*
अच्छी लड़कियाँ	*good girls*

Note that for feminine agreement there is no distinction between singular and plural adjectival forms.

Unmarked adjectives: Unmarked adjectives have a consonant or vowel ending other than an आ in their masculine singular form, e.g., ख़राब *bad*, सुन्दर *beautiful*, लाल *red*, बहुत *many, much*, भारी *heavy*, मुश्किल *difficult*, मज़ेदार *enjoyable*, साफ़ *clean*, दिलचस्प *interesting*, काफ़ी *enough*. Unmarked adjectives do not change to agree with the noun they modify. Thus unmarked adjectives have only one form. Examples:

सुन्दर लड़का	*beautiful boy*	ख़राब केला	*bad banana*
सुन्दर लड़के	*beautiful boys*	ख़राब केले	*bad bananas*
सुन्दर लड़की	*beautiful girl*	ख़राब मिठाई	*bad sweet*
सुन्दर लड़कियाँ	*beautiful girls*	ख़राब मिठाइयाँ	*bad sweets*

<u>Word order:</u> The word order of nouns and adjectives is the same in Hindi as in English. Generally an adjective precedes the noun it modifies. When an adjective is used as a predicate adjective, it comes after the noun it modifies and before the verb. In both cases adjectives agree in number and gender with the noun they refer to. Examples:

छोटी लड़की वहाँ है ।	*The small/young girl is there.*
क्या ये ताज़े संतरे हैं ?	*Are these fresh oranges?*
वह लड़की छोटी है ।	*That girl is small/young.*
ये संतरे ताज़े हैं ।	*These oranges are fresh.*

Note:

(1) In dictionaries adjectives appear in their masculine singular form.

(2) Several adjectives can be used together to modify a single noun. Example:

वे दो सुन्दर लाल हिन्दुस्तानी साड़ियाँ दीजिये ।
Please give (me) those two beautiful red Indian saris.

(3) When used to modify two or more inanimate things of different genders, an adjective agrees with the noun closest to it.Examples:

ये ताज़ी मिठाइयाँ और फल लीजिये ।	*Please take these fresh sweets and fruits.*
वे साड़ियाँ और जूते सस्ते हैं ।	*Those saris and shoes are cheap.*

(4) When used to modify two or more people of different gender, an adjective takes the masculine plural form.Example:

ये सब लड़के और लड़कियाँ अच्छे हैं ।	*All these boys and girls are good.*

(5) A very few adjectives, although ending in the vowel आ, do not change to agree with the noun they modify.Examples:

बढ़िया खाना	*excellent food*	ज़्यादा दूध	*too much milk*
बढ़िया कपड़े	*excellent clothes*	ज़्यादा केले	*too many bananas*
बढ़िया साड़ी	*excellent sari*	ज़्यादा चाय	*too much tea*
बढ़िया मिठाइयाँ	*excellent sweets*	ज़्यादा मिठाइयाँ	*too many sweets*

(6) Some adjectives are formed by adding the suffix ई to certain nouns (especially relating to place names).Examples:

बनारस	*Banaras*	->	बनारसी	*of/from Banaras*
हिन्दुस्तान	*Hindustan*	->	हिन्दुस्तानी	*of/from Hindustan*
पाकिस्तान	*Pakistan*	->	पाकिस्तानी	*of/from Pakistan*

These adjectives are unmarked and do not change to agree with the noun they modify. Examples:

बनारसी कपड़ा	*cloth from Banaras*
बनारसी कपड़े	*clothes from Banaras*
बनारसी साड़ी	*sari from Banaras*
बनारसी साड़ियाँ	*saris from Banaras*

Exercises

1. Transformation drill

This orange is good.	These oranges are good.
यह संतरा अच्छा है ।	ये संतरे अच्छे हैं ।
यह मिठाई अच्छी है ।	
यह छात्र अच्छा है ।	
यह पपीता अच्छा है ।	
यह पेंसिल अच्छी है ।	

यह बेर अच्छा है ।
यह फल अच्छा है ।
यह साड़ी अच्छी है ।
यह किताब अच्छी है ।
यह लड़का अच्छा है ।
यह क्लास अच्छी है ।

2. <u>Substitution drill</u>

These fruits are good.
ये फल अच्छे हैं ।

ताज़े
मीठे
बड़े
छोटे
सस्ते
महँगे
ख़राब
पक्के
काफ़ी
कच्चे
अच्छे और मीठे

3. <u>Substitution drill</u>

How are these fruits?
ये फल कैसे हैं ?

book
sweet
students
books
oranges
sweets

teacher
shop
class
mangoes
saris

4. Chain drill

Q: How is this student?
यह छात्र कैसा है ?

A: He is good.
अच्छा है ।

Q: How are these books?
ये किताबें कैसी हैं ?

A: They are expensive.
महँगी हैं ।

5. Substitution drill

These sweets are cheap.
ये मिठाइयाँ सस्ती हैं ।

expensive
fresh
sweet
big
good
small
bad
cheap
good and fresh
enough

6. Substitution drill

Please take this sari. It's very good.
यह साड़ी लीजिये, बहुत अच्छी है ।
this pretty sari
these sweet oranges
these cheap bananas
these fresh sweets
this small book
this big chair
these sweet mangoes
these small fruits
these shoes
these pretty shirts

7. Individual conversational response drill
(Answer the following questions with appropriate adjectives.)

How is this book?	It's big.
यह किताब कैसी है ?	बड़ी है ।

ये छात्र कैसे हैं ?
यह क्लास कैसी है ?
यह मेज़ कैसी है ?
ये फल कैसे हैं ?
ये कुरसियाँ कैसी हैं ?
ये साड़ियाँ कैसी हैं ?
ये जूते कैसे हैं ?
यह यूनिवर्सिटी कैसी है ?
ये मिठाइयाँ कैसी हैं ?
ये कमीज़ें कैसी हैं ?
यह कहानी कैसी है ?
ये चीज़ें कैसी हैं ?
ये दुकानें कैसी हैं ?
यह देश कैसा है ?

8. <u>Chain drill</u>

Q: What is this?
यह क्या है ?

A: This is a table.
यह मेज़ है ।

Q: How is it? (i.e., What's it like?)
कैसी है ?

A: It's big.
बड़ी है ।

9. <u>Transformation drill</u>

India	Indian
हिन्दुस्तान	हिन्दुस्तानी
जयपुर	
बंगाल	
मद्रास	
गुजरात	
बनारस	
पाकिस्तान	

10. <u>Transformation drill</u>

These shoes are from India.	These are Indian shoes.
ये जूते हिन्दुस्तान से हैं ।	ये हिन्दुस्तानी जूते हैं ।
ये जूते पाकिस्तान से हैं ।	
ये जूते मद्रास से हैं ।	
ये जूते गुजरात से हैं ।	
ये जूते बंगाल से हैं ।	

ये जूते जापान से हैं ।
ये जूते बनारस से हैं ।
ये जूते जयपुर से हैं ।

11. Substitution drill

Please take these clothes from Pakistan.
ये पाकिस्तानी कपड़े लीजिये ।
clothes from Bengal
clothes from Banaras
clothes from Gujarat
clothes from Jaipur
clothes from India
clothes from Madras

12. Translation exercise

1. This Indian sari is pretty.
2. These students are good.
3. This university is very big.
4. These oranges are fresh and very sweet.
5. That table is expensive.
6. How are the fruits? They are very cheap.
7. Please give that pretty sari from Banaras.
8. Those sweets are cheap and good.
9. How is the class? The class is very interesting.
10. This city is big.
11. That book is very difficult.
12. Please take these shirts from Madras.

4. PRONOUNS AND THE VERB होना *TO BE*

The grammatical pattern of Hindi pronouns is similar to that of English pronouns:

	Singular		**Plural**	
1st person	I	मैं	we	हम
2nd person	you	तू	you	आप, तुम
3rd person	he, she, it	यह, वह	they	ये, वे

First person pronouns: In Hindi the first person singular pronoun is मैं *I*. The form of the verb "to be" used with मैं is हूँ *am*. मैं is always treated as singular and is used by both men and women.

मैं अच्छा हूँ।	*I* (M) *am good/fine.*
मैं अच्छी हूँ।	*I* (F) *am good/fine.*

The first person plural pronoun is हम *we*. It takes the plural form of the verb "to be," हैं *are*. Sometimes in colloquial Hindi हम may be used by one person (instead of मैं). This is especially true in Eastern Uttar Pradesh and Bihar. Whether used by one person or more, हम is always treated grammatically as plural as far as agreement is concerned.

हम अच्छे हैं। *We are good/fine*, or *I am good/fine.*

Note:

(1) Often women, when using हम instead of मैं for themselves, use masculine plural forms. Example:

हम अच्छे हैं। *I am good/fine* instead of हम अच्छी हैं।

(2) Since हम can be used by one person or more than one person, in order to make the plurality clear, the word लोग *people* may be used with हम. Example:

हम लोग भारत से हैं।	*We (people) are from India.*

Second person pronouns: In contrast to English, where there is only one second person pronoun, "you," Hindi speakers use three second person pronouns depending on the degree of closeness in the relationship and on the age and relative social position of the person being addressed in relation to the speaker.

आप हैं	*you are*	Formal and honorific
तुम हो	*you are*	Familiar and informal
तू है	*you are*	Intimate

आप: The use of आप is respectful and formal. It is used for elders, seniors, superiors, and for equals with respect. It is used to indicate rather formal relationships and is very common among educated urban people.

आप can be used to address one person or more than one person. Grammatically आप is always treated as plural; therefore the adjectives and verb forms used with आप are in the plural.

आप कैसे हैं ?	*How are you?*	(For masc. sg./pl.)
आप कैसी हैं ?	*How are you?*	(For fem. sg./pl.)

Again लोग can be used with आप to make the plurality explicit. आप is the safest form to use when one is new to the culture and not sure of which form will be appropriate to use.

तुम: The second equivalent of the English "you" is the familiar pronoun तुम. तुम is generally employed with one's equals as a sign of familiarity and informality. तुम is used mostly with close friends and colleagues in informal situations and among family members as a sign of close relationship. In situations of social inequality, a speaker would use तुम for people who are younger in age or lower in social position.

A special form of the verb "to be," हो, is employed with तुम. Like आप, तुम may refer to one person or more than one person. Whether तुम is used for one person or more than one person, grammatically it is always treated as plural.

तुम अच्छे छात्र हो । *You (M) are a good student.*
You (M) are good students.
तुम अच्छी छात्र हो । *You (F) are a good student.*
You (F) are good students.

As with आप, लोग can be used with तुम to make it clear that more than one person is being referred to.

तुम लोग अच्छे छात्र हो । *You people are good students.*

The use of तुम is very common, especially in rural areas. Students who are not familiar with the culture should use तुम only when they are sure of the informality in the relationship.

तू: The third equivalent of the English "you" is the intimate pronoun तू. Since the use of तू is also a sign of great intimacy, close friends and some family members use तू for each other. It is also used for small children. In religious contexts, तू is often used to address God.

The use of the intimate pronoun तू is more common in rural areas than in cities. In rural areas it is also used in asymmetrical relationships, e.g., parents using it for children, and master for servant.

The pronoun तू can also be used to express anger or insult. Foreigners should be cautious in using this pronoun unless they understand the culture of the area well.

तू is always treated as singular, and the form of the verb "to be" used with तू is है *is*. Since तू is always used in the singular, it never refers to more than one person. In order to refer to more than one person, one has to use तुम or तुम लोग instead of तू.

Note: English sentences using the second person pronoun "you" can be translated into Hindi in several ways depending on the gender and familiarity or formality one wishes to convey.

How are you?	आप कैसे हैं ?	आप कैसी हैं ?
	तुम कैसे हो ?	तुम कैसी हो ?
	तू कैसा है ?	तू कैसी है ?

You are a good student.	आप अच्छे छात्र हैं ।	आप अच्छी छात्र हैं ।
	तुम अच्छे छात्र हो ।	तुम अच्छी छात्र हो ।
	तू अच्छा छात्र है ।	तू अच्छी छात्र है ।

Third person pronouns:

यह and वह: The third person singular pronouns for the English "he, she, it" are यह and वह in Hindi. यह and वह are always treated as singular. While English forms distinguish between genders in third person pronouns, Hindi has the same form for masculine and feminine. The form of the verb "to be" used with यह and वह is है *is*.

Since both यह and वह can be used for "he, she, or it," students should learn the situations where the use of यह is more appropriate and where the use of वह is more natural.

यह is used mostly for a person or thing that is physically close to the speaker. वह, on the other hand, is used for a person or thing that is not in the immediate proximity of the speaker. When the distance is not specified, वह is the more appropriate form to use.

ये and वे: The third person plural pronouns for the English "they" are ये and वे. ये is the plural form of यह, and वे is the plural form of वह. The form of the verb "to be" used with ये or वे is हैं *are*.

Although ये and वे are grammatically always plural, they can also be used to refer to a singular person as a sign of respect or deference. Whether used for a single person or more than one person, agreement is always in the plural. In order to make the plurality unambiguous, one may use लोग with ये or वे.

ये लोग अमरीकन हैं । *These people are Americans.*
वे लोग अमरीकन हैं । *Those people are Americans.*

while

ये अमरीकन हैं । could mean: *He/She is an American.* (respectful)
They are Americans.

Summary

Pronouns		The verb होना *to be*	
मैं	*I*	हूँ	*am*
हम	*we*	हैं	*are*
आप	*you*	हैं	*are*
तुम	*you*	हो	*are*
तू	*you*	है	*are*
यह	*he, she, it*	है	*is*
वह	*he, she, it*	है	*is*
ये	*they*	हैं	*are*
वे	*they*	हैं	*are*

Note:

(1) In normal daily speech, both यह and ये are pronounced as ये and both वह and वे are pronounced as वो. However, in standard written Hindi, the spellings यह and वह are used for singular forms and ये and वे for plural forms. In formal speech, some people pronounce these pronouns as written.

(2) यह, ये, वह, and वे are used as personal pronouns as well as demonstrative pronouns and adjectives with the meanings "this," "these," "that," and "those" respectively.

वह अच्छा छात्र है ।	*He is a good student.*
ये हिन्दुस्तान से हैं ।	*They are from India.*
वह लड़का अमरीकन है ।	*That boy is an American.*
ये लोग कौन हैं ?	*Who are these people?*

Although the basic pattern of Hindi pronouns is similar to that of English, there are some important differences between the two:

(a) Since Hindi uses plural forms for singular references in order to show respect, often only context shows whether a pronoun refers to one person or more than one person. In order to clarify the plural reference, लोग may be added to the pronoun, e.g., हम लोग, आप लोग, तुम लोग, ये लोग, वे लोग.

(b) The proper use of Hindi pronouns can reveal the relative age and social status of the speaker and the person spoken to or about. It can also indicate whether the relationship among the two parties is formal or informal, intimate or distant.

(c) There are three second person pronouns in Hindi while English has only one. The correct use of these three second person pronouns requires great sensitivity and understanding of the culture of the area. When choosing an appropriate second person pronoun, one has to consider several factors such as age, social status, and the degree of familiarity and intimacy one wants to convey. Also, as mentioned earlier, आप is used more among educated urban people. आप and तुम are heard more often in cities while तुम and तू are more common in rural areas.

Respectful terms of address: As noted with the pronouns, Hindi uses plural forms in singular reference to show respect or honor for an individual. The following titles and suffixes are commonly used in Hindi as a mark of respect and honorific reference and therefore always require plural agreement:

(1) The honorific particle जी is commonly used to show respect for an individual. It can be used with a person's first or last name, with a kinship term, or with the title of a person, e.g., गाँधी जी, सुषमा जी, पिता जी, प्रधान मंत्री जी.

(2) The Hindi word साहब is equivalent to "sir" in English, and is often used alone for strangers, foreigners, and westernized Indians. साहब can also be added to a man's last name (and sometimes first name) in order to accord respect, e.g., स्मिथ साहब, इक़बाल साहब.

The feminine counterpart of साहब is मेमसाहब. The use of मेमसाहब is limited to foreign women or westernized Indian women. Compared to साहब, मेमसाहब is less commonly used.

श्री, श्रीमती, and कुमारी correspond to English "Mr.," "Mrs.," and "Miss" respectively, and are used in formal reference, e.g., श्री सुरेन्द्र गुप्ता or श्री गुप्ता, श्रीमती वाइली, or श्रीमती क्रिस्टी वाइली.

Note: Whenever plural forms are used in a singular reference for expressing respect, pronouns, adjectives, and verbs always take plural forms of agreement but only marked masculine nouns take plural forms to express respect; unmarked masculine nouns and feminine nouns do not take plural forms.

आपकी पत्नी अच्छी हैं ।	(sg. polite)	*Your wife is fine.*

and not

आपकी पत्नियाँ अच्छी हैं ।		*Your wives are fine.*
आपके भाई अच्छे हैं ।	(sg. polite)	*Your brother is fine.*
	(pl.)	*Your brothers are fine.*
ये शिक्षक अच्छे हैं ।	(sg. polite)	*This teacher is good.*
	(pl.)	*These teachers are good.*

आपके बेटे होशियार हैं।	(sg. polite)	*Your son is smart.*
	(pl.)	*Your sons are smart.*

Exercises

1. Substitution drill

I am a shopkeeper.
मैं दुकानदार हूँ।
गाहक
साहब
मेमसाहब
अमरीकन
अच्छी लड़की
बड़ा लड़का
अच्छा छात्र
बड़ा साहब
हिन्दुस्तानी
अच्छा शिक्षक
छोटा दुकानदार
विदेशी

2. Substitution drill

I am from India.
मैं हिन्दुस्तान से हूँ।
पाकिस्तान
अमरीका
यहाँ
वहाँ
दिल्ली
बम्बई

जापान
कराची
न्यू यॉर्क

3. Chain drill

Q: Where are you from?
आप कहाँ से हैं ?

A: I am from America.
मैं अमरीका से हूँ।

4. Substitution drill

We (M/M & F) are customers.
हम गाहक हैं।
अमरीकन
छात्र
शिक्षक
बड़े लोग
अच्छे लोग
अच्छे छात्र
अच्छे शिक्षक
क्लास में
बाज़ार में

5. Substitution drill

We (F) are good.
हम अच्छी हैं।
अच्छी लड़कियाँ
बड़ी
छोटी
गाहक

बर्कली में
मेमसाहब
बड़ी मेमसाहब
हिन्दुस्तानी लड़कियाँ
अमरीका में

6. Substitution drill

Are you a student?
क्या आप छात्र हैं ?
अमरीका से
गाहक
अच्छे छात्र
शिक्षक
बड़े
छोटे
सुन्दर
भारत से
छात्रा
अच्छी
छोटी

7. Conversational response drill

Are you (people) students?
क्या आप लोग छात्र हैं ?

Yes, we (people) are students.
जी हाँ, हम लोग छात्र हैं ।

अमरीका से
बर्कली में
अच्छे छात्र
कमरे में
क्लास में
कुरसी पर
गाहक
दुकानदार

8. Chain drill

Q: What is your name?
आपका नाम क्या है ?

A: My name is Sharon.
मेरा नाम शैरन है ।

Q: Where are you from?
आप कहाँ से हैं ?

A: I am from Berkeley.
मैं बर्कली से हूँ ।

9. Substitution drill

You are an American.
तुम अमरीकन हो ।
गाहक
बर्कली में
अच्छे
कहाँ से
सुन्दर
छोटे
बड़े
कौन
कहाँ

10. Substitution drill

You people (M/M & F) are good students.
तुम लोग अच्छे छात्र हो ।
बड़े
सुन्दर

अमरीकन
छोटे
क्लास में
कौन
कहाँ से
कहाँ
विदेशी
हिन्दुस्तानी
पाकिस्तान से

11. Substitution drill

How are you?
तू कैसा है ?
अच्छा छात्र
कहाँ से
सुन्दर
कौन
बड़ा लड़का
कहाँ
छोटी लड़की
अमरीकन
बर्कली में
अच्छा छात्र
सुन्दर लड़की

12. Substitution drill
(Assume all subjects are male.)

This boy is good.
यह लड़का अच्छा है ।
ये साहब
हम
मैं

तुम
आप
तू
वे लड़के
वे आदमी
वे लोग
तुम लोग
आप लोग
ये छात्र

13. Substitution drill
(Assume all subjects are female.)

Those girls are small.
वे लड़कियाँ छोटी हैं।
यह छात्रा
तू
वे औरतें
यह लड़की
मैं
आप
वह अमरीकन औरत
तुम
ये हिन्दुस्तानी औरतें
हम

14. Translation exercise

1. I am a good student.
2. You are a small girl. (intimate form)
3. We (M & F) are in the class.
4. Who are you? I am a foreigner. (familiar form)
5. These people are from India.
6. How are you? I am fine. (polite form)
7. He is a big boy.

8. Who is she? She is an Indian student.
9. They are good people.
10. We (F) are not girls. We are women.
11. He is not a teacher. He is a student.
12. Where is he from? He is from Pakistan.

5. IMPERATIVE FORMS

Imperative forms are the verbal forms used in commands and requests. Imperative forms in Hindi do not change to agree in number and gender with the subject. Hindi has four types of imperatives commonly used in everyday speech:

(1) Formal
(2) Familiar/Informal
(3) Intimatc
(4) Neutral

Formal imperative: The formal imperative is formed by adding the suffix इये (इए) to the verb stem. A verb stem is the infinitive form of the verb without the final ना ending.

Note that a verb stem is the basic element of the Hindi verb pattern, and all verb forms are created by adding different suffixes to the verb stem. Examples:

Infinitive		Stem	Formal Imperative
खाना	*to eat*	खा	खाइये (खाइए)
पढ़ना	*to read/study*	पढ़	पढ़िये (पढ़िए)
जाना	*to go*	जा	जाइये (जाइए)
सुनना	*to listen*	सुन	सुनिये (सुनिए)

The formal imperatives of the following four verbs are somewhat irregular:

Infinitive		Stem	Formal Imperative
लेना	*to take*	ले	लीजिये (लीजिए)
देना	*to give*	दे	दीजिये (दीजिए)
करना	*to do*	कर	कीजिये (कीजिए)
पीना	*to drink*	पी	पीजिये (पीजिए)

If a verb stem ends in ऊ, ऊ is shortened to उ before adding the इये (इए) ending:

Infinitive		Stem	Formal Imperative
छूना	*to touch*	छू	छुइये (छुइए)

Formal imperatives are used for people to whom one wishes to convey respect on account of age, seniority, or social status and among equals in formal situations. In short, these are the appropriate forms to use for people whom one would normally address as आप.

Familiar/Informal imperative: The familiar imperative is formed by adding the suffix ओ to the verb stem.

Infinitive		Stem	Familiar Imperative
आना	*to come*	आ	आओ
बैठना	*to sit*	बैठ	बैठो

Two verbs have irregular familiar imperative forms:

Infinitive		Stem	Familiar Imperative
लेना	*to take*	ले	लो
देना	*to give*	दे	दो

If a verb stem ends in ऊ, it is shortened to उ before adding the suffix ओ:

Infinitive		Stem	Familiar Imperative
छूना	*to touch*	छू	छुओ

If a verb stem ends in ई, the ई is shortened to इ and often य is inserted before adding the familiar imperative suffix ओ to the stem:

Infinitive		Stem	Familiar Imperative
पीना	*to drink*	पी	पियो (पिओ)
सीना	*to sew*	सी	सियो (सिओ)

Familiar imperatives are used in informal situations and with people of equal or lower social status. These forms are generally used for people whom one would normally address as तुम. Familiar imperatives convey familiarity and informality and are commonly used among friends and for people of lower social status.

Intimate imperative: Intimate imperatives are identical in form to the verb stem.

Infinitive		Stem	Intimate Imperative
जाना	*to go*	जा	जा
पढ़ना	*to read/study*	पढ़	पढ़

Intimate imperatives are generally used for small children. Since these forms show maximum intimacy, they are also used among people who feel very close to each other and sometimes when addressing God. Intimate imperatives are used in the same situations where one would use the pronoun तू and are more common in rural areas than in cities. Since these forms can also be used to express anger or contempt, students should avoid using them.

Neutral imperative: Neutral imperatives and infinitive forms of verbs are the same.

Infinitive		Neutral Imperative
पूछना	*to ask*	पूछना
सुनना	*to listen*	सुनना

Neutral imperatives are generally employed in impersonal situations such as giving directives and also when giving commands with no specific reference to the relative status of both parties. These forms can be used for people whom one would address as either तुम or आप. Sometimes neutral imperatives are also used when the command is not to be carried out right away. Example:

तुम कल दफ़्तर जाना और शर्मा जी से मिलना ।
Tomorrow you go to the office and meet Mr. Sharma.

Negative: The negative particles used with imperatives are generally न or मत. Since मत is a stronger negative than न, it is more frequently used with familiar and intimate imperatives. In certain situations, however, one can use मत with formal and neutral imperatives, especially if one wants to emphasize the negation or to warn the person.

ये सस्ते कपड़े न ख़रीदिये ।	*Please don't buy these cheap clothes.*
यह गन्दा पानी मत पीजिये ।	*Please don't drink this dirty water.*
अन्दर न जाना ।	*Don't go inside.*
मेज़ पर मत बैठ ।	*Don't sit on the table.*

Note:

(1) In colloquial language people often use करिये as the formal imperative of करना, but this form is never used in standard written language.

(2) By adding the suffix गा to a formal imperative, another type of imperative is formed. Examples:

जाइये	->	जाइयेगा
बैठिये	->	बैठियेगा

This type of imperative is very formal and is not used in ordinary daily speech. Since this form is used only in situations where one wants to show great deference for the person addressed, the subject of this form is always आप.

(3) Students should realize that in Hindi the different types of imperatives represent different levels of social relationships rather than different degrees of politeness. Generally when giving a command or making a request, politeness is conveyed by the tone of the voice. Therefore, if used in proper reference, each of these commands conveys proper politeness.

(4) Although Hindi speakers do not use a word equivalent to the English word "please" in everyday speech, there are many ways to make a command or request more gentle:

(a) A softer tone of voice is used.

(b) The adverb ज़रा (lit., "just, a little") is often used at the beginning of a command or request in order to make it softer.

ज़रा वह किताब दीजिये ।	*Please give that book.*
ज़रा एक कुरसी लाना ।	*Bring a chair.*
ज़रा वहाँ जाओ और कुछ फल लाओ ।	*Go there and bring some fruit.*

(c) Sometimes in a very formal situation the adverb कृपया (lit., "kindly") is used with formal imperatives. Such usage is not common in daily speech and is limited to business letters, public notices, and extremely formal situations.

कृपया इस कुरसी पर बैठिये ।	*Please (kindly) sit on this chair.*
कृपया घास पर न चलिये ।	*Please (kindly) do not walk on the grass.*

(5) The subject of an imperative is always a second person pronoun, which is often not expressed in the sentence.

आप यहाँ आइये ।	*You please come here.*
यहाँ बैठिये ।	*Please sit here.*

Exercises

1. Substitution drill

Look at these books.
ये किताबें देखना ।

buy
sell
give
take
read
bring

2. Substitution drill

Please go there.
आप वहाँ जाइये ।

यह खाइये
यहाँ आइये
कुरसी लाइये
यह सुनिये
पत्र लिखिये
किताब पढ़िये
ये चीज़ें बेचिये
कपड़े ख़रीदिये
हिन्दी बोलिये

3. Substitution drill

Please give this.
आप यह दीजिये ।

please take
please do

please begin
please drink
please work
please talk

4. Transformation drill

Read this book.	Please read this book.
यह किताब पढ़ना ।	यह किताब पढ़िये ।
चार कुरसियाँ लाना ।	
एक कलम देना ।	
एक मिठाई खाना ।	
दो कलम ख़रीदना ।	
चाय पीना ।	
यह काम करना ।	
यह काम शुरू करना ।	
ये किताबें बेचना ।	
दो रुपये देना ।	
ये कपड़े लेना ।	
एक कहानी सुनाना ।	
हिन्दी में बात करना ।	
घर जाना ।	

5. Substitution drill

You come here.
तुम यहाँ आओ ।
फल खाओ
किताब लाओ
यह लो
पैसा दो
बात करो
पेंसिल ख़रीदो
अख़बार बेचो

किताब पढ़ो
काम करो
चाय पियो

6. Transformation drill

Buy two books. (neutral form)	Buy two books. (familiar form)
दो किताबें ख़रीदना ।	दो किताबें ख़रीदो ।
एक पेंसिल देना ।	
कहानी शुरू करना ।	
दूध पीना ।	
ये रुपये लेना ।	
वह किताब पढ़ना ।	
ये मीठे और ताज़े सन्तरे ख़रीदना ।	
ये मिठाइयाँ खाना ।	
हिन्दी पढ़ना ।	
बाज़ार जाना ।	
एक कुरसी लाना ।	

7. Transformation drill

Begin. (familiar form)	Begin. (intimate form)
शुरू करो ।	शुरू कर ।
घर जाओ ।	
दो कुरसियाँ लाओ ।	
ठीक कहो ।	
सवाल पूछो ।	
जवाब दो ।	
किताब पढ़ो ।	
ये किताबें लो ।	
जल्दी करो ।	
हिन्दी बोलो ।	

8. Transformation drill

Please go there.	Please don't go there.
वहाँ जाइये ।	वहाँ न जाइये ।
	वहाँ मत जाइये ।

ये सस्ती मिठाइयाँ खाओ ।
यह काम कर ।
वे महँगे फल ख़रीदो ।
चार रुपये दीजिये ।
वह किताब पढ़ ।
यह चाय पीजिये ।
बाज़ार जाना ।
बड़ी कुरसी पर बैठो ।
ये सस्ते फल लीजिये ।
शराब पीना ।
ये महँगे कपड़े ख़रीद ।

9. Translation exercise

1. Please eat these sweets. They are very fresh.
2. Don't sit on the big chair. (intimate form)
3. Buy these good and fresh fruits. (neutral form)
4. Please don't buy these shoes. They are very expensive.
5. Please begin the story.
6. Read these books. They are very interesting. (neutral form)
7. This milk is not good. Don't drink it. (intimate form)
8. Please buy this pretty sari from Jaipur.
9. Don't go there. (familiar form)
10. Bring those papers and books here. (familiar form)

6. INTERROGATIVES

All interrogatives in Hindi begin with the consonant क. While in English question words always come at the beginning of the sentence, in Hindi the word order is rather flexible. Generally the word order for questions is the same as for statements, and a question word normally occurs in the same place in the question as the word that answers that question does in the reply.

There are two types of questions in Hindi: (1) yes or no questions and (2) information questions.

The question word क्या: The interrogative क्या is unique because it is used in both yes or no and information questions.

क्या in yes or no questions: In English, yes or no questions do not use any interrogative word. They are formed simply by using the verb or part of the verb at the beginning of the question. Example:

Is he an Indian?
Do you study here?

In Hindi, this type of question is formed by adding the question word क्या at the beginning of the sentence. The word order of such questions is the same as that of a statement. The interrogative क्या is not stressed, but the voice is raised at the end of the sentence. This unstressed क्या serves simply as a question marker and cannot be translated into English. It is often dropped in colloquial speech, and in that case the question is distinguished from the statement only by rising intonation. Examples:

वह अच्छा छात्र है ।	*He is a good student.*
क्या वह अच्छा छात्र है ?	*Is he a good student?*
वह अच्छा छात्र है ?	*Is he a good student?*

<u>क्या in information questions:</u> The question word क्या when used in information questions comes directly before the verb and is the equivalent of the English "what." In this type of question the question word क्या is stressed, but there is no rise in voice inflection at the end of the sentence. Examples:

वह क्या है ?	*What is that?*
आपका नाम क्या है ?	*What is your name?*
साड़ी क्या है ?	*What is a sari?*

<u>The question word कैसा:</u> Another interrogative that conveys two different meanings depending on its location in the sentence is कैसा. When used attributively (i.e., right before the noun it modifies), कैसा has the general meaning "what sort of," "what kind of"; but when used predicatively (i.e., right before the verb) it is translated as "how" in English. Examples:

वह कैसा फल है ?	*What kind of fruit is that?*
वह फल कैसा है ?	*How is that fruit?*

The interrogative adjective कैसा declines like a marked adjective (कैसा, कैसे, कैसी) and agrees with the noun it modifies in number and gender. Examples:

वह केला कैसा है ?	*How is that banana?*
वे संतरे कैसे हैं ?	*How are those oranges?*
यह किताब कैसी है ?	*How is this book?*
ये किताबें कैसी हैं ?	*How are these books?*

<u>Other interrogatives:</u> The other commonly used information question words in Hindi are कहाँ *where*, किधर *in which direction*, कौन *who*, कब *when*, क्यों *why*, and कितना / कितने / कितनी *how much/many*.

Note that like कैसा, the interrogative adjective कितना also functions as a marked adjective and agrees with the noun it modifies in number and gender.

Exercises

1. Individual conversational response drill

What is "book" in Hindi?	It is "किताब."
हिन्दी में book क्या है ?	किताब है ।
हिन्दी में table क्या है ?	मेज़ है ।
हिन्दी में chair क्या है ?	कुरसी है ।
हिन्दी में door क्या है ?	दरवाज़ा है ।
हिन्दी में floor क्या है ?	फ़र्श है ।
हिन्दी में window क्या है ?	खिड़की है ।
हिन्दी में pencil क्या है ?	पेंसिल है ।
हिन्दी में paper क्या है ?	कागज़ है ।
हिन्दी में wall क्या है ?	दीवार है ।
हिन्दी में bag क्या है ?	थैला है ।
हिन्दी में notebook क्या है ?	कापी है ।
हिन्दी में pen क्या है ?	कलम है ।

2. Chain drill

(Students should point out some object in the classroom while asking the question.)

Q: What is this?
यह क्या है ?

A: This is a book.
यह किताब है ।

Q: What is that?
वह क्या है ?

A: That is a window.
वह खिड़की है ।

3. Transformation drill

This book is good. यह किताब अच्छी है ।	Is this book good? क्या यह किताब अच्छी है ?

यह पेंसिल छोटी है ।
यह छात्र अच्छा है ।
वह राम है ।
राम बड़ा लड़का है ।
ये लड़के अच्छे छात्र हैं ।
यह साड़ी महँगी है ।
ये कमीज़ें सस्ती हैं ।
वह होटल अच्छा है ।

4. Individual conversational response drill

Are these clothes expensive? क्या ये कपड़े महँगे हैं ?	Yes, they are expensive. जी हाँ, महँगे हैं ।
	No, they are cheap. जी नहीं, सस्ते हैं ।

क्या यह यूनिवर्सिटी बड़ी है ?
क्या बर्कली शहर सुन्दर है ?
क्या अमरीका बड़ा देश है ?
क्या यह किताब अच्छी है ?
क्या वह अच्छा छात्र है ?
क्या यह मेज़ बड़ी है ?
क्या वे मिठाइयाँ सस्ती हैं ?
क्या ये फल ताज़े हैं ?
क्या यह बाज़ार बड़ा है ?
क्या यह दुकान छोटी है ?
क्या वह लड़की सुन्दर है ?

5. Chain drill

Q: What is this?
यह क्या है ?

A: This is an orange.
यह सन्तरा है ।

Q: Is it sweet?
मीठा है ?

A: Yes, it is very sweet.
जी हाँ, बहुत मीठा है ।

6. Substitution drill

Where is Delhi?
दिल्ली कहाँ है ?
मद्रास
बर्कली
बैंगकॉक
होनोलूलू
हौलैंड
रोम
यूनिवर्सिटी
कलकत्ता
बम्बई

7. Individual conversational response drill

Where is Bombay?	It is in India.
बम्बई कहाँ है ?	भारत में है ।
कराची कहाँ है ?	
वाइट हाउस कहाँ है ?	

पेरिस कहाँ है ?
न्यू यॉर्क कहाँ है ?
ऐफ़िल टावर कहाँ है ?
ताज महल कहाँ है ?
ऐम्पायर स्टेट बिल्डिंग कहाँ है ?

8. Chain drill

Q: Where is Athens?
एथेन्स कहाँ है ?

A: It is in Greece.
ग्रीस में है ।

9. Oral questions

मौसम कैसा है ?
फ़िल्म कैसी है ?
लाइब्रेरी कहाँ है ?
वह किताब कैसी है ?
क्लास कैसी है ?
वहाँ कितनी किताबें हैं ?
क्लास में कितनी खिड़कियाँ हैं ?
आपका घर कहाँ है ?
यहाँ कितने छात्र हैं ?
क्लास में कितने शिक्षक हैं ?
सुनिये, पुस्तकालय किधर है ?
बड़ा बाज़ार किधर है ?
वह लड़का कौन है ?
ये लोग कौन हैं ?
वहाँ कौन हैं ?
क्या वे लोग पाकिस्तान से हैं ?
क्या क्लास में बहुत छात्र हैं ?

10. Translation exercise

1. What is "paper" in Hindi?
2. Is this university big?

    Yes, it is big.

    No, it is not big.
3. What is this? It is a notebook.
4. Is she a good student?
5. Are these clothes cheap?

    Yes, they are cheap.

    No, they are expensive.
6. Is America a big country?
7. Where are the students? They are in the class.
8. How is the food? It is good.
9. Where is Madras? It is in India.
10. Who are those people?
11. How is the class? It is interesting.
12. Where is the library? It's over there.

7. POSTPOSITIONS

In Hindi, postpositions function exactly like prepositions in English. A postposition generally helps to determine the exact function of a noun or noun phrase in the sentence. Although they are pronounced as independent words, they can never be used alone and must always follow a noun, pronoun, or noun phrase. The only difference between Hindi postpositions and English prepositions is that Hindi postpositions follow the noun phrase with which they are connected while English prepositions precede the phrase.

Some postpositions in Hindi are only one word. These are called simple postpositions. Some simple postpositions are में *in, among*, पर *on, at*, से *from, by, with, since*, का (possessive postposition) *belonging to, related to* (equivalent to English " 's"), को *to* (and used in various situations with different meanings), तक *up to, until.*

The meanings of the simple postpositions given above are their general meanings. Students will note that the postpositions have different meanings depending on the use or context.

Hindi also has a large number of compound postpositions. These have two or more words and are formed with one of the simple postpositions (generally के, की, or से and some other word). Compound postpositions function in exactly the same way as simple postpositions and follow the words they govern. Some compound postpositions are के लिये *for*, से / के पहले *before*, के बाद *after*, के ऊपर *above, on, on top of*, के नीचे *under, beneath, below*, के बारे में *about*, की तरफ़ *towards*, के सामने *in front of*, के पीछे *behind*, के आगे *ahead of*, के पास *near*, के साथ *together with, with, along with*, के कारण *because of*, की वजह से *because of*, से दूर *far from*, के नज़दीक *near*.

As a writing convention, postpositions are often joined together with pronouns but not with nouns, e.g., तुमसे, आपका, मेज़ पर.

Exercises

1. Substitution drill

We are in the class.
हम क्लास में हैं।

बर्कली
बाज़ार
कैलिफ़ोर्निया
दुकान
अमरीका
यूनिवर्सिटी
शहर

2. Chain drill

Q: Where are you?
तुम कहाँ हो ?

A: I am in the class.
मैं क्लास में हूँ।

3. Substitution drill

Those books are on the table.
वे किताबें मेज़ पर हैं।

on the floor
on the ground
here
there
where
in the class
near the chair

under the table
for you
about India

4. Substitution drill

This student is from India.
यह छात्र भारत से है।

from Delhi
from Bengal
from here
from America
from Pakistan
from where
from there

5. Chain drill

Q: Where are you from?
आप कहाँ से हैं ?

A: I am from India.
मैं भारत से हूँ।

6. Substitution drill

What is under the chair?
कुरसी के नीचे क्या है।

के ऊपर
के पास
के सामने
के पीछे
के नज़दीक
से दूर

7. Transformation drill

There are some books on the table.	Are there some books on the table?
मेज़ के ऊपर कुछ किताबें हैं ।	क्या मेज़ के ऊपर कुछ किताबें हैं ?

किताब के नीचे अख़बार है ।
किताब के पास कलम है ।
शिक्षक के सामने छात्र हैं ।
घर के नज़दीक कुछ दुकानें हैं ।
पुस्तकालय यहाँ से दूर है ।
यह किताब भारत के बारे में है ।
घर के सामने पेड़ है ।
यह किताब छात्र के लिये है ।
घर के पीछे बगीचा है ।

8. Oral questions

ये लोग कहाँ से हैं ?
खिड़की के पास कौन है ?
आपकी किताबें कहाँ हैं ?
क्या पुस्तकालय यहाँ से बहुत दूर है ?
छात्र के सामने कौन है ?
शिक्षक के पीछे क्या है ?
मेज़ के ऊपर कितनी किताबें हैं ?
शिक्षक के सामने कौन हैं ?
कुरसी के नीचे क्या है ?
क्या विश्वविद्यालय के नज़दीक अच्छी दुकानें हैं ?
क्या आपका घर कैम्पस से दूर है ?
क्या यह किताब भारत के बारे में है ?

9. Translation exercise

1. Where are the students? They are in the class.
2. Please don't sit on the table.
3. That book is under the table.
4. Are you from Pakistan? No, I am from India.
5. Is the university far from here?
6. Don't sit near the window.
7. Who is behind you?
8. Please bring two chairs from the class.
9. Please read this book. It is about India.
10. There is a big tree in front of the library.

8. POSSESSIVE FORMS

The postposition का is the only postposition in Hindi that has more than one form. This is due to the fact that when a noun, pronoun, or adverb is followed by the postposition का, it, along with the following postposition का, grammatically becomes an adjective. This marked adjective agrees with the noun it modifies in number and gender. Therefore, like any marked adjective, का has three forms: का, के, and की.

लड़की का घर	*the girl's house*
लड़की के जूते	*the girl's shoes*
लड़की की साड़ी	*the girl's sari*
लड़की की किताबें	*the girl's books*

In the above phrases लड़की का, लड़की के, and लड़की की grammatically are adjectives, agreeing with the following nouns. Similarly, in आप का दोस्त *your friend,* the pronoun आप with the postposition का is functioning as a possessive adjective. In कल का अख़बार *yesterday's newspaper* and यहाँ का मौसम *the weather (of) here* the adverbs कल *yesterday* and यहाँ *here,* together with the postposition का, form adjectival phrases.

Like other adjectives, those formed with the postposition का either precede the noun they modify or come after the noun and before the verb if they are used predicatively. In either case these adjectives always agree with the noun they refer to in number and gender. Examples:

जॉन की किताब यहाँ है ।	*John's book is here.*
यह किताब जॉन की है ।	*This book is John's.*
आपके कपड़े महँगे हैं ।	*Your clothes are expensive.*
क्या वे महँगे कपड़े आपके हैं ?	*Are those expensive clothes yours?*

The postposition का is generally used to indicate possession or relationship, for example,

(1) छात्र की किताबें मेज़ पर हैं। *The student's books are on the table.*

Here the postposition का is used to indicate personal possession and can be translated in English with " 's."

(2) साड़ी का दाम दो सौ रुपये है। *The price of the sari is two hundred rupees.*

Notice that in the above example the word order of the "of phrase" in English and the "का phrase" in Hindi is not the same. Since the का phrase indicates possession and comes before the thing or person possessed, the phrase साड़ी का दाम is most directly translated "the sari's price." Note that the word order required by the "of" construction in English is just the opposite of the Hindi का construction:

साड़ी का दाम *price of the sari*

(3) बर्कली के छात्र होशियार हैं। *Berkeley students are smart.*
यह रेशम की साड़ी महँगी है। *This silk sari is expensive.*
यह किताब की दुकान बड़ी है। *This book shop is big.*

The extremely common English pattern of using two nouns together, such as "Berkeley students," "silk sari," or "bookshop" does not occur in Hindi. Instead, the first noun must be followed by का, के, की (depending on the gender of the following noun). Thus, "Berkeley students" in Hindi is "Berkeley's students" (= the students of Berkeley); "silk sari" is "silk's sari" (= sari of silk) and "bookshop" is the "book's shop" (= the shop of books).

Pronouns with the postposition का

Notice that many pronouns with the postposition का / के / की have special forms:

Pronouns		with का		with के	with की
मैं	*I*	मेरा	*my*	मेरे	मेरी
हम	*we*	हमारा	*our*	हमारे	हमारी
आप	*you*	आपका	*your*	आपके	आपकी
तुम	*you*	तुम्हारा	*your*	तुम्हारे	तुम्हारी
तू	*you*	तेरा	*your*	तेरे	तेरी
यह	*he/she/it*	इसका	*his/her/its*	इसके	इसकी
वह	*he/she/it*	उसका	*his/her/its*	उसके	उसकी
ये	*they*	इनका	*their*	इनके	इनकी
वे	*they*	उनका	*their*	उनके	उनकी
कौन	*who* (sg.)	किसका	*whose* (sg.)	किसके	किसकी
कौन	*who* (pl.)	किनका	*whose* (pl.)	किनके	किनकी
क्या	*what* (sg.)	किसका	*of what* (sg.)	किसके	किसकी
क्या	*what* (pl.)	किनका	*of what* (pl.)	किनके	किनकी

Note: (1) The का forms of pronouns (the possessive forms) grammatically are adjectives and agree with the nouns they modify; in Hindi and English grammar these are called possessive adjectives.

(2) Besides being used as possessive adjectives, these forms are also used when का, के, or की follows a pronoun as part of a compound postposition, and their meanings change accordingly.Examples:

मेरे लिये (मैं + के लिये) कुछ चाय लाना। *Bring some tea for me.*
हमारे सामने (हम + के सामने) कौन है ? *Who is in front of us?*

Exercises

1. Substitution drill

What is your name?
आप का नाम क्या है ?
विदेशी
बाज़ार
दुकान
छोटी लड़की
गाहक
शहर
किताब
छात्र

2. Transformation drill

This is the student's book. These are the student's books.
यह छात्र की किताब है। ये छात्र की किताबें हैं।
यह छात्र का कमरा है।
यह छात्र का सवाल है।
यह छात्र की पेंसिल है।
यह छात्र का फल है।
यह छात्र का कपड़ा है।
यह छात्र का जूता है।
यह छात्र की मेज़ है।
यह छात्र का जवाब है।
यह छात्र की कुरसी है।
यह छात्र का कागज़ है।

यह छात्र की मिठाई है ।
यह छात्र का दोस्त है ।
यह छात्र की कमीज़ है ।
यह छात्र की साड़ी है ।

3. <u>Substitution drill</u>

Is this your house?
क्या यह आपका घर है ?

class
shoes
big chair
sister
brother
clothes
question
correct answer
shop

4. <u>Substitution drill</u>

This is Ram's expensive table.
यह राम की महँगी मेज़ है ।

big office
cheap chairs
expensive shirt
good clothes
questions
expensive books
room
small shop
big house
correct answer

5. Substitution drill

This is my small house.
यह मेरा छोटा घर है ।

ठीक जवाब
बनारसी साड़ी
अच्छे कपड़े
बड़ी कुरसी
सस्ती पेंसिलें
महँगे कपड़े
हिन्दी की किताब

6. Substitution drill

These are our books.
ये हमारी किताबें हैं ।

छोटे कमरे
हिन्दी की किताबें
सुन्दर साड़ियाँ
ताज़े फल
अच्छी कुरसियाँ
सस्ते केले
महँगे जूते
दोस्त

7. Substitution drill

Is this your chair?
क्या यह तेरी कुरसी है ?

किताबें
घर
सस्ते फल

सवाल
पेंसिलें
पपीते
रोटी

8. Substitution drill

Where are your books?
तुम्हारी किताबें कहाँ हैं ?
रोटी
बड़े कागज़
सुन्दर साड़ियाँ
मीठे फल
सस्ती पेंसिल
कमरा
दुकान
कापियाँ

9. Substitution drill

Is this your expensive sari?
क्या यह आपकी महँगी साड़ी है ?
कलम
कपड़े
ठीक जवाब
छोटी किताब
दफ़्तर
घर
दोस्त

10. Substitution drill

My books are here.
मेरी किताबें यहाँ हैं ।
His
Our
Your (polite form)
My friend's (F)
Your (familiar form)
Their
My
Your (intimate form)
Ram's

11. Substitution drill

They are our friends.
वे हमारे दोस्त हैं ।
my
his
our
your (familiar form)
their
your (intimate form)
her
your (polite form)

12. Chain drill

Q: Whose book is this?
यह किसकी किताब है ?

A: This is my book.
यह मेरी किताब है ।

Q: Is this your pencil?
क्या यह तुम्हारी पेंसिल है ?

A: No, this is David's pencil.
नहीं, यह डेविड की पेंसिल है ।

13. <u>Translation exercise</u>

1. These Hindi students are smart.
2. Please tell (me) the meaning of the question.
3. Don't buy paper bags.
4. What is the price of the book?
5. This is my pen; that one is yours. (familiar form)
6. These are Sita's pretty saris.
7. Where are my papers? Your papers are on her table.
8. Is this your correct answer? (intimate form)
9. Whose Hindi book is this? This is my Hindi book.
10. Our house is in the city. Where is your house? (polite form)
11. Ram's sister is in your class. What is her name?
12. The foreigner's clothes are expensive.

9. THE PRESENT HABITUAL TENSE

There are three types of present tense in Hindi:

(1) **The simple present:** In simple present tense the verb is simply "to be." Examples:

मैं यहाँ हूँ ।	*I am here.*
तुम छात्र हो ।	*You are a student.*

(2) **The present habitual tense:** This tense indicates frequent, regular, or habitual actions in the present, or general statements in the present (where the verb is not just "to be"). It usually equates with the English present tense. Examples:

वह दफ़्तर में काम करती है ।	*She works in an office.*
वह बर्कली में रहता है ।	*He lives in Berkeley.*
छात्र पुस्तकालय में पढ़ते हैं ।	*Students study in the library.*

(3) **The present progressive tense:** This tense is used when the action is in progress at present. Examples:

हम काम कर रहे हैं ।	*We are working.*
वह पढ़ रही है ।	*She is studying.*

Note: The present progressive tense will be discussed in Section 12.

<u>Formation of the present habitual tense:</u> The present habitual tense consists of two parts. The first part marks the habitual aspect of the verb and is formed by adding the suffix ता, ते, or ती to the stem of the verb. This part of the verb agrees in number and gender with the subject of the sentence. Thus the suffix ता is added to the verb stem if the subject is masculine

singular, ते if the subject is masculine plural, and ती if the subject is feminine singular or plural.

In the second part of the present habitual tense, the appropriate present forms of the verb होना *to be* are used as helping verbs to mark the tense of the action. Thus the basic pattern is:

stem + ता (masculine singular)	है (singular)
+ ते (masculine plural)	हैं (plural)
+ ती (feminine singular and plural)	हूँ (if the subject is मैं)
	हो (if the subject is तुम)

Examples with the verb रहना *to live:*

मैं यहाँ रहता / रहती हूँ ।	*I* (M/F) *live here.*
हम यहाँ रहते / रहती हैं ।	*We* (M/F) *live here.*
आप यहाँ रहते / रहती हैं ।	*You* (M/F) *live here.*
तुम यहाँ रहते / रहती हो ।	*You* (M/F) *live here.*
तू यहाँ रहता / रहती है ।	*You* (M/F) *live here.*
यह यहाँ रहता / रहती है ।	*He/She lives here.*
वह यहाँ रहता / रहती है ।	*He/She lives here.*
ये यहाँ रहते / रहती हैं ।	*They* (M/F) *live here.*
वे यहाँ रहते / रहती हैं ।	*They* (M/F) *live here.*

In negative sentences of the present habitual tense, the negative marker नहीं is added directly before the entire verb, and the present tense forms of the verb होना *to be* are generally dropped. Keeping these forms will imply a special emphasis on negation.

वह लड़का हिन्दी नहीं पढ़ता ।	*That boy does not study Hindi.*
वे लड़के हिन्दी नहीं पढ़ते ।	*Those boys do not study Hindi.*
वह लड़की हिन्दी नहीं पढ़ती ।	*That girl does not study Hindi.*
वे लड़कियाँ हिन्दी नहीं पढ़तीं ।	*Those girls do not study Hindi.*

Notice here a special nasalization is added for the feminine plural form of the verb in order to distinguish it from the feminine singular form. This addition of nasalization for feminine plural is possible only when the present tense form of the verb होना *to be* is dropped in negative statements. Otherwise the plurality of feminine subjects is indicated by the plural form of the verb होना.

Note: Sometimes with the adverb अभी *right now* the present habitual form of the verb is used for an immediate future action. Example:

मैं अभी कॉफ़ी लाती हूँ।	*I will bring the coffee right away.*

Exercises

1. Transformation drill

to go	He goes.
जाना	वह जाता है।
आना	
खाना	
लाना	
ख़रीदना	
बेचना	
लेना	
पढ़ना	
देखना	
दिखाना	

2. Transformation drill

to speak Hindi	We speak Hindi.
हिन्दी बोलना	हम हिन्दी बोलते हैं।
काम करना	
किताबें ख़रीदना	
साड़ियाँ दिखाना	
फल बेचना	
बात करना	
हिन्दी समझना	
बाज़ार जाना	
अख़बार पढ़ना	
फ़िल्म देखना	

3. Substitution drill

I (M) study Hindi.
मैं हिन्दी पढ़ता हूँ।
speak English
write English
understand English
work here
live in America
study in the library
sell books

4. Substitution drill

I (F) live in Berkeley.
मैं बर्कली में रहती हूँ।
study Hindi
write Urdu
understand French

speak Hindi
buy saris
work in the office

5. Individual conversational response drill

Do you live in Berkeley?	Yes, I live in Berkeley.
क्या आप बर्कली में रहते हैं ?	जी हाँ, मैं बर्कली में रहता हूँ ।
क्या आप बर्कली में रहती हैं ?	जी हाँ, मैं बर्कली में रहती हूँ ।
क्या आप अँग्रेज़ी बोलते हैं ?	
क्या आप अँग्रेज़ी समझते हैं ?	
क्या आप हिन्दी पढ़ते हैं ?	
क्या आप उर्दू लिखते हैं ?	
क्या आप फल खाते हैं ?	
क्या आप लाइब्रेरी में पढ़ते हैं ?	
क्या आप विदेशी फ़िल्में देखते हैं ?	
क्या आप बहुत किताबें ख़रीदते हैं ?	
क्या आप यहाँ काम करते हैं ?	

6. Transformation drill

to study	What do you (M) study?
पढ़ना	तुम क्या पढ़ते हो ?
ख़रीदना	
देखना	
समझना	
लिखना	
बेचना	
पीना	
खाना	
दिखाना	
करना	
बोलना	

7. <u>Transformation drill</u>

to go	Where do you (F) go?
जाना	तुम कहाँ जाती हो ?
खाना	
पीना	
ख़रीदना	
बेचना	
बैठना	
काम करना	
पढ़ना	
रहना	

8. <u>Chain drill</u>

Q: What do you (M) study?
तुम क्या पढ़ते हो ?

A: I (M) study Hindi.
मैं हिन्दी पढ़ता हूँ ।

Q: What do you (F) drink?
तुम क्या पीती हो ?

A: I (F) drink tea.
मैं चाय पीती हूँ ।

9. <u>Substitution drill</u>

I go to the market.
मैं बाज़ार जाता हूँ ।
आप (F)
वे लड़कियाँ
हम (M and F)

वे लोग
तुम (F)
वह लड़का
तुम लोग (F)
तू (M)
मेमसाहब
सब छात्र (M and F)
यह लड़की

10. Substitution drill

Where can one get bread? (lit.,Where is bread obtained?)
रोटी कहाँ मिलती है ?
अंडे
मुर्ग़ी / मुरग़ी
हिन्दुस्तानी चाय
अच्छी कॉफ़ी
चावल
दूध
शराब
गोश्त
सब्ज़ियाँ
मिठाइयाँ
मसालेवाला खाना
शाकाहारी खाना

11. Chain drill

Q: Where can one get milk? (lit., Where is milk obtained?)
दूध कहाँ मिलता है ?

A: One can get milk in the shop. (lit., Milk is obtained in the shop.)
दूध दुकान में मिलता है ।

Q: Where can one get sweets? (lit., Where are sweets obtained?)
मिठाइयाँ कहाँ मिलती हैं ?

A: One can get sweets in the market. (lit., Sweets are obtained in the market.)
मिठाइयाँ बाज़ार में मिलती हैं ।

12. <u>Transformation drill</u>

I understand Urdu.	I don't understand Urdu.
मैं उर्दू समझता हूँ ।	मैं उर्दू नहीं समझता ।

मैं फ़्रेंच पढ़ती हूँ ।
वह लड़की हिन्दी बोलती है ।
वे लोग भारत में रहते हैं ।
अमरीकन लड़कियाँ साड़ी पहनती हैं ।
हम लोग क्लास में अँग्रेज़ी बोलते हैं ।
वे लोग यहाँ काम करते हैं ।
वे छात्र यहाँ पढ़ते हैं ।
यह लड़की शराब पीती है ।
ये लड़के पुरानी दिल्ली में रहते हैं ।
वे हिन्दुस्तानी औरतें अँग्रेज़ी बोलती हैं ।

13. <u>Chain drill</u>

Q: Do you (M) study French?
क्या आप फ़्रेंच पढ़ते हैं ?

A: No, I don't study French; I study Hindi.
जी नहीं, मैं फ़्रेंच नहीं पढ़ता; हिन्दी पढ़ता हूँ ।

Q: Do you (F) drink coffee?
क्या तुम कॉफ़ी पीती हो ?

A: No, I don't drink coffee; I drink tea.
नहीं, मैं कॉफ़ी नहीं पीती; चाय पीती हूँ ।

14. Oral questions

आप कहाँ रहते हैं ?
क्या तुम गोश्त खाते हो ?
कौन हिन्दी पढ़ता है ?
हम क्लास में क्या बोलते हैं ?
कौन बहुत सवाल पूछता है ?
अच्छी साड़ियाँ कहाँ मिलती हैं ?
क्या तू उर्दू लिखता है ?
कौन बहुत किताबें ख़रीदता है ?
तुम चाय पीते हो या कॉफ़ी ?
अच्छी और ताज़ी मिठाइयाँ कहाँ मिलती हैं ?
छात्र क्या करते हैं ?
क्या आप लोग मेरी अँग्रेज़ी समझते हैं ?

15. Translation exercise

1. Students ask questions.
2. He tells the right price.
3. I drink tea but my friends drink coffee.
4. Many foreign students study here.
5. She comes into the class.
6. All good students speak Hindi.
7. She doesn't understand French.
8. Do you sell fresh vegetables?

9. We don't drink wine.
10. They live in a village and work in Delhi.
11. American women don't wear saris.
12. Where do you work? I work in an office.
13. They don't eat meat. They only eat vegetarian food.
14. What do you study? I study about India.

10. THE SINGULAR OBLIQUE FORM

There are two cases in Hindi: the direct case and the oblique case. The direct case is used when a noun phrase is not followed by a postposition, and the oblique case is used when a noun phrase is followed by a postposition.

Changes in the singular oblique: When a postposition follows a noun phrase, the whole noun phrase (i.e., a noun or pronoun and all its modifiers) changes into the oblique case. The following are the changes that occur in oblique singular forms:

Nouns: Only marked masculine singular nouns change the - आ ending, becoming - ए in their oblique singular form. Unmarked masculine nouns and marked and unmarked feminine nouns in the singular never change in the oblique case.

लड़का	->	लड़के का नाम	*the boy's name*
छात्र	->	छात्र का नाम	*the student's name*
लड़की	->	लड़की का नाम	*the girl's name*
किताब	->	किताब का नाम	*the name of the book*

Adjectives: Marked adjectives modifying a masculine noun (marked or unmarked) change - आ endings to - ए endings in the oblique case. Marked adjectives modifying feminine nouns and unmarked adjectives do not change in the oblique case.

बड़ा लड़का	->	बड़े लड़के से बात कीजिये । *Talk with the big boy.*
बड़ी लड़की	->	बड़ी लड़की से बात कीजिये । *Talk with the big girl.*

अच्छा छात्र	->	अच्छे छात्र से बात कीजिये ।
		Talk with the good student.
हिन्दुस्तानी छात्र	->	हिन्दुस्तानी छात्र से बात कीजिये ।
		Talk with the Indian student.
पंजाबी औरत	->	पंजाबी औरत से बात कीजिये ।
		Talk with the Punjabi woman.

Note:

(1) Although the singular oblique form and direct plural form of marked masculine nouns and marked adjectives are the same, oblique forms can be recognized by the presence of a following postposition.

(2) A small number of masculine nouns, e.g., पिता *father*, चाचा *uncle*, राजा *king*, etc., although ending in आ, do not change in the oblique case. These same nouns also do not change in plural form.

Pronouns: Like nouns and adjectives, some pronouns take special forms in the oblique case:

Direct form	Oblique form
मैं	मुझ
हम	हम
आप	आप
तुम	तुम
तू	तुझ
यह	इस
वह	उस
ये	इन
वे	उन

Examples:

मुझ से बात कीजिये ।	*Please talk with me.*
उसका नाम बताइये ।	*Please tell (me) his name.*
उस बड़े कमरे में जाइये ।	*Please go in that big room.*

इस सुन्दर साड़ी का दाम बताइये । *Please tell (me) the price of this pretty sari.*
इस छोटी लड़की का नाम क्या है ? *What is the name of this little girl?*

Note: The plural oblique form will be discussed in Section 14.

Exercises

1. Transformation drill

Look at the cloth.	Look at the cloth.
कपड़ा देखिये ।	कपड़े को देखिये ।
किताब देखिये ।	
जूता देखिये ।	
फल देखिये ।	
संतरा देखिये ।	
मेज़ देखिये ।	
दीवार देखिये ।	
कमरा देखिये ।	

2. Substitution drill

We study here.
हम यहाँ पढ़ते हैं ।

in the room
in this room
in this big room
at home
in that city
at (in) the university
at (in) that university
at (in) that famous university
in this library
in this big library

3. Substitution drill

Please call that student.
उस छात्र को बुलाइये ।
that Indian student
that good student
that girl
that pretty girl
that boy
that big boy
that foreigner
that Indian woman
that American woman
that man

4. Transformation drill

That is cheap cloth.	Look at that cheap cloth.
वह सस्ता कपड़ा है ।	उस सस्ते कपड़े को देखिये ।
वह सुन्दर साड़ी है ।	
वह महँगी मेज़ है ।	
वह बड़ा कमरा है ।	
वह मीठा सेब है ।	
वह बड़ी कुरसी है ।	
वह ताज़ा फल है ।	
वह छोटा लड़का है ।	
वह अच्छा छात्र है ।	

5. Substitution drill

Please tell (me) the price of this book.
इस किताब का दाम बताइये ।
this pen
this small chair

that small chair
that sweet apple
this fresh sweet
that good fruit
that pretty sari
this big table
that ripe papaya
this small pencil

6. Substitution drill

What is the name of this Indian boy?
इस हिन्दुस्तानी लड़के का नाम क्या है ?
that student
this good student
that foreigner
this Indian girl
that big man
that American boy
this Pakistani woman
this fruit shop
that beautiful city

7. Translation exercise

1. What is the name of this little girl?
2. My books are on that big table. Bring them here.
3. What is the price of this pretty sari from Banaras?
4. Please call that Indian woman.
5. Bring the newspaper from that room.
6. Don't sit on that big chair near the window.
7. Please tell (me) the name of this small sweet.
8. What is the price of this fresh orange?

9. Your friend works in this big shop.
10. There are many students in this room.
11. My friend lives in that big house.
12. Many foreign students study at (in) this famous university.

11. POSTPOSITIONS को AND से WITH PERSONAL OBJECTS

In Hindi a verb cannot agree with a noun or pronoun followed by a postposition, because a postposition "blocks" the operation of agreement between a noun or pronoun and the verb. In other words, the grammatical subject in Hindi has to be in the direct case for the verb to agree with it.

The object of a sentence, on the other hand, may be marked by the postposition को. If the object is inanimate, that is, not referring to a person, the use of the postposition may add a meaning of definiteness, which is conveyed in English by the definite article "the." The presence or absence of the postposition को is often equivalent to the use of the definite or the indefinite article in English, although this is only an approximate equivalence. Examples:

वह अख़बार ख़रीदती है ।	*She buys a newspaper.*
वह अख़बार को पढ़ती है ।	*She reads the newspaper.*

Sometimes the postposition को is used simply to emphasize the inanimate object. Examples:

किताब पढ़ो ।	*Read the book.*
किताब को पढ़ो ।	*Read the book.*

The meaning of these two sentences is the same, except that in the second sentence the postposition को is used to emphasize the object "book" or to particularize any specific "book" (depending on the context).

If the object of a sentence is animate, that is, if it is a noun or pronoun referring to a human being, then a postposition is generally used with it. If the reference is to a specific person then the use of a postposition is obligatory. This postposition is generally को. Examples:

(आप) उस को बुलाइये ।	*Please call him.*
वह राम को पढ़ाता है ।	*He teaches Ram.*

Some Hindi verbs require the use of the postposition से with an animate object. The most common of these verbs are कहना *to say,* बोलना *to speak,* बात करना *to converse,* पूछना *to ask,* मिलना *to meet.* Examples:

मैं कैम्पस पर दोस्त से मिलती हूँ।	*I meet (my) friend on campus.*
वह छात्र से बात करता है।	*He converses with the student.*

Note:

(1) If a sentence has both an indirect and a direct object, the indirect object (which is generally animate) must be followed by the postposition को or से. The direct object (whether animate or inanimate) will not take any postposition and will therefore not be in the oblique case. Examples:

मैं छात्र को किताब देती हूँ।	*I give the book to the student.*
औरत लड़की को बच्चा देती है।	*The woman gives the child to the girl.*
हम आपसे यह सवाल पूछते हैं।	*We ask you this question.*

(2) When a sentence has both an indirect object and a direct object, the indirect object with the postposition generally precedes the direct object. The standard word order is:

subject indirect object direct object verb

<u>Pronouns with the postposition को</u>

Direct case	Oblique case	With को	Combined form with को
मैं	मुझ	मुझको	मुझे
हम	हम	हमको	हमें
आप	आप	आपको	आपको

Pronouns with the postposition को (contd.)

Direct case	Oblique case	With को	Combined form with को
तुम	तुम	तुमको	तुम्हें
तू	तुझ	तुझको	तुझे
यह	इस	इसको	इसे
वह	उस	उसको	उसे
ये	इन	इनको	इन्हें
वे	उन	उनको	उन्हें
क्या / कौन (sg.)	किस	किसको	किसे
क्या / कौन (pl.)	किन	किनको	किन्हें

Note:

(1) The combined forms of the pronouns with को (extreme right column above) are very frequent in standard Hindi.

(2) The combined forms are possible only when the postposition को directly follows a pronoun. If any other word is used between the pronoun and को, then the combined forms cannot be used. Examples:

आप उसे ये किताबें दीजिये ।	*Please give these books to him.*
आप उस लड़के को ये किताबें दीजिये ।	*Please give these books to that boy.*
आप हमें हिन्दी पढ़ाइये ।	*Teach us Hindi.*
आप हम सब को हिन्दी पढ़ाइये ।	*Teach Hindi to all of us.*

(3) Students should be aware of the distinction between the combined forms of इसको and उसको, which are इसे and उसे, and the oblique forms of these pronouns with the postposition से, which are इससे and उससे respectively.

Exercises

1. Transformation drill

to say	Please say (it) to him.
कहना	उससे कहिये ।
पूछना	
देखना	
बात करना	
सुनना	
बताना	
बुलाना	
बोलना	
मिलना	
सुनाना	

2. Substitution drill

We talk to you.
हम आप से बात करते हैं ।

ask you some questions
speak to you
say this to you
call you
listen to you
see you
understand you
tell you something
tell you a story

3. Substitution drill

Please give him some books.
उसको कुछ किताबें दीजिये ।

me

us
them
him
that girl
her
this student
my friend
this Indian boy
his sister
my brother

4. Substitution drill

We give him some money.
हम उसको कुछ पैसा देते हैं ।

you (polite form)
them
her
you (intimate form)
Ram
his friend
you (familiar form)
his brother's friend

5. Individual conversational response drill

(Add to the basic sentence first the direct object and then the indirect object, if any.)

	Please ask. आप पूछिये ।
this question यह सवाल	Please ask this question. आप यह सवाल पूछिये ।
he वह	Please ask him this question. आप उससे यह सवाल पूछिये ।

आप दीजिये ।

यह किताब
मैं

मैं देता हूँ ।

यह साड़ी
वह लड़की

आप बताइये ।

उसका नाम
हम

आप पढ़ाइये ।

हिन्दी
यह लड़का

फलवाला बेचता है ।

फल
विदेशी

वह बात करती है ।

लड़का

आप देखते हैं ।

कौन

मैं पूछती हूँ ।

सवाल
शिक्षक

तुम मिलते हो ।

कौन

आप यहाँ बुलाइये ।

वह लड़का

आप दीजिये ।

कुछ चाय
मैं

वह सुनाता है ।

कहानी
छोटी लड़की

वह सिखाता है ।

पियानो

हम

मैं कहता हूँ ।

यह

आप

6. Oral questions

तुम किससे सवाल पूछते हो ?
कौन विदेशी को साड़ियाँ दिखाता है ?
आप कैम्पस पर किससे मिलते हैं ?
पिताजी किसको कहानी सुनाते हैं ?
कौन आपको हिन्दी पढ़ाता है ?
तुम किससे हिन्दी बोलते हो ?
फलवाला किसको फल का दाम बताता है ?
क्या तुम रोज़ दोस्त से बात करते हो ?
कौन तुम्हें सितार सिखाता है ?
वह तुम्हें क्या देता है ?

7. Translation Exercise

1. Please tell me his name.
2. Ask the teacher this question.
3. Give these books to Ram.
4. Please tell a story to the little girl.
5. Every day I see your teacher in the library.
6. The fruitseller sells fruits to the American.
7. We meet him every day on the campus.
8. Please give us some Indian tea.
9. To whom does he teach Hindi?
10. We talk to them in Hindi.

12. THE PRESENT PROGRESSIVE TENSE

The present progressive tense in Hindi is used to indicate an action that is actually taking place at the time of speaking, in contrast to the present habitual tense, which refers to a habitual action or state.

Formation: The present progressive tense has three parts: (1) the verb stem; (2) the progressive endings रहा, रहे, or रही, which agree in number and gender with the subject of the verb; thus रहा is used if the subject is masculine singular, रहे if the subject is masculine plural, and रही if the subject is feminine singular or plural; and (3) the appropriate simple present tense form of the verb होना *to be* to mark the tense of the action. The basic pattern is:

stem	रहा (masc. sg.)	है (sg.)
	रहे (masc. pl.)	हैं (pl.)
	रही (fem. sg. or pl.)	हूँ (if the subject is मैं)
		हो (if the subject is तुम)

Examples with the verb पढ़ना *to read, to study*:

मैं किताब पढ़ रहा / रही हूँ ।	*I* (M/F) *am reading a book.*
हम किताब पढ़ रहे / रही हैं ।	*We* (M/F) *are reading a book.*
आप किताब पढ़ रहे / रही हैं ।	*You* (M/F) *are reading a book.*
तुम किताब पढ़ रहे / रही हो ।	*You* (M/F) *are reading a book.*
तू किताब पढ़ रहा / रही है ।	*You* (M/F) *are reading a book.*
यह किताब पढ़ रहा / रही है ।	*He/She is reading a book.*
वह किताब पढ़ रहा / रही है ।	*He/She is reading a book.*
ये किताब पढ़ रहे / रही हैं ।	*They* (M/F) *are reading a book.*
वे किताब पढ़ रहे / रही हैं ।	*They* (M/F) *are reading a book.*

In this verb form the progressive endings are written as separate words and are not joined with the verb stem.

In the present progressive tense, a negative statement can be formed by adding the negative particle नहीं either before or after the verb stem. The present tense forms of the verb होना are not generally dropped in negative statements as they are in the present habitual tense. If these forms are dropped, then, as in the present habitual tense, a special nasalization is added to distinguish feminine plural forms from feminine singular forms. Examples:

आपकी बहनें किताब नहीं पढ़ रही हैं । *Your sisters are not reading the book.*
आपकी बहनें किताब पढ़ नहीं रही हैं ।
आपकी बहनें किताब नहीं पढ़ रहीं ।

Note:

(1) Although the present progressive tense is basically used to talk about an action that is actually in progress at the time of speaking, sometimes this tense is used for future actions also. (The actual future tense can also be used in these situations.) Example:

मेरा दोस्त कल भारत जा रहा है । *My friend is going to India tomorrow.*

This use of the present progressive tense to indicate a future action is most common with verbs of motion, e.g., आना, जाना, etc. English also employs the present progressive tense for future actions as seen in the translation above.

(2) In English sometimes the distinction between the present habitual and the present progressive tense is not clear. For example, the sentence "My father is working in this office" could mean either that he works here regularly or that he is actually working at the time of speaking. In Hindi this distinction is made very clear, and the present progressive tense is used only for those actions that are actually in progress at the time of speaking.

For actions that are performed on a regular basis, the present habitual tense is used.

(3) If the plural pronouns refer to a group of males and females, the masculine plural forms are used. Examples:

आप किताब पढ़ रहे हैं।	*You* (M or M & F) *are reading a book.*
वे किताब पढ़ रहे हैं।	*They* (M or M & F) *are reading a book.*

Exercises

1. Transformation drill

to go home	I am going home.
घर जाना	मैं घर जा रहा हूँ।
फल खाना	
अँग्रेज़ी बोलना	
घर जाना	
दूध पीना	
पत्र लिखना	
काम करना	
किताबें पढ़ना	
सवाल पूछना	
कपड़े ख़रीदना	
हिन्दी पढ़ना	

2. Substitution drill

He is talking with a friend.
वह दोस्त से बात कर रहा है।
हम
वे (M)
यह (M)

तुम (F)
ये (F)
तू (M)
कौन (sg.)
तुम लोग
वे लोग (F)
हम लोग
आप (F)
कौन (pl.)
मेरा दोस्त
हम सब

3. Transformation drill

to do	What are you doing?
करना	तुम क्या कर रहे हो ?
खाना	
देखना	
बोलना	
लिखना	
दिखाना	
सुनना	
बेचना	
ख़रीदना	
पीना	

4. Chain drill

Q: What are you doing?
तुम क्या कर रहे हो ?

A: I am studying Hindi.
मैं हिन्दी पढ़ रहा हूँ ।

5. Transformation drill

The girl writes a letter to a friend.	The girl is writing a letter to a friend.
लड़की दोस्त को पत्र लिखती है ।	लड़की दोस्त को पत्र लिख रही है ।

तुम क्या करते हो ?
आप लोग क्या पढ़ते हैं ?
वे लोग यहाँ कपड़े ख़रीदते हैं ।
मैं लाइब्रेरी जाती हूँ ।
कौन दूध पीता है ?
कौन शिक्षक से सवाल पूछता है ?
तुम काम करती हो ।
हम आपको जवाब देते हैं ।
मेरा दोस्त अख़बार पढ़ता है ।
लड़की कुरसी पर बैठती है ।
हम आपसे हिन्दी बोलते हैं ।

6. Oral questions

तुम क्या कर रहे हो ?
तुम लोग कहाँ जा रहे हो ?
आपके दोस्त क्या पी रहे हैं ?
तू किससे बात कर रहा है ?
आप किसको देख रहे हैं ?
आप लोग कहाँ जा रहे हैं ?
शिक्षक किसको हिन्दी पढ़ा रहे हैं ?
वह किससे सवाल पूछ रहा है ?
कौन लाइब्रेरी जा रहा है ?
आप किससे हिन्दी बोल रहे हैं ?
वह लड़का उस कमरे में क्या कर रहा है ?
वे छात्र कौन-सी किताब पढ़ रहे हैं ?
वह किसको कहानी सुना रहा है ?
कौन भारत के बारे में पढ़ रहा है ?

7. Chain drill

Q: Who is buying books?
कौन किताबें ख़रीद रहा है ?

A: The students are buying books.
छात्र किताबें ख़रीद रहे हैं ।

8. Transformation drill

We are speaking English.	We are not speaking English.
हम अँग्रेज़ी बोल रहे हैं ।	हम अँग्रेज़ी नहीं बोल रहे हैं ।
हम अख़बार पढ़ रहे हैं ।	
हम यूनिवर्सिटी जा रहे हैं ।	
हम उर्दू लिख रहे हैं ।	
हम खाना पका रहे हैं ।	
हम किताबें ख़रीद रहे हैं ।	
हम चाय पी रहे हैं ।	
हम काम कर रहे हैं ।	

9. Individual conversational response drill

Are we speaking French?	No, not French; we are speaking Hindi.
क्या हम फ़्रेंच बोल रहे हैं ?	नहीं, फ़्रेंच नही; हम हिन्दी बोल रहे हैं ।
क्या आप उर्दू लिख रहे हैं ?	
क्या आप चाय पी रहे हैं ?	
क्या ये विद्यार्थी घर जा रहे हैं ?	
क्या तुम जूते ख़रीद रहे हो ?	
क्या आपका दोस्त उर्दू पढ़ रहा है ?	
क्या आप अख़बार पढ़ रहे हैं ?	
क्या फलवाला मिठाई बेच रहा है ?	
क्या ये छात्र उर्दू लिख रहे हैं ?	
क्या तुम अंग्रेज़ी की किताब ख़रीद रहे हो ?	
क्या वे लोग हिन्दुस्तानी संगीत सुन रहे हैं ?	

10. Translation exercise

1. I am listening to Indian music.
2. Are you reading the Hindi newspaper? (polite form)
3. The student is buying books from this bookstore.
4. We are not studying French. We are studying Hindi.
5. She is asking us many questions.
6. What are you doing here in my room? (familiar form)
7. Are you singing a Hindi song? (intimate form)
8. She is not going home. She is going to the party.
9. They are speaking Urdu with that Pakistani man.
10. What are they drinking? They are drinking cold coffee.
11. My friend is studying in that room.
12. Our teacher is telling us about India.

13. INDIRECT VERB CONSTRUCTIONS

Various verbs and expressions in Hindi are used in indirect verb constructions. In these constructions the general connotation is that the subject is not actively involved in the activity of the verb and that the action or condition happens to the subject.

Indirect verb constructions are very common in Hindi and are used in many different situations. The sentence structure of these constructions is very different from the one used in equivalent English sentences. But since all indirect verb constructions follow the same basic pattern, once this pattern is learned it will not be difficult for a non-Hindi speaker to perceive the situation from a Hindi speaker's point of view. The basic pattern is:

(1) The noun or pronoun designating the principal of the action in the English sentence (i.e., the person who likes someone or something, the person who knows about someone or something, the person who knows the skill, the person who gets or obtains the object, the person who experiences the feeling) becomes the indirect object in the corresponding Hindi sentence and is followed by the postposition को.

(2) The direct object of the English sentence functions as the subject in the corresponding Hindi sentence and the verb agrees with it.

Thus, the English sentence "She likes these saris" is expressed in Hindi as:

Indirect object + को	subject	verb
उसको	ये साड़ियाँ	पसन्द हैं
To her	*these saris*	*are pleasing*

In this section four verbs that occur in indirect verb constructions are discussed: (1) पसन्द होना, (2) मालूम होना, (3) आना, and (4) मिलना.

(1) **पसन्द होना:** Although translated into English as "to like," this verb in Hindi literally means "to be pleasing to" and is used in indirect verb constructions. Examples:

उस औरत को बनारसी साड़ियाँ पसन्द हैं ।
That woman likes the Banarasi saris. (lit., *The saris of Banaras are pleasing to that woman.*)
लड़की को कहानियाँ पढ़ना पसन्द है ।
The girl likes to read stories. (Note: Here the verb agrees with the infinitive "पढ़ना.")
उसको मैं पसन्द हूँ ।
He likes me. (or *She likes me.*)

(2) **मालूम होना:** This verb is generally translated as "to know" (lit., "to be known to") but has the general connotation "to have information about something or someone." Examples:

क्या आपको सब जवाब मालूम हैं ।
Do you know all the answers? (lit., *Are all the answers known to you?*)
मुझे उस छात्र का नाम मालूम नहीं है ।
I don't know that student's name.

(3) **आना:** This verb is used in both direct and indirect verb constructions. In direct verb constructions it means "to come." Example:

वह कब घर आता है ? *When does he come home?*

When used in indirect verb constructions, आना is translated as "to know" and is generally used to express the knowledge of learned skills. Because of this special meaning, the verb आना in indirect verb constructions usually indicates knowing some language or knowing how to do something. Examples:

मुझे हिन्दी आती है । *I know Hindi.*

उसको सितार बजाना आता है । *He knows how to play the sitar.*

(4) **मिलना:** This verb expresses different meanings in different contexts. Like आना it is used in both direct and indirect verb constructions.

A. In direct verb constructions the verb मिलना often means "to meet (someone)" with the connotation that the meeting is intentional or arranged.

मैं कॉफ़ी की दुकान में दोस्त से मिलती हूँ ।
I meet with (my) friend in the coffee shop.
हम रोज़ क्लास में आप से मिलते हैं ।
Every day we meet you in the class.

Note: The object (i.e., the person one meets with) takes the postposition से.

B. In indirect verb constructions मिलना has one of the following two meanings:

(1) When the subject in the Hindi sentence is animate, the verb मिलना in indirect verb constructions means "to happen to meet someone," and the implication here is that the mentioned meeting is unexpected and unplanned. Example:

हमें इस दुकान में अक्सर हिन्दुस्तानी लोग मिलते हैं ।
In this shop we often meet (come across) Indian people.

(2) When the subject in the Hindi sentence is inanimate, the verb मिलना has the general meaning "to be available to," "to get," "to receive." Examples:

वहाँ सस्ती किताबें मिलती हैं ।
Inexpensive books are available there.
उस दुकान में सुन्दर साड़ियाँ मिलती हैं ।
In that shop (you) get beautiful saris.

मुझे हर हफ़्ते माँ का पत्र मिलता है ।
Every week I receive mother's letter.

Many other verbs and expressions occur in indirect verb constructions. Some of them will be discussed later.

Exercises

1. Substitution drill

I like Indian food.
मुझे हिन्दुस्तानी खाना पसन्द है ।
ये किताबें
बर्कली
अमरीकन लोग
मद्रासी साड़ियाँ
हिन्दी
हिन्दुस्तानी लोग
हिन्दुस्तानी फ़िल्में
यह शहर
ठंडा मौसम
यह यूनिवर्सिटी

2. Substitution drill

Which book do you like?
तुम्हें कौन-सी किताब पसन्द है ।
शहर
फ़िल्म
संगीत
क्लास

देश
भाषा
अख़बार
मौसम
छात्र

3. Chain drill

Q: Which book do you like?
तुम्हें कौन-सी किताब पसन्द है ?

A: I like this book.
मुझे यह किताब पसन्द है ।

Q: Which girl do you like?
आपको कौन-सी लड़की पसन्द है ?

A: I like Sita.
मुझे सीता पसन्द है ।

4. Substitution drill

We like to see films.
हमें फ़िल्में देखना पसन्द है ।
हिन्दी पढ़ना
गाना गाना
खाना पकाना
पार्टी में जाना
संगीत सुनना
किताब पढ़ना
हिन्दुस्तानी खाना खाना

5. Chain drill

Q: What do you like to do ?
तुम्हें क्या करना पसन्द है ?

A: I like to listen to music.
मुझे संगीत सुनना पसन्द है ।

6. Oral questions

क्या आपको बर्कली पसन्द है ?
तुम्हें कैसा मौसम पसन्द है ?
क्या तुम्हें बनारसी साड़ियाँ पसन्द हैं ?
आपको कैसा संगीत सुनना पसन्द है ?
क्या आपको हिन्दी पसन्द है ?
किसको फ़िल्म देखना पसन्द है ?
तुझे कैसा खाना पसन्द है ?
तुम्हें कहाँ जाना पसन्द है ?
तुम्हें चाय पसन्द है या कॉफ़ी ?
आपको कौन पसन्द है ?
क्या तुम्हें बर्कली का मौसम पसन्द है ?
आपको हिन्दुस्तानी खाना पसन्द है या अमरीकन खाना ?
तुम्हें क्या करना पसन्द है ?
तुम्हें क्या पढ़ना पसन्द है ?

7. Substitution drill

Do you know the answer?
आपको जवाब मालूम है ?
उसका नाम
सवाल
क्या
मेरा नाम
इस शहर का नाम

उस किताब का दाम
उस गाँव का नाम
उस छात्र का नाम
उसकी बहन का नाम
इस सवाल का जवाब

8. Substitution drill

We know everything.
हमें सब कुछ मालूम है ।
I
You (polite form)
This boy
You (intimate form)
They
That girl
This student
You (familiar form)

9. Individual conversational response drill

Who is he ? Do you know ?	Yes, I know. He is David.
वह कौन है ? आपको मालूम है ?	हाँ, मुझे मालूम है । वह डेविड है ।

ये जूते कहाँ से हैं ? आपको मालूम है ?
सस्ता खाना कहाँ मिलता है ? आपको मालूम है ?
यह क्या है ? आपको मालूम है ?
अच्छे हिन्दुस्तानी कपड़े कहाँ मिलते हैं ? आपको मालूम है ?
सुन्दर साड़ियाँ कहाँ मिलती हैं ? आपको मालूम है ?
इस छात्र का नाम क्या है ? आपको मालूम है ?
इस किताब का दाम क्या है ? आपको मालूम है ?

10. Chain drill

Q: What is this? Do you know?
यह क्या है ? आपको मालूम है ?

A: Yes, I know. It's a table.
हाँ, मुझे मालूम है। यह मेज़ है।

Q: Who is he? Do you know?
वह कौन है ? आपको मालूम है ?

A: No, I don't know.
नहीं, मुझे मालूम नहीं।

11. Substitution drill

Indian sweets are obtained there. (i.e., One gets Indian sweets there.)
वहाँ हिन्दुस्तानी मिठाइयाँ मिलती हैं।

सुन्दर साड़ियाँ
हिन्दी की किताबें
अच्छे कपड़े
सस्ते फल
अच्छा खाना
अमरीकन जूते
सस्ती चीज़ें
सुन्दर तसवीरें

12. Individual conversational response drill

What does one get in a bookstore?	One gets books.
किताब की दुकान पर क्या मिलता है ?	किताबें मिलती हैं।
कपड़े की दुकान पर क्या मिलता है ?	
साड़ी की दुकान पर क्या मिलता है ?	
जूते की दुकान पर क्या मिलता है ?	

फल की दुकान पर कौन मिलता है ?
मिठाई की दुकान पर कौन मिलता है ?
विश्वविद्यालय में कौन मिलते हैं ?
हिन्दी की क्लास में कौन मिलते हैं ?
अच्छी मिठाइयाँ कहाँ मिलती हैं ?
सस्ते कपड़े कहाँ मिलते हैं ?
रेशमी साड़ियाँ कहाँ मिलती हैं ?

13. Chain drill

Q: Where does one get good Indian food?
अच्छा भारतीय खाना कहाँ मिलता है ?

A: In that shop.
उस दुकान में ।

14. Substitution drill

The foreigner knows Hindi.
विदेशी को हिन्दी आती है ।
मुझे
आपको
तुम्हें
हमें
तुझे
उसको
इनको
इस छात्र को
इस लड़के को

15. Substitution drill

Do you know Hindi?
क्या आपको हिन्दी आती है ?

how to speak Hindi
Urdu
how to write Urdu
English
how to read English
how to play the sitar
how to play the piano
how to cook Indian food
how to dance
how to swim

16. Chain drill

Q: Do you know French?
क्या आपको फ़्रेंच आती है ?

A: Yes, I know a little French.
हाँ, मुझे थोड़ी फ़्रेंच आती है ।

Q: Do you know how to write Urdu?
क्या आपको उर्दू लिखना आता है ?

A: No, I don't know how to write Urdu.
नहीं, मुझे उर्दू लिखना नहीं आता ।

17. Translation exercise

1. My friend likes Indian films.
2. Do you know that Indian student's name?
3. He likes to read Hindi stories.
4. The foreigner doesn't know the name of this village.

5. We like Indian food. What kind of food do you like?
6. She knows how to speak Urdu, but she doesn't know how to write it.
7. What do you get in this shop?
8. Do you know how to cook Indian food?
9. In this shop we get beautiful silk saris.
10. I like cold weather, but my wife likes hot weather.
11. How many languages do you know?
12. They get a lot of money.
13. I like to play the sitar.
14. That smart student knows all the answers.

14. THE PLURAL OBLIQUE FORM

Plural oblique forms, like singular oblique forms, are used for all the members of a noun phrase (i.e., a noun or pronoun and all its modifiers) when followed by a postposition.

Nouns: All masculine and feminine nouns, whether marked or unmarked, have the ending - ओं for their plural oblique form. Marked masculine nouns change the - आ ending to - ओं while all other masculine and feminine nouns have the oblique plural ending - ओं added to their direct singular form. Examples:

	Singular		Plural	Plural oblique
marked masc. noun	केला	*banana*	केले	केलों का
	लड़का	*boy*	लड़के	लड़कों का
unmarked masc. noun	बाज़ार	*market*	बाज़ार	बाज़ारों का
	फल	*fruit*	फल	फलों का
marked fem. noun	मिठाई	*sweet*	मिठाइयाँ	मिठाइयों का
	कुरसी	*chair*	कुरसियाँ	कुरसियों का
unmarked fem. noun	किताब	*book*	किताबें	किताबों का
	माता	*mother*	माताएँ	माताओं का

Note:

(1) The postposition का is used in the above chart as an example of a Hindi postposition and can be replaced by any other postposition (e.g., लड़कों से, लड़कों को, etc.).

(2) The general spelling rule is that the final long ई is shortened to short इ and य is inserted before adding the endings आ, आँ, ओ, or ओं, and the final long ऊ is shortened to short उ before adding आ, आँ, ओ, or ओं. Examples:

Singular		Plural	Plural oblique
आदमी	*man*	आदमी	आदमियों का
भाई	*brother*	भाई	भाइयों का
धोबी	*washerman*	धोबी	धोबियों का
हिन्दू	*Hindu*	हिन्दू	हिन्दुओं का
डाकू	*dacoit*	डाकू	डाकुओं का
चाकू	*knife*	चाकू	चाकुओं का

Adjectives: Adjectives modifying plural nouns, whether masculine or feminine, marked or unmarked, do not change in plural oblique form. Examples:

अच्छे लड़के	*good boys*	->	अच्छे लड़कों का
अच्छे छात्र	*good students*	->	अच्छे छात्रों का
अच्छी लड़कियाँ	*good girls*	->	अच्छी लड़कियों का
अच्छी औरतें	*good women*	->	अच्छी औरतों का
सुन्दर जूते	*beautiful shoes*	->	सुन्दर जूतों का
सुन्दर पेड़	*beautiful trees*	->	सुन्दर पेड़ों का
सुन्दर साड़ियाँ	*beautiful saris*	->	सुन्दर साड़ियों का
सुन्दर तसवीरें	*beautiful pictures*	->	सुन्दर तसवीरों का

The oblique forms of pronouns have been discussed previously in Section 10.

Exercises

1. Substitution drill

Ask those boys.
उन लड़कों से पूछिये ।

लड़कियों
आदमियों
औरतों
बच्चों
दुकानदारों
फलवालों
विदेशियों
छात्रों
शिक्षकों

2. Transformation drill

Buy these shoes.	Buy these shoes.
ये जूते ख़रीदिये ।	इन जूतों को ख़रीदिये ।
ये साड़ियाँ देखिये ।	
ये कुरसियाँ ठीक कीजिये ।	
ये कपड़े देखिये ।	
ये किताबें पढ़िये ।	
ये कागज़ ख़रीदिये ।	
ये वाक्य पढ़िये ।	
ये चीज़ें ठीक कीजिये ।	
ये फूल देखिये ।	

3. Substitution drill

Please tell (me) the price of these pretty saris.
इन सुन्दर साड़ियों का दाम बताइये ।
these Indian saris

these fresh sweets
these good tables
these Pakistani clothes
these small fruits
these fresh vegetables
these good shoes
these big books
these pretty things
these big papers
these pretty flowers

4. Transformation drill

Look at these Indian saris. ये हिन्दुस्तानी साड़ियाँ देखो ।	Look at these Indian saris. इन हिन्दुस्तानी साड़ियों को देखो ।

ये अच्छी किताबें पढ़ो ।
ये महँगे कपड़े ख़रीदो ।
ये ताज़े फल ख़रीदो ।
ये बंगाली मिठाइयाँ खाओ ।
ये सस्ते कपड़े ख़रीदो ।
ये सुन्दर कमीज़ें धोओ ।
ये दिल्ली के बाज़ार देखो ।
ये ताज़े सन्तरे खाओ ।
ये अच्छे जूते ख़रीदो ।
ये बड़ी कुरसियाँ ठीक करो ।
ये मुश्किल सवाल पूछो ।

5. Individual conversational response drill

(Add to the basic sentence first the direct object and then the indirect object, if any.)

	Please give. आप दीजिये ।
these sweets ये मिठाइयाँ	Please give these sweets. आप ये मिठाइयाँ दीजिये ।

children	
बच्चे	आप बच्चों को ये मिठाइयाँ दीजिये ।
	आप पढ़ाइये ।
हिन्दी	
ये विदेशी	
	वह बेचता है ।
किताबें	
लोग	
	शिक्षक पूछते हैं ।
सवाल	
सब छात्र	
	हम कैम्पस पर मिलते हैं ।
बहुत दोस्त	
	वह दिखाता है ।
ताज महल	
लोग	
	वह बात कर रही है ।
हिन्दुस्तानी लड़कियाँ	
	पिताजी बता रहे हैं ।
भारत के बारे में	
लड़के	
	मेरी माँ सुनाती हैं ।
कहानियाँ	
बच्चे	
	आप बुलाइये ।
वे आदमी	
	वह दिखा रहा है ।
रेशमी साड़ियाँ	
विदेशी औरतें	

6. Translation exercise

1. What is the price of these pretty saris?
2. He is talking with some Indian students.
3. My husband cooks Indian food for my friends.
4. Show these expensive shoes to those foreign customers.
5. Please bring some wine for these people.
6. He teaches Hindi to these foreigners.
7. Give these sweets to those children.
8. Our teacher is asking students some questions.
9. These Indian men know a little Sanskrit.
10. My brothers like to eat Indian food.

15. चाहना AND चाहिये

The verb चाहना *to wish, to want, to desire* is commonly used in Hindi. It indicates either a desire for something or, more frequently, a desire to carry out some action. In the first usage it takes an inanimate noun as its object; in the second situation the object of the verb is always an infinitive representing the desired action or activity. This infinitive comes directly before the verb. Examples:

मैं कुछ आम चाहती हूँ ।
I want (desire) some mangoes.
लड़की नये कपड़े चाहती है ।
The girl wants (desires) new clothes.
ये छात्र भारत जाना चाहते हैं ।
These students want (wish) to go to India.
मेरी बेटी उर्दू सीखना चाहती है ।
My daughter wants (wishes) to learn Urdu.
भारत में हम ताज महल देखना चाहते हैं ।
In India we want (wish) to see the Taj Mahal.

Note: When the verb चाहना has an animate noun as its object, it has the idiomatic meaning "to love (to desire)" that person. Example:

लड़की पीटर को बहुत चाहती है । *The girl loves Peter very much.*

चाहिये (चाहिए): Although the verb चाहिये appears as if it is the polite imperative form of the verb चाहना, it does not function like an imperative at all. It has the general meaning "to be needed," "to be wanted," "to be required." The verb चाहिये always occurs in an indirect verb construction; therefore the subject of a corresponding English sentence (i.e., the person who needs or requires something) becomes the indirect object in Hindi followed by the postposition को, and the object (i.e., the thing that is needed or required) functions as the subject with which the verb agrees. The plural of चाहिये is चाहियें, but some speakers use चाहिये for both singular and plural agreement. Examples:

आपको क्या चाहिये ?
What do you want (need)? (lit., *to you what is needed?*)
उस ग़रीब आदमी को खाना ख़रीदने के लिए कुछ पैसा चाहिये ।
That poor man needs some money to (in order to) buy food.
मुझे दो किताबें चाहियें ।
I need two books.

Note: Although both चाहना and चाहिये can be translated into English as "want," चाहना conveys more of a desire while चाहिये indicates more of a need. Examples:

मुझे नये जूते चाहियें । *I want (need) new shoes.*
मैं नये जूते चाहता हूँ । *I want (desire) new shoes.*

Exercises

1. Substitution drill

We want new books.
हम नई किताबें चाहते हैं ।
ताज़े फल
नये जूते
कुछ पैसा
पुरानी चीज़ें
सुन्दर कपड़े
बहुत चीज़ें
सब कुछ
बहुत पैसा

2. Substitution drill

The girl wants to go to India.
लड़की भारत जाना चाहती है ।

to write a letter
to sleep
to see the film
to buy a sari
to dance
to listen to the music
to work in this office
to learn Hindi
to meet the President

3. Oral questions

तुम क्या चाहते हो ?
तुम क्या करना चाहते हो ?
आप क्या पढ़ना चाहते हैं ?
तू क्या सीखना चाहता है ?
आप किस से मिलना चाहते हैं ?
तुम किस को पत्र लिखना चाहते हो ?
आप क्या ख़रीदना चाहते हैं ?
तू क्या बेचना चाहता है ?
तू कहाँ जाना चाहता है ?
तुम कहाँ रहना चाहते हो ?
आप क्या देखना चाहते हैं ?

4. Chain drill

Q: What do you want?
तुम क्या चाहते हो ?

A: I want some books.
मैं कुछ किताबें चाहता हूँ ।

Q: What do you want to buy?
तुम क्या ख़रीदना चाहते हो ?

A: I want to buy some clothes.
मैं कुछ कपड़े ख़रीदना चाहता हूँ ।

5. Substitution drill

I need a pen.
मुझे एक कलम चाहिये ।
बहुत पैसा
कुछ खाना
चार किताबें
एक कमरा
सब कुछ
कुछ नहीं
बहुत चीज़ें
कुछ पानी
दूध
नये कपड़े
एक बनारसी साड़ी
गरम कॉफ़ी

6. Chain drill

Q: What do you need?
आपको क्या चाहिये ?

A: I need some money.
मुझे कुछ पैसा चाहिये ।

Q: How many books do you need?
तुम्हें कितनी किताबें चाहियें ?

A: I need only one book.
मुझे सिर्फ़ एक किताब चाहिये ।

7. Oral questions

आपको क्या चाहिये ?
आप क्या करना चाहते हैं ?
तुम्हें कितना दूध चाहिये ?
तुम किस से मिलना चाहते हो ?
तुम कहाँ जाना चाहते हो ?
क्या तुझे नये जूते चाहियें ?
आप क्या ख़रीदना चाहते हैं ?
किसको यह किताब चाहिये ?
कौन भारत जाना चाहता है ?
किसको कुछ पैसा चाहिये ?
मुझे कुछ नहीं चाहिये । तुझे क्या चाहिये ?
किनको मदद चाहिये ?

8. Translation exercise

1. We want new clothes and new shoes.
2. These poor people need food and some clothes.
3. My sister wants to learn to play the sitar.
4. What do you need? I don't need anything.
5. Who wants to go with me?
6. He doesn't want to read these books.
7. Why does she need so many expensive clothes?
8. How many books do you need?
9. What do you want to do tonight? I want to see a movie.
10. We want to learn Hindi because we want to go to India.
11. They need some money to buy bread.
12. I want good food and good clothes. What do you want?

16. THE PAST OF होना *TO BE*

The past tense forms of the verb होना *to be* are था, थे, थी, and थीं. These forms agree with their subjects in number and gender.

था is used with a masculine singular subject.
थे is used with a masculine plural subject.
थी is used with a feminine singular subject.
थीं is used with a feminine plural subject.

Note:

(1) In the past tense, the verb होना does not have any special forms for मैं and तुम as it does in the present. Examples:

मैं क्लास में हूँ।	*I am in the class.*
मैं क्लास में था।	*I was in the class.*
तुम कहाँ हो ?	*Where are you?*
तुम कहाँ थे ?	*Where were you?*

(2) Past forms of होना do differentiate between masculine and feminine genders while the present forms do not. Examples:

वह शिक्षक है।	*He/She is a teacher.*
वह शिक्षक था।	*He was a teacher.*
वह शिक्षक थी।	*She was a teacher.*

Exercises

1. Conversational response drill

Where was that boy yesterday?	He was here.
वह लड़का कल कहाँ था ?	यहाँ था ।

सब छात्र कल कहाँ थे ?
यह लड़की कल कहाँ थी ?
ये लड़कियाँ कल कहाँ थीं ?
आप लोग कल कहाँ थे ?
आपका दोस्त कल कहाँ था ?
तुम लोग कल कहाँ थे ?
तू कल कहाँ था ?
तुम कल कहाँ थे ?
आपकी बहनें कल कहाँ थीं ?

2. Individual conversational response drill

(Give any appropriate answer.)

How was that book?	It was good.
वह किताब कैसी थी ?	अच्छी थी ।

वह फ़िल्म कैसी थी ?
वह क्लास कैसी थी ?
राष्ट्रपति का भाषण कैसा था ?
आपके दोस्त कैसे थे ?
वहाँ का मौसम कैसा था ?
तुम्हारा काम कैसा था ?
वे चीज़ें कैसी थीं ?
कल खाना कैसा था ?
वे किताबें कैसी थीं ?
वहाँ सब लोग कैसे थे ?
आपका परिवार कैसा था ?

3. Chain drill

Q: How were those things?
वे चीज़ें कैसी थीं ?

A: They were good.
अच्छी थीं ।

Q: How were the books?
किताबें कैसी थीं ?

A: They were interesting.
दिलचस्प थीं ।

4. Substitution drill

Where was that man the day before yesterday?
वह आदमी परसों कहाँ था ?
आप लोग
छोटी लड़की
वह छात्र
तुम्हारा दोस्त
मेरा भाई
उसकी बहन / बहिन
आपकी पत्नी
आपकी माता जी
आपके पिता जी
उसके माता-पिता
उसकी सहेली
सब लोग
तुम लोग

5. Chain drill

Q: Where were you the day before yesterday in the evening?
तुम परसों शाम को कहाँ थे ?

A: I was on campus.
मैं कैम्पस पर था ।

Q: Where was your brother yesterday in the afternoon?
तुम्हारा भाई कल दोपहर को कहाँ था ?

A: He was in the library.
पुस्तकालय में था ।

Q: Where were you last night?
तुम कल रात को कहाँ थे ?

A: I was at home.
घर में था ।

6. Translation exercise

1. Yesterday those students were not in the room.
2. Last night the food was good.
3. Who were they? They were our friends.
4. Where was she? She was in the office.
5. How was the film? It was very interesting.
6. Yesterday the weather was not good.
7. Where were you the day before yesterday? I was at home.
8. How was his speech? It was not good.
9. How was the party? It was very enjoyable.
10. Yesterday how many people were at the meeting?

17. THE PAST HABITUAL TENSE

The past habitual tense is used to describe frequent, regular, or habitual actions in the past, corresponding to "used to" in English sentences. Often the past habitual tense is not used in English in situations where it would normally be used in Hindi. For example, "Last year he used to study at this university" is grammatically correct for a Hindi speaker although in English one would say, "Last year he studied at this university."

Formation: The formation of the past habitual tense is identical to the formation of the present habitual tense except that the appropriate past forms of the verb होना are used instead of their present forms. Examples:

मेरा भाई यहाँ पढ़ता है ।	*My brother studies here.*
मेरा भाई यहाँ पढ़ता था ।	*My brother used to study here.*
वे लड़के इस पार्क में खेलते हैं ।	*Those boys play in this park.*
वे लड़के इस पार्क में खेलते थे ।	*Those boys used to play in this park.*

Note: In negative statements, नहीं is used directly before the entire verb, but the past tense form of the verb होना is not dropped as is done in the negative of the present habitual tense.

वे बच्चे इस पार्क में नहीं खेलते थे ।
Those children did not (used to) play in this park.

Exercises

1. Substitution drill

Those boys used to live here.
वे लड़के यहाँ रहते थे ।

used to work
used to study
used to play
used to sing
used to eat
used to sit
used to come
used to sleep

2. Substitution drill

Last year I used to work here.
पिछले साल मैं यहाँ काम करता था ।

हम
वह लड़की
वे लोग
तुम (F)
वे औरतें
मेरे पिता
सैली और मार्था
जॉन
आप लोग
मेरा भाई
उसकी सहेली
आप

3. Transformation drill

We study Hindi. हम हिन्दी पढ़ते हैं।	We used to study Hindi. हम हिन्दी पढ़ते थे।

ये लड़कियाँ यहाँ रहती हैं।
मैं अँग्रेज़ी बोलता हूँ।
वे औरतें इस दफ़्तर में काम करती हैं।
तुम कहाँ रहती हो ?
मैं यहाँ पढ़ती हूँ।
बच्चे इस पार्क में खेलते हैं।
तू क्या करती है ?
मेरी दोस्त तबला बजाती है।
उसका भाई यहाँ काम करता है।
आपके माता-पिता कहाँ रहते हैं ?
मेरी बहन इस यूनिवर्सिटी में पढ़ती है।

4. Chain drill

Q: Where did you used to live?
तुम कहाँ रहते थे ?

A: I used to live in Delhi.
मैं दिल्ली में रहता था।

Q: Where did you used to work?
आप कहाँ काम करती थीं ?

A: I used to work in this office.
मैं इस दफ़्तर में काम करती थी।

5. Translation exercise

1. They used to study in the library.
2. Last year I used to live in a big house near the university.
3. She used to buy books from this store.
4. Who used to work here? My brother used to work here.
5. He used to ask the teacher many questions.
6. Last year we used to study at (in) this university.
7. They (F) used to buy saris from this shop.
8. The children used to play in this park.
9. Ram and I used to see many Hindi films.
10. Last year her brother used to work in this office.

18. THE PAST PROGRESSIVE TENSE

The past progressive tense is used to indicate an action that was in progress at a certain time in the past.

Formation: The formation of the past progressive tense is the same as the formation of the present progressive tense except that the simple present forms of the verb होना are replaced by their corresponding past forms. Examples:

कल हम लाइब्रेरी में पढ़ रहे थे ।	*Yesterday we were studying in the library.*
आपके पिता दोस्तों से बात कर रहे थे ।	*Your father was talking with friends.*
बच्चा कमरे में सो रहा था ।	*The child was sleeping in the room.*
वे लड़कियाँ कहाँ खेल रही थीं ।	*Where were those girls playing?*
यहाँ कल बारिश हो रही थी ।	*It was raining here yesterday.*

In negative statements, the negative particle नहीं is added either before or after the verb stem. Examples:

वे छात्र क्लास नहीं जा रहे थे ।	*Those students were not going to the class.*
वे छात्र क्लास जा नहीं रहे थे ।	*Those students were not going to the class.*

Exercises

1. Substitution drill

He was going to the market.
वह बाज़ार जा रहा था ।
मैं (M)
हम लोग

आप (F)
जॉन और जिम
वे लोग
तू (F)
तुम (M)
वह आदमी
कौन
लीसा और जेन
तुम लोग

2. Transformation drill

I am buying fruits.	I was buying fruits.
मैं फल ख़रीद रहा हूँ ।	मैं फल ख़रीद रहा था ।

लड़की दोस्त से सवाल पूछ रही है ।
बच्चे पार्क में खेल रहे हैं ।
वह भाषण दे रहा है ।
वह सितार बजा रहा है ।
हम खाना खा रही हैं ।
कौन भारत जा रहा है ?
मेरी पत्नी खाना पका रही है ।
आप क्या कर रहे हैं ?
हम लोग हिन्दुस्तानी संगीत सुन रहे हैं ।
वह बच्चा कमरे में सो रहा है ।
पिता जी हमें कहानी सुना रहे हैं ।
तुम कहाँ जा रहे हो ?
वे लड़कियाँ क्लास जा रही हैं ।

3. Oral questions

आप कल दोपहर को कहाँ जा रहे थे ?
तुम कल सवेरे क्या ख़रीद रहे थे ?
आप कल शाम को कौन-सी किताब पढ़ रहे थे ?
तू कल किसको पत्र लिख रही थी ?

क्या तुम आज सवेरे हिन्दी का अख़बार पढ़ रहे थे ?
बच्चे दोपहर को कहाँ खेल रहे थे ?
तुम लोग किस से बात कर रहे थे ?
छात्र किस से सवाल पूछ रहे थे ?
क्या ये छात्र कल शराब पी रहे थे ?
तुम कल क्लास के बाद क्या बजा रहे थे ?
आप लोग कल किसका भाषण सुन रहे थे ?

4. Chain drill

Q: What were you reading yesterday?
तुम कल क्या पढ़ रहे थे ?

A: This book.
यह किताब ।

Q: To whom were you writing a letter yesterday?
आप कल किस को पत्र लिख रही थीं ?

A: To a friend.
दोस्त को ।

5. Translation exercise

1. He was speaking Hindi with an Indian woman.
2. Where were you going? I was going home.
3. To whom was she writing the letter?
4. Yesterday he was working in the office.
5. What were you people doing there? We were watching a Hindi film.
6. The children were listening to the story.
7. Who was singing? Those children were singing.
8. In the morning my father was reading a Hindi newspaper.
9. Those foreign students were not speaking English.
10. These students were asking many questions in the class.

19. EQUIVALENT OF THE ENGLISH VERB "TO HAVE"

In Hindi there is no single verb corresponding to the English verb "to have." This concept of possession is conveyed in Hindi in three different ways depending on what is possessed.

The basic structure of such sentences is:

subject	a postposition	object	the verb होना
(the possessor)		(what is possessed)	*to be*

Since the subject (i.e., the noun or pronoun expressing the possessor) is always followed by a postposition, which "blocks" the agreement of the verb with it, the verb agrees with the direct object (i.e., the noun representing what is possessed).

(1) The postposition के पास *near* is used with the subject (possessor) to express the possession of tangible, movable, and material objects (i.e., things that can be separated or given away). Examples:

शिक्षक के पास बहुत किताबें हैं। *The teacher has many books.*
(lit., *Near the teacher there are many books.*)
उस आदमी के पास सिर्फ़ एक रुपया है। *That man has just one rupee.*

(2) The postpositions का, के, की *of, belonging to, related to* are used with the subject to express kinship relationships or any other human relationship, to indicate ownership of immovable objects, legal ownership, and possession of parts of the body. Examples:

उसके तीन भाई हैं। *He/She has three brothers.*
(lit., *There are three brothers of him/her.*)
हमारे दो हिन्दी के शिक्षक हैं। *We have two Hindi teachers.*

मेरे पिता के दो मकान हैं।	*My father has two houses.*
उसका सिर्फ़ एक हाथ है।	*He has only one hand.*

Note: Some speakers, when referring to relatives, only use के irrespective of the number and gender of the following noun.

(3) When the thing possessed is an abstract entity, the postposition को *to* is used with the subject. Examples:

मुझे आज कुछ फ़ुरसत है।	*I have some free time today.* (lit., *To me there is some free time today.*)
क्या आपको आज बहुत काम है।	*Do you have a lot of work today?*
बच्चे को बुख़ार है।	*The child has fever.*
मेरे दोस्त को किताब की ज़रूरत है।	*My friend has need of the book.*

Note: When the verb "to have" is used in English with an inanimate subject, Hindi uses the postposition में with it. Examples:

इस कमरे में सिर्फ़ एक खिड़की है।	*This room has only one window.* (lit., *In this room there is only one window.*)
उस घर में दो गुसलख़ाने हैं।	*That house has two bathrooms.*

Exercises

1. Substitution drill

I have many books.
मेरे पास बहुत किताबें हैं।

- three pens
- some papers
- one small pencil
- one red sari
- many shoes

everything
nothing
some dollars
some money
one yellow shirt

2. Chain drill

Q: What do you have?
आपके पास क्या है ?

A: I have two books.
मेरे पास दो किताबें हैं ।

Q: What do you have?
आपके पास क्या है ?

A: I have nothing.
मेरे पास कुछ नहीं है ।

3. Substitution drill

We have some money.
हमारे पास कुछ पैसा है ।
I
You (familiar form)
He
Those people
This student
Who (singular)
You (intimate form)
She
Those women
You (polite form)
Who (plural)

4. Chain drill

Q: Do you have the Hindi book?
क्या आपके पास हिन्दी की किताब है ?

A: Yes, I have the Hindi book.
जी हाँ, मेरे पास हिन्दी की किताब है ।

Q: Does John have a yellow pencil?
क्या जॉन के पास पीली पेंसिल है ?

A: No, John doesn't have a yellow pencil.
जी नहीं, जॉन के पास पीली पेंसिल नहीं है ।

5. Substitution drill

I have three brothers.
मेरे तीन भाई हैं ।

one sister
two sisters
many friends
four children
two eyes
only one daughter
two hands
three teachers
one house
one old car

6. Substitution drill

I have two children.
मेरे दो बच्चे हैं ।

You (polite form)
He
We
You (familiar form)
She
They
You (intimate form)
My brother
His friend
My sister

7. Chain drill

Q: How many brothers do you have?
आपके कितने भाई हैं ?

A: I have two brothers.
मेरे दो भाई हैं ।

Q: How many sisters does that man have?
उस आदमी की कितनी बहनें हैं ?

A: He has one sister.
उसकी एक बहन है ।

8. Substitution drill

That student had a lot of work yesterday.
उस छात्र को कल बहुत काम था ।

We
They

You (familiar form)
Our teacher
Those people
You (intimate form)
He
I
You (polite form)
These students
Who

9. Substitution drill

Yesterday that boy had some free time.
कल उस लड़के को थोड़ी फ़ुरसत थी ।

ज़ुकाम
बुख़ार
किताब की ज़रूरत
थोड़ा समय
थोड़ा काम
थोड़ी जल्दी

10. Chain drill

Q: Do you have a lot of work today?
क्या आपको आज बहुत काम है ?

A: Yes, I have a lot of work today.
जी हाँ, मुझे आज बहुत काम है ।

Q: Who has need of this book? (i.e., Who needs this book?)
किसको इस किताब की ज़रूरत है ?

A: I have need of this book. (i.e., I need this book.)
मुझे इस किताब की ज़रूरत है ।

11. Oral questions

आपके कितने भाई हैं ?
आपके पास कितनी हिन्दी की किताबें हैं ?
आपकी बहन के कितने बच्चे हैं ?
क्या तुम्हारे माता-पिता के पास बहुत पैसा है ?
क्या तुझे आज बहुत काम है ?
किसको आज फ़ुरसत है ?
आपके कितने भारतीय दोस्त हैं ?
क्या आपको आज कुछ समय है ?
आपके पास क्या है ?
किसको हमेशा जल्दी है ?
क्या छात्रों को आजकल बहुत काम है ?
किसको कल ज़ुकाम था ?
किसके पास बहुत पैसा है ?
मेरे पास कुछ नहीं है । आपके पास क्या है ?
क्या आपके दोस्त को कल बुख़ार था ?
किसको इस कलम की ज़रूरत है ?

12. Translation exercise

1. She has two brothers, one older and one younger.
2. How many Hindi books do you have?
3. He doesn't have anything. Please give him something.
4. My sister has many expensive clothes.
5. He has one older sister.
6. I have only two good friends.
7. I don't have any brothers.
8. How many Indian friends do you have?
9. Please come tomorrow. Today we have a lot of work.
10. How much money do you have? I have only ten dollars.
11. These days my husband doesn't have any free time.
12. My mother has many beautiful silk saris.
13. These people have everything, but we have nothing.
14. Yesterday my friend had a fever.

20. THE REFLEXIVE POSSESSIVE अपना

If the subject of a sentence or clause and the possessor in a possessive phrase refer to the same person, Hindi uses अपना instead of possessive forms of pronouns in the possessive phrase. Examples:

मैं अपनी किताब पढ़ रहा था ।	*I was reading my book.*
मोहन अपनी बहन से बात कर रहा है ।	*Mohan is talking with his sister.*
मुझे अपना पैसा चाहिये ।	*I want (need) my money.*
वह अपने कपड़े धोता है ।	*He washes his clothes.*
वह अपने कमरे में काम कर रही है ।	*She is working in her room.*

Thus in the first sentence अपनी is used with किताब instead of मेरी because the possessor of the book and the subject of the sentence are the same person.

अपना functions like a marked adjective and agrees with the noun it modifies in number and gender. Examples:

वह अपनी किताबें पढ़ता है ।	*He reads his books.*
वह अपने कपड़े धो रहा है ।	*He is washing his clothes.*
वह अपना काम कर रहा है ।	*He is doing his work.*
वह अपने भाई से पूछ रहा है ।	*He is asking his brother.*

Note:

(1) The reflexive possessive अपना refers to the subject of the sentence or clause whether it is expressed or understood. Thus, in imperative sentences where the subject "you" is generally understood, अपना refers to the person addressed and is equivalent to "your." Examples:

(आप) अपनी साड़ी लीजिये ।	*(You) Take your sari.*
(तुम) अपना काम करो ।	*(You) Do your work.*
(तू) अपनी रोटी खा ।	*(You) Eat your bread.*

(2) अपना can never be used with the subject of the sentence or clause. Examples:

वह और उसका भाई यहाँ रहते हैं ।	*He and his brother live here.*
मैं कहता हूँ कि यह मेरी किताब है ।	*I say that this is my book.*

In the first example above, अपना भाई is not possible because both वह and उसका भाई are subjects of the sentence. Similarly, अपना is not used with किताब in the second example above because किताब is the subject of the second clause.

(3) The translation of अपना in English will be different in different contexts depending on whom or what it refers to in any particular sentence. Examples:

वे अपने दोस्तों से बात कर रहे हैं ।	*They are talking with their friends.*
तुम अपने कमरे में जाओ ।	*Go to (in) your room.*
मुझे अपना परिवार पसन्द है ।	*I like my family.*

(4) Note that the spelling of अपना has अ rather than आ as its first letter. It is not related to the second person pronoun आप.

Exercises

1. Substitution drill

Please take your book.
अपनी किताब लीजिये ।

pencil
papers
newspaper
bag

shoes
clothes
money
saris
books

2. <u>Individual conversational response drill</u>

Are you reading my book?	No, I'm reading my (own) book.
क्या आप मेरी किताब पढ़ रहे हैं ?	नहीं, मैं अपनी किताब पढ़ रहा हूँ ।
क्या आप मेरे घर जा रहे हैं ?	
क्या आप मेरा काम कर रहे हैं ?	
क्या आप मेरी कुरसी पर बैठ रहे हैं ?	
क्या आप मेरी मिठाई खा रहे हैं ?	
क्या आप मेरे कमरे में पढ़ रहे हैं ?	
क्या आप मेरे कागज़ पर लिख रहे हैं ?	
क्या आप मेरी किताबें बेच रहे हैं ?	
क्या आप मेरी पेंसिल से लिख रहे हैं ?	
क्या आप मेरी चाय पी रहे हैं ?	
क्या आप मेरे दोस्त से बात कर रहे हैं ?	
क्या आप मेरे भाई को पत्र लिख रहे हैं ?	

3. <u>Individual conversational response drill</u>

Do you like my house?	No, I like my (own) house.
क्या तुम्हें मेरा घर पसन्द है ?	नहीं, मुझे अपना घर पसन्द है ।
क्या तुम्हें मेरा कमरा पसन्द है ?	
क्या तुम्हें मेरा स्कूल पसन्द है ?	
क्या तुम्हें मेरे कपड़े पसन्द हैं ?	
क्या तुम्हें मेरी किताब पसन्द है ?	
क्या तुम्हें हमारी क्लास पसन्द है ?	
क्या तुम्हें हमारा देश पसन्द है ?	
क्या तुम्हें हमारा शहर पसन्द है ?	
क्या तुम्हें हमारी भाषा पसन्द है ?	

4. Substitution drill

This man is selling his (own) house.
यह आदमी अपना घर बेच रहा है ।

our house
his books (his own books)
her books
his clothes (his own clothes)
your clothes
his shoes (his own shoes)
my shoes
his chairs (his own chairs)
their chairs

5. Individual conversational response drill

Please give me my notebook.
मेरी कापी दीजिये ।

All right, please take your notebook.
अच्छा, अपनी कापी लीजिये ।

मेरी किताब दीजिये ।
मेरे कागज़ दीजिये ।
मेरे जूते दीजिये ।
मेरी साड़ी दीजिये ।
मेरी पेंसिल दीजिये ।
मेरे कपड़े दीजिये ।
मेरा थैला दीजिये ।

6. Chain drill

Q: What are you doing?
तुम क्या कर रहे हो ?

A: I am reading my book.
मैं अपनी किताब पढ़ रहा हूँ ।

Q: Where were you yesterday evening?
आप कल शाम को कहाँ थीं ?

A: I was in my room.
मैं अपने कमरे में थी ।

7. Translation exercise

1. Please tell me your address.
2. Eat your orange. Don't eat mine (my orange).
3. The little boy was drinking his milk.
4. I love my family and my family also loves me.
5. Are they selling their books?
6. She tells us about her country.
7. Sit down on your chair and do your work.
8. Take your book and read it.
9. He wants to play with his friends.
10. We are doing our work. What are you doing?
11. Go in your room and do your work.
12. They like their country.

21. THE FUTURE TENSE

The future tense is used to describe an action or an event that will take place in the future. It is formed by adding two sets of suffixes directly to the verb stem. The first set of suffixes is:

ए	if the subject of the verb is singular
एँ	if the subject of the verb is plural
ऊँ	if the subject of the verb is the first person singular pronoun मैं
ओ	if the subject of the verb is the second person familiar pronoun तुम

The second set of the suffixes is:

गा	if the subject of the verb is masculine singular
गे	if the subject of the verb is masculine plural
गी	if the subject of the verb is feminine singular or plural

Note that the first set of suffixes agrees with the subject in number and person while the second set of suffixes agrees with the subject in number and gender.

Thus the basic pattern of future tense forms is:

मैं	verb stem + ऊँगा / ऊँगी
हम	verb stem + एँगे / एँगी
आप	verb stem + एँगे / एँगी
तुम	verb stem + ओगे / ओगी
तू	verb stem + एगा / एगी
यह	verb stem + एगा / एगी
वह	verb stem + एगा / एगी

ये verb stem + एँगे / एँगी
वे verb stem + एँगे / एँगी

Examples with the verbs जाना *to go* and लिखना *to write*:

मैं जाऊँगा / जाऊँगी ।	*I* (M/F) *will go.*
हम जाएँगे / जाएँगी ।	*We* (M/F) *will go.*
आप जाएँगे / जाएँगी ।	*You* (M/F) *will go.*
तुम जाओगे / जाओगी ।	*You* (M/F) *will go.*
तू जाएगा / जाएगी ।	*You* (M/F) *will go.*
यह जाएगा / जाएगी ।	*He/She will go.*
वह जाएगा / जाएगी ।	*He/She will go.*
ये जाएँगे / जाएँगी ।	*They* (M/F) *will go.*
वे जाएँगे / जाएँगी ।	*They*(M/F) *will go.*
मैं लिखूँगा / लिखूँगी ।	*I* (M/F) *will write.*
हम लिखेंगे / लिखेंगी ।	*We* (M/F) *will write.*
आप लिखेंगे / लिखेंगी ।	*You* (M/F) *will write.*
तुम लिखोगे / लिखोगी ।	*You* (M/F) *will write.*
तू लिखेगा / लिखेगी ।	*You* (M/F) *will write.*
यह लिखेगा / लिखेगी ।	*He/She will write.*
वह लिखेगा / लिखेगी ।	*He/She will write.*
ये लिखेंगे / लिखेंगी ।	*They* (M/F) *will write.*
वे लिखेंगे / लिखेंगी ।	*They* (M/F) *will write.*

Note that if the verb stem ends in a vowel (e.g., जा), the vowel of the first set of suffixes is written in its independent form, but if the stem of the verb ends in a consonant (e.g., लिख), the vowel of the first set of suffixes is written in its मात्रा (dependent) form.

Irregular future forms: The future forms of three verbs, लेना *to take,* देना *to give,* and होना *to be,* are somewhat irregular.

	लेना	देना	होना
मैं	लूँगा / लूँगी	दूँगा / दूँगी	हूँगा / हूँगी (होऊँगा / होऊँगी)
हम	लेंगे / लेंगी	देंगे / देंगी	होंगे / होंगी
आप	लेंगे / लेंगी	देंगे / देंगी	होंगे / होंगी
तुम	लोगे / लोगी	दोगे / दोगी	होगे / होगी
तू	लेगा / लेगी	देगा / देगी	होगा / होगी
यह	लेगा / लेगी	देगा / देगी	होगा / होगी
वह	लेगा / लेगी	देगा / देगी	होगा / होगी
ये	लेंगे / लेंगी	देंगे / देंगी	होंगे / होंगी
वे	लेंगे / लेंगी	देंगे / देंगी	होंगे / होंगी

If the stem of a verb ends in ई or ऊ as in the verbs पीना *to drink* or छूना *to touch*, then ई or ऊ is shortened to इ or उ before adding the verbal suffixes. Examples:

मैं पिऊँगा / पिऊँगी ।	*I* (M/F) *will drink.*
मैं छुऊँगा / छुऊँगी ।	*I* (M/F) *will touch.*
हम पिएँगे / पिएँगी ।	*We* (M/F) *will drink.*
हम छुएँगे / छुएँगी ।	*We* (M/F) *will touch.*

When conjugating the verbs with stems ending in ई, some people also insert a य before adding the verbal suffixes. Examples:

मैं पियूँगा / पियूँगी।	*I* (M/F) *will drink.*
हम पियेंगे / पियेंगी ।	*We* (M/F) *will drink.*

For negative statements, नहीं is used directly before the verb.

मैं कल नहीं आऊँगा ।	*I will not come tomorrow.*
अगले साल वह यहाँ नहीं पढ़ेगी ।	*Next year she will not study here.*

Exercises

1. Transformation drill

to go	When will you (M) go?
जाना	आप कब जाएँगे ?
खाना	
पीना	
ख़रीदना	
बेचना	
पढ़ना	
लिखना	
देखना	
लेना	
देना	
बताना	

2. Substitution drill

I will go there tomorrow.
मैं कल वहाँ जाऊँगा (जाऊँगी) ।

will read this book
will come here
will write a story
will give the money

will buy books
will take some sweets
will see a film
will meet Ram

3. Substitution drill

Will you go there tomorrow?
क्या तुम कल वहाँ जाओगे (जाओगी) ?

will write the letter
will study Hindi
will buy shoes
will come to my house
will bring my book
will give him some money
will do this work
will play with friends

4. Substitution drill

I (M) will go to India.
मैं भारत जाऊँगा ।

तुम (M)
वह (M)
हम (M)
वे (M)
आप (M)
तू (M)
यह लड़का
हमारे शिक्षक
आपका भाई
आपके पिता
मेरा दोस्त

5. Substitution drill

I (F) will talk with a friend.
मैं दोस्त से बात करूँगी ।
तुम (F)
वह (F)
हम (F)
वे (F)
आप (F)
तू (F)
यह लड़की
मेरी बहनें
वे लड़कियाँ
मेम साहब

6. Transformation drill

He studies Hindi.	He will study Hindi.
वह हिन्दी पढ़ता है ।	वह हिन्दी पढ़ेगा ।
क्या तुम यहाँ काम करते हो ?	
मैं बर्कली में रहती हूँ ।	
वह बहुत पैसा लेता है ।	
हमारे शिक्षक हम से सवाल पूछते हैं ।	
आपका भाई वहाँ क्यों जाता है ?	
क्या तुम्हारा दोस्त हिन्दी पढ़ता है ?	
वे लोग मेरी भाषा नहीं समझते ।	
मेरा दोस्त रोज़ यूनिवर्सिटी आता है ।	
हम लोग हिन्दी की फ़िल्में देखते हैं ।	
तुम कहाँ रहते हो ?	

7. Transformation drill

I am studying Hindi.	I will study Hindi.
मैं हिन्दी पढ़ रही हूँ।	मैं हिन्दी पढ़ूँगी।

वे लोग यह घर नहीं ख़रीद रहे हैं।
आपकी बहन काम कर रही है।
उन के पिता कहानी सुना रहे हैं।
हम कुछ साड़ियाँ ख़रीद रही हैं।
तुम कहाँ जा रहे हो ?
तू अपनी किताब क्यों नहीं पढ़ रहा है ?
छात्र जवाब दे रहे हैं।
तुम लोग क्या कर रहे हो ?
मोहन दफ़्तर में काम कर रहा है।
सीता और शीला शिक्षक से सवाल पूछ रही हैं।

8. Oral questions

आप क्लास में कहाँ बैठेंगे ?
तुम अगले साल कहाँ जाओगे ?
क्या आप आज हमारे साथ खाना खाएँगे ?
तुम आज शाम को कौन-सी फ़िल्म देखोगे ?
ये छात्र अगले साल कहाँ काम करेंगे ?
तुम क्या पियोगे, चाय या कॉफ़ी ?
आपकी बहन किस विश्वविद्यालय में पढ़ेगी ?
क्या विदेशी टैक्सीवाले को बहुत पैसा देगा ?
तू अगले साल कहाँ काम करेगा ?
आप लोग इस क्लास में कौन-सी भाषा बोलेंगे ?
कौन हमारे लिये चाय लाएगा ?
लड़की कौन-सी साड़ी ख़रीदेगी, लाल या पीली ?
तुम कब न्यू यॉर्क जाओगे ?
तू कल किससे मिलेगा ?
कौन जल्दी जवाब देगा ?
आप कब राष्ट्रपति को पत्र लिखेंगे ?

9. Chain drill

Q: What will you do tomorrow?
तुम कल क्या करोगे ?

A: Tomorrow I will go to the market.
मैं कल बाज़ार जाऊँगा ।

Q: What will you read?
तुम क्या पढ़ोगे ?

A: I will read this book.
मैं यह किताब पढ़ूँगा ।

10. Translation exercise

1. I will go home in the evening and (will) study.
2. She will come tomorrow in the afternoon.
3. Next year my brother will live in New York.
4. What will you do about this? (familiar form)
5. They will see a film tonight.
6. We will meet you tomorrow.
7. In India, we will only speak Hindi.
8. To whom will you sell these cheap vegetables? (familiar form)
9. Will you people drink tea? No, we will drink coffee. (polite form)
10. Who will give the answer? That smart student will give the answer.
11. How many questions will you ask? (intimate form)
12. How much money will you take? (polite form)

22. USE OF THE VERB सकना *TO BE ABLE TO*

When used with a verb stem, the auxiliary verb सकना corresponds to the English "to be able to," "can."

सकना can only be used with the stem of another verb; it cannot occur independently as it does in English. For example, in English if someone asks, "Can you write Urdu?," one may answer, "Yes, I can." But in Hindi one has to say, "Yes, I can write (Urdu)." (हाँ, मैं लिख सकता हूँ). Examples:

मैं हिन्दी बोलती हूँ।	*I speak Hindi.*
मैं हिन्दी बोल सकती हूँ।	*I can speak Hindi.*
मेरा दोस्त सितार बजाता है।	*My friend plays the sitar.*
मेरा दोस्त सितार बजा सकता है।	*My friend can play the sitar.*
क्या तुम अगले साल भारत जाओगे ?	*Will you go to India next year?*
क्या तुम अगले साल भारत जा सकोगे ?	*Will you be able to go to India next year?*
हम इतना पैसा नहीं देंगे।	*We will not give this much money.*
हम इतना पैसा नहीं दे सकेंगे।	*We will not be able to give this much money.*

Since the main verb always remains in stem form, all the changes due to number, gender, and person agreement occur in the auxiliary सकना. The auxiliary सकना can be used with any verb stem and is found in all tenses with the exception of the progressive tense. If the sentence with सकना is negative, the negative particle नहीं can come either before or after the verb stem. Examples:

मेरी बहन गा नहीं सकती।	*My sister cannot sing.*
मेरी बहन नहीं गा सकती।	*My sister cannot sing.*

Exercises

1. Substitution drill

I can sing a song.
मैं गाना गा सकता हूँ।
अँग्रेज़ी पढ़
उर्दू लिख
हिन्दी बोल
फ़्रेंच समझ
काम कर
घर जा
खाना पका

2. Chain drill

Q: What can you do?
आप क्या कर सकते हैं ?

A: I can cook Indian food.
मैं भारतीय खाना पका सकता हूँ।

3. Transformation drill

He is singing.	Can you sing too?
वह गा रहा है।	क्या आप भी गा सकते हैं ?
वह सितार बजा रहा है।	
वह फ़्रेंच बोल रहा है।	
वह हिन्दी का अख़बार पढ़ रहा है।	
वह उर्दू लिख रहा है।	
वह तैर रहा है।	
वह टेनिस खेल रहा है।	
वह भारतीय खाना पका रहा है।	

4. Individual conversational response drill

Who will be able to go to the market?	I will be able to go to the market.
कौन बाज़ार जा सकेगा ?	मैं बाज़ार जा सकूँगा ।
कौन जवाब दे सकेगा ?	
कौन हिन्दी बोल सकेगा ?	
कौन कुरसी ठीक कर सकेगा ?	
कौन अख़बार पढ़ सकेगा ?	
कौन पत्र लिख सकेगा ?	
कौन कपड़े धो सकेगा ?	
कौन यह काम कर सकेगा ?	
कौन यहाँ आ सकेगा ?	
कौन फ़िल्म देख सकेगा ?	

5. Substitution drill

He will be able to go to India next year.
वह अगले साल भारत जा सकेगा ।
हम
आप (F)
तुम (M)
हमारा दोस्त
वे लोग
वे औरतें
मैं (F)
तू (F)
सब लोग
ये हिन्दी के छात्र

6. Substitution drill

We can't do this much work.
हम इतना काम नहीं कर सकते ।

can't eat this much food
can't drink this much wine
can't go there
can't study today
can't play here
can't give this much money
can't write Urdu
can't work here
can't buy these books

7. Oral questions

क्या आप आज बाज़ार जा सकते हैं ?
क्या तुम सितार बजा सकते हो ?
कौन गा सकता है ?
तुम क्या क्या कर सकते हो ?
क्या तुम हिन्दी में पत्र लिख सकते हो ?
क्या तुम हमारे लिए कुछ चाय ला सकते हो ?
आज शाम को कौन आ सकता है ?
कौन इस सवाल का जवाब दे सकता है ?
कौन अच्छा भारतीय खाना पका सकता है ?
आज मेरे घर कौन आ सकता है ?
आप कितनी मिठाइयाँ खा सकते हैं ?
तुम कितनी भाषाएँ बोल सकते हो ?
क्या आप लोग मेरी हिन्दी समझ सकते हैं ?

8. Translation exercise

1. I can read this Hindi newspaper.
2. We can sing and dance.
3. Will you be able to go to India next year?

4. My sister can play the sitar.
5. How many languages can your friend speak?
6. My sister can cook good Indian food.
7. I will be able to finish this work by tomorrow.
8. When can you come to my house?
9. I can come to your house tomorrow. Will you be at home?
10. I can't go there today, but I can go tomorrow.
11. How many letters can you write in an hour?
12. Where can we play? You can play in the park.
13. When can we meet? We can meet this evening at (in) my house.
14. Can you buy this book for me? Yes, I can.

23. THE PERFECT TENSE

The perfect tense in Hindi is employed to describe an action that is completed. It usually equates with the English simple past tense, e.g., "Yesterday my father went to India" or "We saw him on campus." The difference between the perfect tense and the past habitual tense is important to understand. The past habitual tense is used to describe frequent, regular, or habitual actions in the past (the "used to" construction in English) while the perfect tense is used for a single completed action. Examples:

मेरा दोस्त आठ बजे स्कूल गया ।	*My friend went to school at 8 o'clock.*
मेरा दोस्त आठ बजे स्कूल जाता था।	*My friend used to go to school at 8 o'clock.*
लड़की किताबें लाई ।	*The girl brought the books.*
लड़की किताबें लाती थी ।	*The girl used to bring the books.*

Formation: The formation of the perfect tense is very simple. It is formed by adding the endings आ, ए, ई, ईं directly to the verb stem. These endings agree with the subject in number and gender.

आ is added to the verb stem for a masculine singular subject.
ए is added to the verb stem for a masculine plural subject.
ई is added to the verb stem for a feminine singular subject.
ईं is added to the verb stem for a feminine plural subject.

Examples with the verb बैठना *to sit*:

मैं बैठा / बैठी ।	*I* (M/F) *sat.*
हम बैठे / बैठीं ।	*We* (M/F) *sat.*

आप बैठे / बैठीं ।	*You* (M/F) *sat.*
तुम बैठे / बैठीं ।	*You* (M/F) *sat.*
तू बैठा / बैठी ।	*You* (M/F) *sat.*
यह बैठा / बैठी ।	*He/She sat.*
वह बैठा / बैठी ।	*He/She sat.*
ये बैठे / बैठीं ।	*They* (M/F) *sat.*
वे बैठे / बैठीं ।	*They* (M/F) *sat.*

If the verb stem ends in आ, ए, or ओ, the consonant य is added to the stem before adding the masculine singular endings. It is also frequently added before masculine plural endings but less frequently before feminine singular and plural endings. Examples with the verb खाना *to eat* and सोना *to sleep*:

masc. sg.	खाया	सोया
masc. pl.	खाये / खाए	सोये / सोए
fem. sg.	खाई / खायी	सोई / सोयी
fem. pl.	खाईं / खायीं	सोईं / सोयीं

If the verb stem ends in ई, it is shortened to इ and य is added to the stem before adding masculine singular and plural endings, but the stem and ending coalesce in feminine singular and plural forms. Examples with the verbs पीना *to drink* and सीना *to sew*:

masc. sg.	पिया	सिया
masc. pl.	पिये / पिए	सिये / सिए
fem. sg.	पी	सी
fem. pl.	पीं	सीं

If the verb stem ends in ऊ, it is shortened to उ before adding the regular endings. Examples with the verb छूना *to touch*:

masc. sg.	छुआ
masc. pl.	छुए
fem. sg.	छुई
fem. pl.	छुईं

The following five verbs have irregular perfective forms:

	जाना *to go*	होना *to occur/ become*	लेना *to take*	देना *to give*	करना *to do/ make*
masc. sg.	गया	हुआ	लिया	दिया	किया
masc. pl.	गये / गए	हुए	लिये / लिए	दिये / दिए	किये / किए
fem. sg.	गई / गयी	हुई	ली	दी	की
fem. pl.	गईं / गयीं	हुईं	लीं	दीं	कीं

Note:

(1) The verb होना can mean "to be," "to become," or "to occur." The perfective forms हुआ, हुए, हुई, and हुईं represent only "to become" or "to occur." होना with the meaning "to be" cannot be used in the perfect tense. It has only simple past forms: था, थे, थी, and थीं.

(2) The stems of the verbs लेना *to take*, देना *to give,* and करना *to do* do not end in ई, but in their perfective forms these verbs follow the pattern as if their stems ended in ई.

(3) The irregular forms of करना given above are the only forms accepted in standard Hindi, but one might encounter the regular forms करा, करे, करी, and करीं in colloquial speech.

Exercises

1. Substitution drill

My friend arrived in Delhi yesterday.
मेरा दोस्त कल दिल्ली पहुँचा ।

Those students
These girls
We
I (F)
My sisters
His parents
Ram
Who (plural)
Your brother
You (familiar form)
My friends

2. Substitution drill

I (M) came here on Monday.
मैं सोमवार को यहाँ आया ।

तुम (F)
आप (M)
वह (F)
राम
सीता और शीला
कौन
तू (M)
मेरे दोस्त
मेरे माता-पिता
मेरी बहनें

3. Transformation drill

He will come tomorrow.	He came yesterday.
वह कल आएगा ।	वह कल आया ।
वह कल किताब लाएगा ।	
वह कल बर्कली पहुँचेगा ।	
वह कल दिल्ली जाएगा ।	
वह कल यहाँ रुकेगा ।	
वह कल आपसे मिलेगा ।	
वह कल इस होटल में रहेगा ।	
वह कल यहाँ बैठेगा ।	
वह कल यहाँ सोएगा ।	

4. Substitution drill

When did Ram go home?
राम कब घर गया ?
they
Sita
those students
your friend
the children
my brother
his sisters
your parents
our teacher
those girls
she

5. Substitution drill

My friend didn't come to class yesterday.
मेरा दोस्त कल क्लास नहीं आया ।

didn't go home
didn't bring his book
didn't meet his sister
didn't arrive on time
didn't sit here
didn't stay in this hotel
didn't sleep here
didn't come to the party
didn't meet his parents
didn't go to the library

6. Transformation drill

I go to Delhi. मैं दिल्ली जाता हूँ ।	I went to Delhi. मैं दिल्ली गया ।

वह यहाँ आता है ।
तू कहाँ बैठती है ?
वे लोग आगरा पहुँचते हैं ।
हम इस कमरे में बैठते हैं ।
कौन किताबें लाता है ?
तुम कहाँ जाती हो ?
शीला और सीता क्लास से आती हैं ।
आप अपने कमरे से कुरसी लाते हैं ।
तुम कहाँ सोते हो ?
मैं उस कमरे में नहीं लेटता ।
वह इस शहर में रहता है ।
हम इस होटल में रुकते हैं ।

7. Chain drill

(Using one of the following verbs, student A should make up a question, which student B should answer: बोलना, बैठना, आना, जाना, लाना, रुकना, सोना, पहुँचना, रहना, मिलना, हँसना, रोना, उठना.)

verb: पहुँचना *to arrive*

Q: When did your brother arrive in Delhi?
तुम्हारा भाई कब दिल्ली पहुँचा ?

A: Yesterday afternoon.
कल दोपहर को ।

verb: रुकना *to stay*

Q: Where did you stay in Delhi?
आप दिल्ली में कहाँ रुके ?

A: In the Ashoka Hotel.
अशोका होटल में ।

8. Translation exercise

1. Yesterday we met them on campus.
2. He came from the shop at five o'clock.
3. Yesterday we slept late.
4. She and her friends went to see a Hindi film.
5. Where did you stay in Delhi? We stayed in a big hotel.
6. When did your sisters go? They went the day before yesterday.
7. He got up and went out to drink some coffee.
8. The little children ran towards the street.
9. Why didn't you bring my books?
10. Mr. Sharma came and sat on the chair.
11. They didn't arrive there on time due to the bad weather.
12. Our father brought some sweets from the market for us.

24. THE PERFECT TENSE OF TRANSITIVE, OR ने, VERBS

In perfective tenses, Hindi distinguishes between transitive and intransitive verbs. Transitive verbs are verbs that can take a direct object while intransitive verbs are never used with a direct object.

In Hindi when a transitive verb is used in the perfective tenses (perfect, present perfect, and past perfect), the subject of the sentence is always marked by the postposition ने, which has no English equivalent and cannot be translated into English. The subject of an intransitive verb, on the other hand, is never marked by the postposition ने in the perfective tenses. Therefore, transitive verbs in Hindi may be referred to as ने verbs since the occurrence of the postposition ने in the perfective tenses is what distinguishes them from intransitive verbs.

In the perfective tenses of transitive verbs, the verb agrees in number and gender with the direct object, if one is present, because the postposition ने "blocks" the agreement of the verb with the subject. Examples:

मैंने किताब पढ़ी ।	*I read the book.*
मैंने अख़बार पढ़ा ।	*I read the newspaper.*

If, however, there is no direct object in the sentence, whether expressed or understood, or if the object of the sentence is followed by a postposition (generally को), then the verb takes the neutral form (i.e., masculine singular form). Examples:

लड़की ने देखा ।	*The girl saw (something).*
उसने अपने दोस्तों को बुलाया ।	*He/She called his/her friends.*

Since ने is a postposition, all nouns and pronouns that are marked by ने take the oblique form, with the exception of मैं and तू; while ये, वे, and कौन (pl.) take special forms when followed by the postposition ने.

Personal Pronouns with ने

Direct form	Oblique form	With ने
मैं	मुझ	मैंने *
हम	हम	हमने
आप	आप	आपने
तुम	तुम	तुमने
तू	तुझ	तूने *
यह	इस	इसने
वह	उस	उसने
ये	इन	इन्होंने *
वे	उन	उन्होंने *
कौन (sg.)	किस	किसने
कौन (pl.)	किन	किन्होंने *

Note: The forms with * are somewhat irregular.

Most of the verbs that are transitive in English are also transitive in Hindi. However, there are a few verbs in Hindi that, although they are transitive, are not used with ने in the perfective tenses. These are:

ले जाना	*to take something/someone somewhere*
ले चलना	*to take something/someone along*
ले आना	*to bring something/someone*
लाना	*to bring*
भूलना	*to forget*
से डरना	*to fear, to be afraid of*
से मिलना	*to meet someone*

Any verb whether transitive or intransitive when used with सकना is treated as a non-ने verb in the perfective tenses. Example:

उस छात्र ने कल हिन्दी पढ़ी ।	*That student studied Hindi yesterday.*
वह छात्र कल हिन्दी पढ़ सका ।	*That student could study Hindi yesterday.*

In the case of a few verbs, the use of the postposition ने in the perfect tense is optional. The most common of these verbs are बोलना *to speak,* समझना *to understand,* खेलना *to play.* Examples:

वह कुछ नहीं बोला ।	*He did not say (speak) anything.*
विदेशी ने थोड़ी हिन्दी बोली ।	*The foreigner spoke a little Hindi.*
हम शिक्षक का सवाल नहीं समझे ।	*We did not understand the teacher's question.*
हमने शिक्षक का सवाल नहीं समझा ।	*We did not understand the teacher's question.*
वह दोस्त के साथ फुटबॉल खेला ।	*He played football with a friend.*
उसने दोस्त के साथ फुटबॉल खेली ।	*He played football with a friend.*

Note:

(1) It is important to remember that the postposition ने is used with the subject of a transitive verb only in the perfective tenses.

(2) Keep in mind that all the verbs that are used in indirect verb constructions, e.g., पसन्द होना *to like,* मालूम होना *to know*, etc., take the postposition को in all tenses with the subject of the corresponding English sentence, making it an indirect object. Example:

कल उसको कुछ पैसा मिला ।	*He got some money yesterday.*

Exercises

1. Substitution drill

I bought a book.
मैंने एक किताब ख़रीदी ।

नया घर
कुछ कपड़े
ताज़ी सब्ज़ियाँ
दाल
मसाले
नये जूते
बहुत चीज़ें
चावल
कुछ नहीं

2. Chain drill

Q: What did you buy yesterday?
तुमने कल क्या ख़रीदा ?

A: I bought some clothes.
मैंने कुछ कपड़े ख़रीदे ।

3. Substitution drill

Ram saw this film.
राम ने यह फ़िल्म देखी ।

I
Who (singular)
They
You (familiar form)
We
Who (plural)
Those women

My younger brother
You (intimate form)
This boy

4. <u>Substitution drill</u>

We saw Ram there.
हमने वहाँ राम को देखा ।
उस आदमी को
फ़िल्म
उसका नया घर
उन लड़कियों को
एक सुन्दर तसवीर
आपके भाई को
हिन्दी की किताबें
उन लोगों को
बहुत चीज़ें

5. <u>Transformation drill</u>

The boy was doing his work.	The boy did his work.
लड़का अपना काम कर रहा था ।	लड़के ने अपना काम किया ।

वह पत्र लिख रहा था ।
छात्र जवाब दे रहा था ।
हम बहुत सवाल पूछ रहे थे ।
सीता किसको देख रही थी ?
वे लड़कियाँ कपड़े ख़रीद रही थीं ।
वे किताब पढ़ रहे थे ।
कौन फ़िल्म देख रहे थे ?
ये गाना सुन रहे थे ।
हम लोग कॉफ़ी पी रहे थे ।
वे शाकाहारी खाना खा रहे थे ।
पिताजी अख़बार पढ़ रहे थे ।

6. Chain drill

Q: What did you do yesterday?
तुमने कल क्या किया ?

A: I saw a film yesterday.
मैंने कल एक फ़िल्म देखी ।

7. Transformation drill

I will cook Indian food tomorrow. मैं कल हिन्दुस्तानी खाना पकाऊँगा ।	I cooked Indian food yesterday. मैंने कल हिन्दुस्तानी खाना पकाया ।

मैं कल आप से मिलूँगा ।
मैं कल आपके साथ खाना खाऊँगा ।
मैं कल दो कमीज़ें ख़रीदूँगा ।
मैं कल अपना कमरा साफ़ करूँगा ।
मैं कल दोस्त को पत्र लिखूँगा ।
मैं कल ये किताबें पढ़ूँगा ।
मैं कल अपने कपड़े धोऊँगा ।
मैं कल यह फ़िल्म देखूँगा ।
मैं कल अपना काम करूँगा ।
मैं कल आपको पैसा दूँगा ।

8. Substitution drill

He didn't get those things.
उसको वे चीज़ें नहीं मिलीं ।

money
good oranges
cheap vegetables
my letter
good tea
that book
good and cheap clothes
Indian sweets

9. <u>Transformation drill</u>

I read the book.	I was able to read the book.
मैंने किताब पढ़ी ।	मैं किताब पढ़ सका ।
हमने बहुत चीज़ें ख़रीदीं ।	
क्या तुमने कल फ़िल्म देखी ?	
लड़की ने दोस्त को पत्र लिखा ।	
तुमने कल क्या ख़रीदा ।	
उसने अपनी मोटर नहीं बेची ।	
सैली ने हिन्दी का अख़बार पढ़ा ।	
मैंने अपना काम ख़त्म किया ।	
उसने पैसा दिया ।	
मैंने आज खाना नहीं पकाया ।	
छात्रों ने कल अपना निबन्ध नहीं लिखा ।	

10. <u>Individual conversational response drill</u>

I saw the Taj Mahal. What did you see?	I saw the Red Fort.
मैंने ताज महल देखा । आपने क्या देखा ?	मैंने लाल किला देखा ।
मैंने केला खाया । आपने क्या खाया ?	
मैंने कल एक किताब पढ़ी । आपने क्या पढ़ा ?	
मैंने कल दाल पकाई । आपने क्या पकाया ?	
मैंने अपनी गाड़ी बेची । आपने क्या बेचा ?	
मैंने दो कमीज़ें ख़रीदीं । आपने क्या ख़रीदा ?	
मैंने कल अपने कपड़े धोये । आपने क्या धोया ?	
मैंने कल अपना कमरा साफ़ किया । आपने क्या साफ़ किया ?	
मैंने कल एक पत्र लिखा । आपने क्या लिखा ?	
मैंने कल एक फ़िल्म देखी । आपने क्या देखा ?	
मैंने कल अपना काम किया । आपने क्या किया ?	
मैंने कल दोस्त को फ़ोन किया । आपने किसको फ़ोन किया ?	
मैंने कल एक कविता लिखी । आपने क्या लिखा ?	

11. Chain drill

Q: I did my work yesterday. What did you do?
मैंने कल अपना काम किया । तुमने क्या किया ?

A: I did my work too.
मैंने भी अपना काम किया ।

12. Oral questions

आपने कल क्या किया ?
क्या तुमने कल हिन्दी की किताब पढ़ी ?
तुमने कल क्या पकाया ?
तुमने कल क्या ख़रीदा ?
तुमने कल क्या साफ़ किया ?
क्या तुम कल हिन्दी पढ़ सके ?
क्या तुमने कल बहुत काम किया ?
तुमने कल क्या पढ़ा ?
क्या तुमने कल हिन्दी का अख़बार पढ़ा ?
तुमने कल किसको पत्र लिखा ?

13. Translation exercise

(Translate each of these sentences into Hindi twice, using the object in parentheses the second time.)

1. I saw some Indian women. (your parents)
2. We ate some oranges. (some sweets)
3. They read a Hindi book. (a Hindi newspaper)
4. I drank cold water. (wine)
5. Did you meet them at the party? (her brother)
6. Yesterday she wrote an essay. (a story)
7. They cooked Indian food. (some vegetables)
8. The women washed their clothes. (their saris)
9. Who took my book? (my money)
10. He gave me some money. (these books)

25. THE PRESENT PERFECT TENSE

The present perfect tense in Hindi is used to express an action that is completed by the present time, and that completed action has some link, effect, or relevance in the present. Examples from English are "He has seen the film," or "I have read the book." Note that English uses "has" and "have" as auxiliary verbs to indicate the present perfect tense.

Formation: The present perfect tense is formed by using the perfective forms of the main verb followed by the simple present forms of the verb होना *to be* (है, हैं, हूँ, or हो). The rules of agreement are the same as for the perfect tense. The postposition ने is not used with the subject of an intransitive verb, and the verb (the perfective form of the main verb + simple present form of the verb होना) agrees with the subject in number and gender. The postposition ने is used with the subject of a transitive verb, and the verb agrees with the object. If there is no object in the sentence or if the object is followed by a postposition, then the verb takes the neutral (i.e., masculine singular) form. Examples:

वह बाज़ार गया है ।	*He has gone to the market.*
मैं पहले यहाँ आई हूँ ।	*I have come here before.*
छात्र ने ये किताबें ख़रीदी हैं ।	*The student has bought these books.*
हमने कुछ हिन्दी की फ़िल्में देखी हैं ।	*We have seen some Hindi movies.*

Note: If the verb agreement is feminine plural, only the auxiliary verb (i.e., the simple present form of the verb होना) shows the plurality. The main verb is in feminine singular form (see the last two example sentences).

Exercises

1. Substitution drill

Those boys have gone there.
वे लड़के वहाँ गये हैं ।
मैं
मेरी पत्नी
मेरा भाई
उसके दोस्त
उसकी बहनें
हम लोग
तेरा दोस्त
वे भारतीय लड़कियाँ
हमारे शिक्षक
वे छात्र

2. Substitution drill

What has he eaten today?
उसने आज क्या खाया है ?
सब्ज़ियाँ
वे फल
भारतीय खाना
गोश्त
मुर्ग़ी
चावल
बहुत आम
शाकाहारी खाना
कुछ नहीं
बहुत खाना
सिर्फ़ एक सेब

3. Substitution drill

I have read two newspapers.
मैंने दो समाचारपत्र पढ़े हैं ।
वह चिट्ठी
यह किताब
इसके बारे में
आपकी किताब
उसका लेख
आपका निबन्ध
आपकी कहानी
आपकी कविताएँ
यह समाचार
हिन्दी का अख़बार

4. Substitution drill

Why has he taken my book?
उसने मेरी किताब क्यों ली है ?
हमारी किताबें
तुम्हारी चीज़ें
तेरी पेंसिल
छुट्टी
आपकी कार
राम के कपड़े
बहुत पैसा
आपका समाचारपत्र
मेरा कलम
हमारी कुरसियाँ
मेरी मिठाई
वे सब तसवीरें

5. Individual conversational response drill

Have you ever seen a Hindi film? क्या आपने कभी हिन्दी की फ़िल्म देखी है ?	Yes, I have. हाँ, देखी है ।
	No, I haven't. नहीं, नहीं देखी है ।

क्या आपके माता-पिता कभी भारत गये हैं ?
क्या आपने कभी हिन्दुस्तानी खाना खाया है ?
क्या आपने कभी बस चलाई है ?
क्या आप कभी मेरे भाई से मिले हैं ?
क्या आपके भाई ने कभी हिन्दी सीखी है ?
क्या आपने कभी लस्सी पी है ?
क्या आपने कभी मेज़ बनाई है ?
क्या आपने कभी साड़ी पहनी है ?
क्या आपने कभी रविशंकर का सितार सुना है ?
क्या आपने कभी बच्चों को कहानी सुनाई है ?
क्या आपने कभी अमरीका के राष्ट्रपति को देखा है ?

6. Chain drill

Q: Have you ever gone to New York?
क्या आप कभी न्यू यॉर्क गये हैं ?

A: Yes, I have.
जी हाँ, गया हूँ ।

7. Oral questions

आपने आज क्या खाया है ?
आप यहाँ कब आए हैं ?
क्या आपने यह ख़बर सुनी है ?
तुम हमारे लिये क्या लाये हो ?
तुमने किसको पत्र लिखा है ?
आपको किस दुकान में यह चीज़ मिली है ?

तुमने बाज़ार में क्या ख़रीदा है ?
क्या तुमने आज का समाचारपत्र पढ़ा है ?
आपने आज क्या पकाया है ?
उसने आपको क्या दिया है ?
आपने अपने भाई से क्या लिया है ?
क्या तुमने ताज महल देखा है ?
क्या तुमने यह हिन्दी की फ़िल्म देखी है ?
किसने मेरी मिठाई खाई है ?
आपने यह किताब कहाँ से ख़रीदी है ?
क्या तुम आज अपने दोस्त से मिले हो ?

8. Translation exercise

1. She has written a novel about her life.
2. Have you seen this movie? Yes, we have seen it.
3. They have finished their work.
4. Have you ever lived in an Indian village?
5. What have you cooked today? I have not cooked anything.
6. He has gone to Delhi and has not come back yet.
7. Have you seen all the famous temples in Banaras?
8. They have brought these books for you.
9. We have written letters to our friends.
10. Have we ever met before? No, we are meeting today for the first time.

26. THE PAST PERFECT TENSE

The past perfect tense in Hindi can be used in three situations:

(1) The first roughly corresponds to the English past perfect tense, which uses "had" as an auxiliary verb to refer to an action that was completed before some other action in the past. Examples:

बर्कली आने से पहले वह न्यू यॉर्क गया था ।
He had gone to New York before he came to Berkeley.
जब हम घर पहुँचे तब तक पिता जी दफ़्तर से नहीं आये थे ।
By the time we arrived home, father had not come back from the office.

(2) The past perfect tense is also used in Hindi for actions in the remote past. Example:

शाहजहाँ ने ताज महल बनवाया था । *Shah Jahan had the Taj Mahal built.*

(3) The past perfect tense is sometimes used in Hindi where English would simply use the perfect tense. Examples:

मैं वहाँ रहा ।	*I lived there.*
मैं वहाँ रहा हूँ ।	*I have lived there.*
मैं वहाँ रहा था ।	*I had lived there (or) I lived there.*

Notice that in the English translation of the last sentence, the perfect tense is more common than the past perfect. In Hindi, on the other hand, the past perfect tense is used in such situations to specify that some action occurred at some time before the immediate past (from the speaker's point of view), the था form stressing the time reference.

Formation: The past perfect is formed with the perfective forms of the main verb followed by the simple past forms of the verb होना *to be* (था, थे, थी, थीं).

The rules for agreement and for the use of the postposition ने with the subject are exactly the same as in the perfect and present perfect tenses. Also, as with the present perfect tense, if the verb agreement is feminine plural, only the second part of the verb phrase (i.e., the auxiliary verb) shows the plurality. The main verb is in the feminine singular form. Examples:

वह आगरा गया था ।	*He had gone to Agra.*
हम आगरा गये थे ।	*We had gone to Agra.*
मेरी बहन आगरा गई थी ।	*My sister had gone to Agra.*
वे लड़कियाँ आगरा गई थीं ।	*Those girls had gone to Agra.*
मैंने अख़बार पढ़ा था ।	*I had read the newspaper.*
मैंने दो अख़बार पढ़े थे ।	*I had read two newspapers.*
मैंने वह किताब पढ़ी थी ।	*I had read that book.*
मैंने वे किताबें पढ़ी थीं ।	*I had read those books.*

Exercises

1. Substitution drill

I had gone there.
मैं वहाँ गया था ।
हम लोग
लड़की
कौन
वह आदमी
पिता जी

हमारे दोस्त
मेरे माता-पिता
मेरी बहनें

2. <u>Substitution drill</u>

I had seen this room.
मैंने यह कमरा देखा था ।
वे कमरे
उस लड़के को
दो फ़िल्में
उन आदमियों को
वह सुन्दर तसवीर
आपका घर
वह मशहूर मन्दिर
ताज महल

3. <u>Substitution drill</u>

Ram had brought these books.
राम ये किताबें लाया था ।
मेरी माता जी
आपका दोस्त
हम
आप (F)
वे छात्र
तू (M)
कौन
तुम लोग
तेरा भाई
वे लड़कियाँ

4. Transformation drill

She was going home.	She had gone home.
वह घर जा रही थी ।	वह घर गई थी ।
वे बाज़ार से किताबें ला रहे थे ।	
मैं कुछ कपड़े ख़रीद रहा था ।	
मेरे दोस्त फ़िल्म देख रहे थे ।	
वे लोग काम शुरू कर रहे थे ।	
वह अशोका होटल में रुक रही थी ।	
हम फल खा रहे थे ।	
तुम किताब पढ़ रहे थे ।	
लड़की पत्र नहीं लिख रही थी ।	
कौन सवाल पूछ रहा था ।	
हम घर आ रहे थे ।	

5. Translation exercise

I gave Ram two hundred bananas. He went to Delhi. In Delhi, he sold those bananas to the fruitseller. Sita came into the fruitseller's shop. She bought some mangoes. Then she went to the bookstore. There she bought three books. Then Sita went home. She called her brother. She said to him, "Come out! Look, I have bought some books for you. Read them!" Sita's brother Mohan came outside. Sita gave Mohan the books. He looked at them. He said, "You have brought English books. I have learned English in school. I will read these books."

27. TIME EXPRESSIONS

Fractions:

चौथाई = quarter
आधा = half
पौन / पौना = three-quarters
पौने + numeral = numeral less a quarter (e.g, पौने तीन = two and three-quarters, i.e., a quarter less than three)
सवा = one and a quarter
सवा + numeral = numeral plus a quarter (e.g., सवा चार = four and a quarter)
डेढ़ = one and a half
ढाई = two and a half
साढ़े = plus a half (starting from three and a half)
साढ़े + numeral = numeral plus half (e.g., साढ़े पाँच = five and a half)

Note:

(1) चौथाई, आधा, and पौन are only used with nouns and never with numerals, e.g.,

चौथाई मील है। *It is one-quarter of a mile.*
आधा सेब लो। *Take half an apple.*
वह पौन घंटे में आएगा। *He will come in three-quarters of an hour.*

पौने and साढ़े are only used with numerals, never with nouns, e.g.,

पौने दो गज़ कपड़ा दीजिये।
Please give (me) one and three-quarters yards of cloth.
स्कूल यहाँ से साढ़े तीन मील है।
The school is three and a half miles from here.

(2) In English any number greater than one takes plural agreement, but in Hindi, डेढ़ (one and a half) is considered singular and takes singular agreement. For numbers greater than डेढ़ plural agreement is needed.

Telling Time: Hindi uses the intransitive verb बजना *to sound, to chime, to strike* to express time by the clock. It is used where English uses "o'clock." There are three possible ways one can ask, "What time is it?":

क्या बजा है ?	(lit., *What has struck?*)
कितने बजे हैं ?	(lit., *How many have struck?*)
क्या समय / वक़्त है ?	(lit., *What time is (it)?*)

The pattern used to state the time of the day in full hours is:

एक बजा है ।	*It's one o'clock.* (lit., *It has struck one.*)
दो बजे हैं ।	*It's two o'clock.* (lit., *It has struck two.*)
पाँच बजे हैं ।	*It's five o'clock.* (lit., *It has struck five.*)

Fractions are used in Hindi for quarter-hour and half-hour time expressions. The pattern for quarter past the hour is:

सवा बजा है ।	*It's a quarter past one.*
सवा तीन बजे हैं ।	*It's a quarter past three.*
सवा सात बजे हैं ।	*It's a quarter past seven.*

The pattern for half past the hour is:

डेढ़ बजा है ।	*It's half past one.*
ढाई बजे हैं ।	*It's half past two.*
साढ़े तीन बजे हैं ।	*It's half past three.*
साढ़े चार बजे हैं ।	*It's half past four.*

The pattern used for quarter to the hour is:

पौन बजा है ।	*It's a quarter to one.*
पौने तीन बजे हैं ।	*It's a quarter to three.*
पौने सात बजे हैं ।	*It's a quarter to seven.*

The pattern used to state time in minutes before and after the hour is:

चार बजने में एक मिनट (बाक़ी) है ।	*It's one minute to four o'clock.* (lit., *One minute [remains] before it strikes four.*)
पाँच बजने में दस मिनट (बाक़ी) हैं ।	*It's ten minutes to five o'clock.*
तीन बजकर दो मिनट (हुए) हैं ।	*It's two minutes after three o'clock.* (lit., *After striking three, two minutes have elapsed.*)
दस बजकर दस मिनट (हुए) हैं ।	*It's ten minutes past ten o'clock.*

When time expressions by the clock are used adverbially, Hindi uses the postposition पर. This postposition is generally understood. Examples:

वह कितने बजे (पर) आएगा ?	*At what time will he come?*
हम साढ़े सात बजे (पर) खाना खाएँगे ।	*We will eat at half past seven.*
वह एक बजे (पर) जाएगी ।	*She will go at one o'clock.*

When specific minutes are stated in an adverbial expression, the postposition पर is always expressed after the number of minutes. Examples:

मैं नौ बजकर दस मिनट पर काम शुरू करूँगी ।
I will begin the work at ten minutes after nine o'clock.
मैं तुम से चार बजने में पाँच मिनट पर मिलूँगी ।
I will meet you at five minutes to four o'clock.

When exact time is stated, ठीक is used before the time expressions. Example:

वह ठीक पाँच बजे पहुँचा ।   *He arrived exactly at five o'clock.*

Parts of the day:

सुबह (F)/ सवेरा (M)	*morning*	सवेरे / सुबह को	*in the morning*
दोपहर (F)	*afternoon*	दोपहर को	*at noon; in the afternoon*
शाम (F)	*evening*	शाम को	*in the evening*
रात (F)	*night*	रात को	*at night*

When these nouns are used adverbially, the postposition को is either used or understood with them. It may be omitted in colloquial speech if the context makes the adverbial use clear.

आप दोपहर को आइये ।
Please come in the afternoon.
मैं कल सवेरे (को) दस बजे यह काम ख़त्म करूँगा ।
I will finish this work tomorrow at ten o'clock in the morning.
वह कल शाम (को) पाँच बजे आया ।
He came yesterday at five o'clock in the evening.

Other words commonly used in time expressions:

आज (adv.)	*today*
कल (adv.)	*tomorrow; yesterday*
परसों (adv.)	*day after tomorrow; day before yesterday*
आजकल (adv.)	*these days*
रात (F)	*night*
दिन (M)	*day*
साल (M)	*year*
महीना (M)	*month*
हफ़्ता / सप्ताह (M)	*week*

तारीख़ (F)/ दिनांक (M)	*date*
घंटा (M)	*hour*
क़रीब / लगभग (adv.)	*approximately*
घड़ी (F)	*clock, watch*

Days of the week: (हफ़्ते / सप्ताह के दिन)

सोमवार	*Monday*
मंगलवार	*Tuesday*
बुधवार	*Wednesday*
बृहस्पतिवार / वीरवार / गुरूवार	*Thursday*
शुक्रवार	*Friday*
शनिवार	*Saturday*
रविवार / इतवार	*Sunday*

Note:

(1) All days of the week are treated as masculine nouns.

(2) In colloquial speech the suffix - वार is sometimes dropped after the days of the week, e.g., मैं मंगल को आई । *I came on Tuesday.*

(3) With the days of the week, when used adverbially, the postposition को is used, e.g., वह सोमवार को जाएगा । *He will go on Monday.*

Months and seasons of the year: The Western calendar is the most commonly used calendar in India today. Hindu and Islamic calendars are used mostly in religious and ceremonial contexts by Hindus and Muslims respectively.

Months: (महीने)

जनवरी (F)	*January*
फ़रवरी (F)	*February*
मार्च (M)	*March*

अप्रेल (M)	*April*
मई (F)	*May*
जून (M)	*June*
जुलाई (F)	*July*
अगस्त (M)	*August*
सितम्बर (M)	*September*
अक्टूबर (M)	*October*
नवम्बर (M)	*November*
दिसम्बर (M)	*December*

Seasons:

जाड़ा (M)	*winter*
गरमी / गर्मी (F)	*summer*
बरसात (F)	*rainy season; rain*
वसन्त (M)	*spring*
पतझड़ (M)	*fall*

Note:

(1) A.D. in Hindi is ईसवी (abbreviated as ई०) and B.C. is ईसा पूर्व (abbreviated as ई० पू०). When using the Christian era, the word सन् (year) is often also used before the number of the year, e.g.,

सन् १९४७ ई० में   *in 1947 A.D.*

(2) Dates in Hindi are expressed in the following sequence: day, month, year, e.g.,

१२ अप्रेल १९९०   *12 April 1990*

(3) When used adverbially, the postposition को is used with specific dates, e.g.,

वे पाँच जून को आएँगे ।   *They will come on the fifth of June.*

(4) The pronunciation of English months is slightly changed in Hindi and this is reflected in the Hindi spellings.

Summary of postpositions used in time expressions:

When stating the time something took place or will take place (i.e., when time expressions are used adverbially):

1. For times longer than a day, the postposition में is either used or understood much as it is in English, and therefore preceding nouns and adjectives are in the oblique case. Examples:

१९९० में *in 1990*, दो साल में *in two years*, एक हफ़्ते में *in one week*, अगले साल *next year*, पिछले महीने *last month*

2. For a specific day, always use the postposition को. Example:

हम शुक्रवार को आपसे मिलेंगे। *We will meet you on Friday.*

3. For a specific date, always use the postposition को. Example:

३१ मई को उसका जन्म-दिन है। *His birthday is on May 31.*

4. For parts of a day, the postposition को is either expressed or understood. Examples:

मैं आज रात को जाऊँगी। *I will go tonight.*
वह कल सवेरे आ सकता है। *He can come tomorrow morning.*

5. When parts of the day are used with clock-time expressions, a possessive form is sometimes used to express a.m. and p.m. Examples:

रात के दस बजे *10 p.m.* सवेरे के सवा आठ बजे *8:15 a.m.*

6. For exact time by the clock when specific minutes are given, always use the postposition पर. Example:

रेलगाड़ी दस बजकर दस मिनट पर आएगी ।	*The train will come at ten minutes after ten o'clock.*

7. The use of other postpositions with time expressions is much the same as in English. Examples:

मैं आज दोपहर तक यह काम ख़त्म करूँगी ।	*I will finish this work by this afternoon.*
मैं रविवार (इतवार) के बाद आ सकती हूँ ।	*I can come after Sunday.*
कल शाम से पहले (के पहले) यह पत्र लिखिये ।	*Please write this letter before tomorrow evening.*
हम रात में यह काम करेंगे ।	*We will do this work during the (at) night.*
मैं पिछले दो साल से इस दफ़्तर में काम कर रहा हूँ ।	*I have been working in this office for the last two years.*

8. The order of time phrases in the sentence is the largest unit first, then the second largest, etc. Example:

वह अगले सोमवार को सवेरे सात बजे आएगा ।	*Next Monday he will come at seven o'clock in the morning.*

Exercises

1. Substitution drill

It's one o'clock.
एक बजा है ।
four
seven
twelve

two
five
ten

2. Substitution drill

It's half past three (three-thirty).
साढ़े तीन बजे हैं ।
half past one
half past five
half past two
half past four
half past six
half past eight

3. Substitution drill

It's a quarter after eleven.
सवा ग्यारह बजे हैं ।
a quarter after two
a quarter after seven
a quarter after ten
a quarter after one
a quarter after five
a quarter after three

4. Substitution drill

It's a quarter to five.
पौने पाँच बजे हैं ।
a quarter to one
a quarter to six
a quarter to four

a quarter to eight
a quarter to eleven
a quarter to nine

5. Substitution drill

It's four o'clock.
चार बजे हैं।
half past four
a quarter to two
half past one
a quarter after four
half past seven
a quarter to one
a quarter after six
half past two
a quarter to eleven
half past eleven
a quarter after one

6. Chain drill

(Each student should add a quarter hour to the time given by the previous student.)

Q: What time is it?
क्या बजा है ?

A: It's twelve o'clock.
बारह बजे हैं।

Q: What time is it?
कितने बजे हैं ?

A: It's a quarter after twelve.
सवा बारह बजे हैं।

7. Substitution drill

We will come at five o'clock.
हम पाँच बजे (पर) आएँगे ।

at half past six
at one o'clock
at half past three
at a quarter after two
at eleven o'clock
at a quarter to one
at half past four
at a quarter after nine

8. Chain drill

Q: At what time will you come?
आप कितने बजे आएँगे ?

A: At six o'clock.
छह बजे ।

Q: At what time will you go to the library?
आप कितने बजे लाइब्रेरी जाएँगे ?

A: At half past twelve.
साढ़े बारह बजे ।

9. Substitution drill

It's ten minutes after two (o'clock).
दो बजकर दस मिनट (हुए) हैं ।
seven minutes after four
two minutes after three
five minutes after six

ten minutes after ten
twenty minutes after nine
twenty-five minutes after seven
one minute after nine

10. <u>Substitution drill</u>

It's five minutes to one (o'clock).
एक बजने में पाँच मिनट (बाक़ी) हैं ।
seven minutes to five
one minute to two
five minutes to four
ten minutes to one
two minutes to eleven
twenty minutes to nine

11. <u>Chain drill</u>

(Each student should add five minutes to the time given by the previous student.)

Q: What time is it?
क्या बजा है ?

A: It's two o'clock.
दो बजे हैं ।

Q: What time is it?
क्या समय है ?

A: It's five minutes after two.
दो बजकर पाँच मिनट हैं ।

12. Substitution drill

He arrived there at five minutes to two (o'clock).
वह दो बजने में पाँच मिनट पर वहाँ पहुँचा ।

at five minutes after seven
at one o'clock
at half past five
at ten minutes to nine
at twenty minutes after three
at a quarter after one
at a quarter to eight
at seven o'clock

13. Substitution drill

My friend will come tomorrow at five o'clock in the evening.
मेरा दोस्त कल शाम को पाँच बजे आएगा ।

on Monday
the day after tomorrow at one o'clock
on Wednesday
today in the afternoon
tomorrow morning
tomorrow at ten o'clock
by tomorrow night
next week
next month
next year
next Sunday
on the seventh of May
by five o'clock

14. Oral questions

आप रोज़ कितने बजे विश्वविद्यालय आते हैं ?
आप आज दस बजकर दस मिनट पर क्या करेंगे ?
अगले साल तुम कहाँ पढ़ोगे ?
तुम आज शाम को सात बजे किससे मिलोगे ?
तुम रोज़ कितने बजे सोते हो ?
आपका दोस्त कब भारत जाएगा ?
आज कौन-सा दिन है ?
क्या तुम हर रविवार को अपने कपड़े धोते हो ?
आपकी बहन कौन-सी तारीख़ को आएगी ?
तुम अगले शनिवार को क्या करोगे ?
पिछले हफ़्ते तुमने कौन-सी फ़िल्म देखी ?
पिछले सोमवार को तुम किससे मिले ?
आजकल तुम्हारा दोस्त कहाँ काम करता है ?
हमारी हिन्दी की क्लास रोज़ कितने बजे शुरू होती है ?

15. Translation exercise
(Write out all numbers in full.)

1. I will come tomorrow at 8:55 in the morning.
2. What time is it? It's half past one.
3. At what time will you go to San Francisco?
4. My parents will come to Berkeley next Friday.
5. Every day she goes to the office at 8:20 in the morning.
6. Last Wednesday I saw a good movie.
7. Next month I want to go to Chicago.
8. My father will come on the fifth of March.
9. Tomorrow we will meet you at 2:30 in the afternoon.
10. Our Hindi class starts at 9:10 in the morning.
11. What is the date today? Today is the twenty-seventh of July.
12. Every Sunday he cooks dinner for his family.

28. COMPARATIVE AND SUPERLATIVE CONSTRUCTIONS

Unlike English, Hindi adjectives do not have any special comparative or superlative forms. When a comparison between two nouns or pronouns is made, the general sentence structure in Hindi is:

subject	comparative phrase (i.e., the noun or pronoun with which the subject is compared + the postposition से)	adjective	verb

Note:

(1) The postposition से in a comparative construction is equivalent to the English "than."

(2) In contrast to English, where adjectives take special comparative forms (e.g., big -> bigger, good -> better), an adjective in a Hindi comparative construction simply agrees with the subject in number and gender. Examples:

राम सीता से लम्बा है।	*Ram is taller than Sita.* (i.e., *Ram compared to Sita is tall.*)
सीता राम से छोटी है।	*Sita is shorter/smaller/younger than Ram.*
वे कपड़े इन कपड़ों से महँगे हैं।	*Those clothes are more expensive than these clothes.*

Sometimes the word order between the subject and comparative phrase can be reversed. This change of word order does not affect the meaning of the sentence because the noun or pronoun with which the subject is compared is always followed by the postposition से. Example:

अमरीका भारत से बड़ा है।	*America is bigger than India.*
भारत से अमरीका बड़ा है।	*America is bigger than India.*

The adjectives ज़्यादा *more* and कम *less* are generally used when comparing amounts or numbers. Examples:

एक किलो एक पौंड से ज़्यादा है ।	*One kilogram is more than one pound.*
एक किलोमीटर एक मील से कम है ।	*One kilometer is less than a mile.*
एक रुपये से ज़्यादा न दीजिये ।	*Please don't give more than one rupee.*
दस डॉलर्स से कम न लूँगा ।	*I will not accept (take) less than ten dollars.*

Note:

(1) If ज़्यादा and कम are used in a sentence (either alone or with a following adjective) without any specific comparison, then they have the general meaning "too much/many" and "too little" respectively. Examples:

मेरे लिये यह खाना ज़्यादा है ।	*This food is too much for me.*
यह किताब ज़्यादा महँगी है ।	*This book is too expensive.*
एक रुपया कम है, कुछ और पैसे दीजिये ।	*One rupee is too little; please give some more money.*

(2) ज़्यादा (although ending in - आ) is an unmarked adjective and does not change to agree with the noun it modifies. Examples:

ज़्यादा पैसा	*much/too much money*
ज़्यादा लोग	*many/too many people*
ज़्यादा शराब	*much/too much liquor*

As mentioned previously, there are no special superlative forms for adjectives in Hindi. Superlative adjectives are formed by adding सबसे before the adjective. Examples:

सुन्दर	*pretty*	सबसे सुन्दर	*prettiest* (i.e., *prettier than all*)
बड़ा	*big*	सबसे बड़ा	*biggest* (i.e., *bigger than all*)
अच्छा	*good*	सबसे अच्छा	*best* (i.e., *better than all*)

The sentence structure of the superlative construction in Hindi is similar to the comparative construction except that the comparison is made with सब *all*. Examples:

मैं आप से छोटी हूँ।	*I am younger/smaller than you.*
मैं सबसे छोटी हूँ।	*I am the youngest/smallest.*
	(i.e., *younger/smaller than all*)
आपकी बहन सीता से सुन्दर है।	*Your sister is prettier than Sita.*
आपकी बहन सबसे सुन्दर है।	*Your sister is the prettiest.*

Note that सबसे is usually written as one word.

Exercises

1. Substitution drill

This house is bigger than that house.
यह घर उस घर से बड़ा है।
छोटा
अच्छा
सुन्दर
महँगा
सस्ता
नया
पुराना

2. Individual conversational response drill

What is Hindi easier than?	Hindi is easier than Sanskrit.
हिन्दी किससे आसान है ?	हिन्दी संस्कृत से आसान है।
भारत किससे बड़ा है ?	
श्री लंका किससे छोटा है ?	

अमरीका किससे बड़ा है ?
सैन फ्रैन्सिस्को शहर किस शहर से सुन्दर है ?
तुम किससे छोटे हो ?
आप किससे बड़े हैं ?
संस्कृत किससे मुश्किल है ?
आपका भाई किससे लम्बा है ?
यह यूनिवर्सिटी किससे बड़ी है ?

3. Chain drill

Q: Who are you younger (smaller) than?
आप किससे छोटे हैं ?

A: I'm younger (smaller) than my sister.
मैं अपनी बहन से छोटा हूँ ।

4. Substitution drill

His shoes are more expensive than mine.
उसके जूते मेरे जूतों से महँगे हैं ।

Her sari
His book
Their house
His bag
Their clothes
His shirt
Her car

5. Substitution drill

Don't give him more than three books.
उसको तीन किताबों से ज़्यादा न दो ।

more than five rupees
more than two pencils
more than ten dollars
less than two books

less than four sweets
less than five dollars

6. Substitution drill

This is my cheapest book.
यह् मेरी सबसे सस्ती किताब है ।

most expensive
best
smallest
biggest
most difficult
easiest
newest

7. Substitution drill

Which language do you like best?
आपको कौन-सी भाषा सबसे अच्छी लगती है ?

देश
मौसम
शहर
लड़का
लड़की
छात्र
किताब
संगीत
फूल
रंग

8. Chain drill

Q: Which sweet do you like best?
आपको कौन-सी मिठाई सबसे अच्छी लगती है ?

A: I like rasgulla best.
मुझे रसगुल्ला सबसे अच्छा लगता है ।

9. Oral questions

क्या अमरीका भारत से बड़ा है ?
क्या भारत पाकिस्तान से छोटा है ?
क्या बर्कली सैन फ़्रैन्सिस्को से बड़ा है ?
क्या हिमालय पहाड़ सबसे ऊँचा पहाड़ है ?
क्या ताज महल भारत की सबसे सुन्दर इमारत है ?
क्या सैन फ़्रैन्सिस्को सबसे सुन्दर शहर है ?
भारत में कौन-सा प्रदेश सबसे बड़ा है ?
दुनिया में कौन-सा पहाड़ सबसे ऊँचा है ?
बर्कली में सबसे पुरानी इमारत कहाँ है ?
अमरीका में कौन-सी नदी सबसे चौड़ी है ?
अमरीका में कौन-सी नदी सबसे लम्बी है ?
दुनिया में कौन-सा देश सबसे बड़ा है ?
दुनिया में कौन-सा देश सबसे छोटा है ?
आपको कौन-सा मौसम सबसे अच्छा लगता है ?
आपको कौन-सी किताब सबसे दिलचस्प लगती है ?

10. Translation exercise

1. My room is bigger than your room.
2. This book is better than the old book.
3. What kind of food do you like best?
4. That smart student wrote the best essay.
5. I am the youngest in my family, but my husband is the oldest in his family.
6. I will not give him more than two hundred dollars for this work.
7. This university is the best in America.
8. Tamil is easier than Sanskrit, but Hindi is easier than Tamil.
9. Which country is the biggest in the world?
10. I am taller than my sister, but my brother is the tallest in the family.

29. THE VERB होना

The verb होना is unique in Hindi because in its infinitive form it represents two different verbs. One of these verbs means "to be" and the other has a range of meanings suggested by the English verbs "to occur," "to happen," "to become."

(1) होना with the meanings "to occur," "to happen," "to take place," "to become" is a regular intransitive verb. It is conjugated like an ordinary intransitive verb. The masculine singular forms are:

होता है	present habitual tense
हो रहा है	present progressive tense
होता था	past habitual tense
हो रहा था	past progressive tense
होगा	future tense
हुआ	perfect tense
हुआ है	present perfect tense
हुआ था	past perfect tense

Examples:

कल यहाँ एक भाषण हुआ ।	*Yesterday a lecture took place (happened) here.*
फल ख़राब हुआ ।	*The fruit became rotten (bad).*
बच्चे बड़े हो रहे हैं ।	*The children are getting (becoming) big.*
यहाँ रोज़ क्लास होती है ।	*Every day the class is held here.*
कल यहाँ मीटिंग होगी ।	*Tomorrow a meeting will take place here.*

(2) होना meaning "to be" is the only verb in Hindi that has both simple present and present habitual forms. All other verbs in Hindi have only present habitual forms.

The simple present forms of the verb होना *to be* are used to make specific statements, while the present habitual forms are employed for general, usual, or habitual statements. The verb होना with the meaning "to be" does not have progressive and perfect forms.

The following are the different tenses of the verb होना *to be* showing only the masculine singular third person forms:

	होना *to be* for specific statements	होना *to be* for general statements
Present	है	होता है
Past	था	होता था
Future/presumptive	होगा	होता होगा

Examples:

ये लखनऊ के आम मीठे हैं ।	*These mangoes from (of) Lucknow are sweet.*
यह विदेशी अख़बार महँगा है ।	*This foreign newspaper is expensive.*
यह सन्तरा बड़ा है ।	*This orange is big.*
ये अमरीकन लम्बे हैं ।	*These Americans are tall.*
लखनऊ के आम मीठे होते हैं ।	*Mangoes from Lucknow are (usually) sweet.*
विदेशी अख़बार महँगे होते हैं ।	*Foreign newspapers are (generally) expensive.*
कैलिफ़ोर्निया के संतरे बड़े होते हैं ।	*California oranges are (usually) big.*
अमरीकन लम्बे होते हैं ।	*Americans are (usually) tall.*

Summary

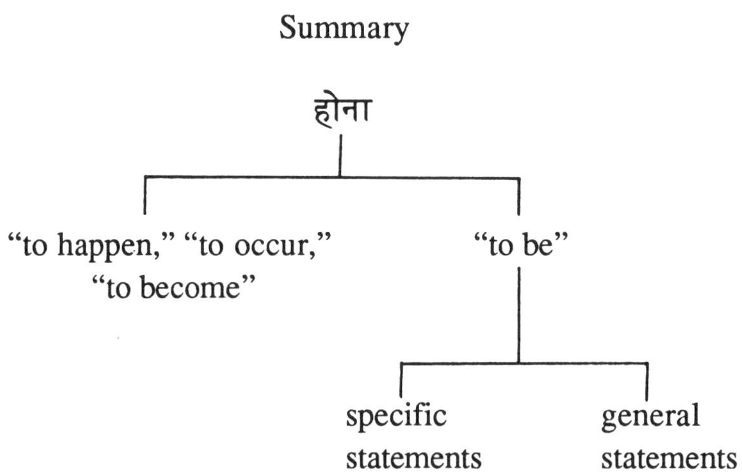

The exact meaning of the verb होना depends on the context.

Examples:

कल वहाँ पार्टी थी ।	*There was a party there yesterday.*
कल वहाँ पार्टी हुई ।	*A party took place there yesterday.*
कमरा साफ़ था ।	*The room was clean.*
कमरा साफ़ हुआ ।	*The room was cleaned (became clean).*
आज यहाँ का मौसम अच्छा है ।	*Today the weather is good here.*
यहाँ का मौसम अच्छा होता है ।	*The weather here is (generally) good.*
ये रेशमी साड़ियाँ महँगी हैं ।	*These silk saris are expensive.*
रेशमी साड़ियाँ महँगी होती हैं ।	*Silk saris are (generally) expensive.*

Exercises

1. Transformation drill

These California oranges are sweet.
ये कैलिफ़ोर्निया के संतरे मीठे हैं ।

California oranges are (generally) sweet.
कैलिफ़ोर्निया के संतरे मीठे होते हैं ।

ये कानपुर की चप्पलें अच्छी हैं ।
इस देश के फल बहुत अच्छे हैं ।
ये लखनऊ के खिलौने बहुत सुन्दर हैं ।
आज बर्कली का मौसम अच्छा है ।
ये बनारस की साड़ियाँ सुन्दर हैं ।
आज उसके फल महँगे हैं ।
ये अमरीकन लोग लम्बे हैं ।
ये बंगाली रसगुल्ले अच्छे हैं ।
आज उसके फूल बहुत सुन्दर हैं ।
ये रेशमी कपड़े महँगे हैं ।

2. Substitution drill

In this country, houses are (generally) big.
इस देश में मकान बड़े होते हैं ।

फूल सुन्दर
मिठाइयाँ अच्छी
हड़तालें बहुत
भाषण ज़्यादा
लोग लम्बे
फल मीठे
मौसम ठंडा
चीज़ें सस्ती

3. Substitution drill

What is happening (going on) here?
यहाँ क्या हो रहा है ?

भाषण
क्लास
पार्टी
मीटिंग
हड़ताल
हंगामा
गड़बड़
कुछ नहीं
तमाशा

4. Chain drill

Q: What was going on here?
यहाँ क्या हो रहा था ?

A: A meeting was going on here.
यहाँ मीटिंग हो रही थी ।

5. Substitution drill

A party took place there yesterday.
कल वहाँ एक पार्टी हुई ।

एक घटना
हड़ताल
पार्टी
भाषण
क्लास
हंगामा
कुछ गड़बड़

6. Chain drill

Q: What happened here the day before yesterday?
परसों यहाँ क्या हुआ ?

A: Nothing happened here the day before yesterday.
परसों यहाँ कुछ नही हुआ ।

7. Transformation drill

He is becoming old.	He became old.
वह बूढ़ा हो रहा है ।	वह बूढ़ा हुआ ।
बच्चे बड़े हो रहे हैं ।	
कमरा साफ़ हो रहा है ।	
खाना तैयार हो रहा है ।	
रोटी बासी हो रही है ।	
यह गाड़ी पुरानी हो रही है ।	
उसके बाल सफ़ेद हो रहे हैं ।	
वह मोटा हो रहा है ।	
बच्चे तैयार हो रहे हैं ।	
उसके कपड़े गन्दे हो रहे हैं ।	

8. Translation exercise

1. The flowers of this country are very pretty.
2. The saris from Madras are expensive.
3. We are all becoming old.
4. What is happening in this class?
5. The weather of Berkeley is (generally) good.
6. Yesterday a lecture took place in this big room.
7. Last year a lot of unrest took place in this city.
8. Because of his illness, he became fat.
9. Buildings in this country are (usually) big.
10. These children are getting ready for the party.

30. COMPULSION AND OBLIGATION

Hindi distinguishes between various degrees of compulsion and obligation by using three different auxiliary verbs with the infinitive of the main verb. The basic structure of a sentence that expresses the idea of compulsion or obligation is:

the person who + को is under an obligation	object	infinitive of the main verb	चाहिये (need to, ought to, should) होना (have/has to) पड़ना (must)

Example:

आपको ये किताबें ख़रीदनी चाहियें ।
You should buy these books.

Thus, in a construction of compulsion or obligation the subject of the equivalent English sentence (i.e., the person who is under a compulsion or obligation) is always followed by the postposition को, which "blocks" the agreement of the verb with it. The verb (both parts, the infinitive of the main verb and the auxiliary verb) agrees with the direct object of the infinitive. If there is no such object in the sentence or if the object is also followed by a postposition, then the verb takes the neutral form (i.e., masculine singular form).

Infinitive of the main verb + चाहिये: The construction using चाहिये as an auxiliary verb with the infinitive of the main verb has meanings similar to the English "ought to" and "should." Examples:

लड़के को अपना काम करना चाहिये ।	*The boy should/ought to do his work.*
आपको ये किताबें पढ़नी चाहियें ।	*You should/ought to read these books.*

उसको कहानियाँ लिखनी चाहियें । *He should/ought to write stories.*
तुम्हें सिगरेट नहीं पीनी चाहिये । *You shouldn't smoke cigarette(s).*

Note: Some speakers use चाहिये for both singular and plural agreement.

In the past tense, appropriate simple past forms of होना *to be* (i.e., था, थे, थी, or थीं) are used with चाहिये. Examples:

उसको घर जाना चाहिये था ।
He should have gone home.
आपको दो पत्र लिखने चाहिये थे ।
You should have written two letters.
छात्र को कहानी पढ़नी चाहिये थी ।
The student should have read the story.
लड़की को अपनी साड़ियाँ धोनी चाहिये थीं ।
The girl should have washed her saris.

Note: There is no special future form for this type of compulsion since the present tense with चाहिये / चाहियें also has a future implication. Example:

मुझे जाना चाहिये ।
I should go (now or in future).

Infinitive of the main verb + होना: This type of compulsion construction conveys a different type of obligation than the previous one and is equivalent to the English "have to." Examples:

मुझे अपना निबन्ध लिखना है । *I have to write my essay.*
हमें अपने शिक्षक से मिलना है । *We have to meet our teacher.*
उसको यह किताब पढ़नी है । *He has to read this book.*

For the past and future tenses, the past and the future forms of the verb होना *to be* are used with the infinitive of the main verb. Examples:

छात्रों को कल हिन्दी पढ़नी थी ।
Yesterday the students had to study Hindi.
आपको उर्दू सीखनी होगी ।
You will have to learn Urdu.
मेरे दोस्त को कल बहुत चिट्ठियाँ लिखनी थीं ।
Yesterday my friend had to write many letters.
हमें कल क्या करना होगा ।
What will we have to do tomorrow?

Infinitive of the main verb + पड़ना: Such sentences indicate a stronger sense of compulsion or obligation and are usually equivalent to the English "must," "have to." The use of the verb पड़ना in a compulsion construction often implies that it is necessary for the person to perform the action of the infinitive because of either some circumstantial or external pressure. Since the verb पड़ना can be conjugated in all tenses, this construction is found in all tenses. Examples:

उनको रोज़ काम करना पड़ता है ।	*They must work every day.*
छात्रों को किताबें ख़रीदनी पड़ेंगी ।	*The students will have to (must) buy the books.*
कल उसको एक निबन्ध लिखना पड़ा ।	*Yesterday he had to write an essay.*
आज उसको बहुत काम करना पड़ रहा है ।	*Today he is having to do a lot of work.*
उनको विदेशियों से लड़ना पड़ा था ।	*They had to fight with the foreigners.*

Note: The distinction between the infinitive + होना and the infinitive + पड़ना is one of degree only. While the infinitive + होना is similar to the English "has/have to," the infinitive + पड़ना is closer to the English "must," "to be obliged to," "to be forced to." But "must" in English has no future and past forms; therefore "will have to" or "had to" can be translated into Hindi with either होना or पड़ना depending on the degree of obligation one wants to convey.

Exercises

1. Substitution drill

The boy has to buy some books.
लड़के को कुछ किताबें ख़रीदनी हैं ।

एक साड़ी
नये जूते
एक फल
बहुत चीजें
नई कार
दो कमीज़ें
कुछ कपड़े
कुछ चीज़ें

2. Substitution drill

I have to study Hindi.
मुझे हिन्दी पढ़नी है ।

to eat an orange
to buy a new car
to sell ten saris
to finish this work
to ask some questions
to write a letter
to meet Mr. Miller
to go home
to bring some things
to read this story
to write an essay

3. <u>Chain drill</u>

Q: What do you have to do today?
आपको आज क्या करना है ?

A: I have to study Hindi today.
मुझे आज हिन्दी पढ़नी है ।

4. <u>Oral questions</u>

आपको आज क्या करना है ?
तुम्हें आज कहाँ जाना है ?
उसको आज क्या धोना है ?
उसको आज क्या बेचना है ?
किसको घर जाना है ?
तुम्हें आज क्या पढ़ना है ?
छात्र को आज क्या लिखना है ?
किसको यह मेज़ ठीक करनी है ?
किसको आज पत्र लिखना है ?
उसको कब आना है ?
आपको अपने दोस्तों से कब मिलना है ?
छात्रों को आज क्या करना है ?

5. <u>Substitution drill</u>

Where did you have to go yesterday?
तुम्हें कल कहाँ जाना था ?
क्या पढ़ना
क्या लिखना
क्या ख़रीदना
किससे मिलना
क्या पकाना

क्या करना
क्या साफ़ करना
क्या ठीक करना

6. <u>Transformation drill</u>

He was going home.	He had to go home.
वह घर जा रहा था ।	उसको घर जाना था ।
लड़की काम कर रही थी ।	
राम अख़बार पढ़ रहा था ।	
छात्र लेख लिख रहा था ।	
लड़का कमरा साफ़ कर रहा था ।	
वह लड़की कपड़े ख़रीद रही थी ।	
वे छात्र बहुत सवाल पूछ रहे थे ।	
तुम किताबें बेच रहे थे ।	
वे छात्र हिन्दी बोल रहे थे ।	
हम लाइब्रेरी जा रहे थे ।	

7. <u>Chain drill</u>

Q: What did you have to do yesterday?
आपको कल क्या करना था ?

A: I had to read a book.
मुझे एक किताब पढ़नी थी ।

Q: You weren't home yesterday. Why?
तुम कल घर में नहीं थे । क्यों ?

A: I had to go to the library.
मुझे लाइब्रेरी जाना था ।

8. Transformation drill

He will go to the office.	He will have to go to the office.
वह दफ़्तर जाएगा ।	उसको दफ़्तर जाना होगा ।
लड़की अपने कपड़े धोएगी ।	
हम यह काम करेंगे ।	
तुम क्या करोगे ?	
तू क्या पढ़ेगा ?	
आपका भाई कहाँ जाएगा ?	
वह लड़की किससे मिलेगी ?	
मैं बहुत काम करूँगी ।	
मैं राम को ये किताबें दूँगा ।	
मैं दोस्त को पत्र लिखूँगी ।	
वे लोग कैम्पस नहीं आएँगे ।	

9. Substitution drill

He has to (must) do a lot of work.
उसको बहुत काम करना पड़ता है ।

बहुत पत्र लिखने
रोज़ क्लास जाना
रोज़ खाना पकाना
बहुत पैसे देने
अपने कपड़े धोने
अपना कमरा साफ़ करना
हिन्दी पढ़नी
क्या करना

10. Substitution drill

We had to (were forced to) study Hindi yesterday.
हमें कल हिन्दी पढ़नी पड़ी ।

to give the answers
to buy some books

to go to the library
to do their work
to do a lot of work
to write the letters
to read two stories
to give a lot of money

11. Transformation drill

I will come to campus.	I will have to (will be forced to) come to campus.
मैं कैम्पस आऊँगी ।	मुझे कैम्पस आना पड़ेगा ।
लड़का हिन्दी पढ़ेगा ।	
हम किताबें ख़रीदेंगे ।	
तुम क्या करोगे ?	
वह पत्र लिखेगा ।	
हम बहुत काम करेंगे ।	
मैं खाना पकाऊँगी ।	
वह जवाब देगी ।	
छात्र लेख लिखेगा ।	

12. Chain drill

Q: What did you have to (were you forced to) do yesterday?
आपको कल क्या करना पड़ा ?

A: I had to (was forced to) cook food.
मुझे खाना पकाना पड़ा ।

Q: What will you have to (will you be forced to) do tomorrow?
तुम्हें कल क्या करना पड़ेगा ?

A: I will have to (will be forced to) read this book.
मुझे यह किताब पढ़नी पड़ेगी ।

Q: What do you have to (must you) do these days?
आपको आजकल क्या करना पड़ता है ?

A: I have to (must) do a lot of work.
मुझे बहुत काम करना पड़ता है ।

13. <u>Substitution drill</u>

We ought to study.
हमें पढ़ना चाहिये ।
घर जाना
सवाल पूछना
हिन्दी बोलनी
छुट्टी मिलनी
दुनिया देखनी
भारत जाना
हँसना
रोना नहीं
बहुत किताबें पढ़नी
अपने दोस्तों से मिलना
सच बोलना
रोज़ अख़बार पढ़ना
झूठ नहीं बोलना

14. <u>Transformation drill</u>

Students read books. छात्र किताबें पढ़ते हैं ।	Students should read books. छात्रों को किताबें पढ़नी चाहियें ।

हम हिन्दी बोलते हैं ।
हम झूठ नहीं बोलते ।
तुम लाइब्रेरी जाते हो ।
बच्चे दूध पीते हैं ।
बच्चे पार्क में खेलते हैं ।
लड़की पत्र लिखती है ।

हम हिन्दी की फ़िल्में देखते हैं ।
कौन यह काम करता है ?

15. Substitution drill

He should have (ought to have) gone home yesterday.
उसको कल घर जाना चाहिये था ।

काम ख़त्म करना
माता-पिता को पत्र लिखना
लाइब्रेरी जाना
किताबें पढ़नी
ये सवाल पूछने
शराब नहीं पीनी
अपने दोस्त से मिलना
अपने कपड़े धोने

16. Chain drill

Q: What should I do?
मुझे क्या करना चाहिये ?

A: You should finish this work.
आपको यह काम ख़त्म करना चाहिये ।

Q: What should you have done yesterday?
आपको कल क्या करना चाहिये था ?

A: I should have met my friend.
मुझे अपने दोस्त से मिलना चाहिये था ।

17. Oral questions

तुम्हें आज क्या करना है ?
आपको हर दिन क्या करना पड़ता है ?

किसको दूध पीना चाहिये ?
छात्रों को क्या करना पड़ता है ?
बच्चों को कहाँ नहीं खेलना चाहिये ?
आपको हर रोज़ कितने बजे कैम्पस आना पड़ता है ?
आपको आज कहाँ जाना है ?
आपको भारत में कौन-सी भाषा बोलनी पड़ेगी ?
हमें कल क्या करना होगा ?
आपको कल कहाँ जाना था ?
मुझे कब आना चाहिये था ?
किसको भारत जाना है ?
आपको क्या करना चाहिये ?
मुझे कितना पैसा देना चाहिये था ?
छात्रों को क्या ख़रीदना पड़ता है ?
आप लोगों को क्या पढ़ना चाहिये ?

18. Translation exercise

1. I have to go home to meet my parents.
2. Who had to read this book? All Hindi students had to read this book.
3. Tomorrow we will have to do a lot of work.
4. You will have to finish this work today.
5. She should have (ought to have) written the letter to her friend.
6. He should take a vacation and (should) see the world.
7. Little children should drink milk.
8. What should I have done? You should have gone there.
9. You should have (ought to have) finished your work.
10. The students had to (were forced to) give many speeches in Hindi class.
11. We have to (must) ask some questions in Hindi.
12. Next year I will have to (will be forced to) earn some money.
13. The students had to (were forced to) buy a lot of books.
14. Examinations are near; therefore we will have to (will be forced to) study a lot now.
15. What was he forced to do? He was forced to leave the university and start working.

31. CONJUNCT VERBS WITH करना

There are many verbs in Hindi that are created by combining a noun or an adjective with a verb (generally करना *to do; to make*). Such verbs are called conjunct verbs. In a conjunct verb, both the non-verbal element and the verb are needed to convey a single verbal idea. In a conjunct verb, the non-verbal element (i.e., the noun or adjective) always remains invariant, and all the changes due to number, gender, and tense agreement occur in the second element of the verb.

There are two types of conjunct verbs: adjectival conjunct verbs and nominal conjunct verbs.

Adjectival conjunct verbs: Such verbs are formed by combining an adjective with करना. Although the adjectival element is necessary to render the meaning of the verb, grammatically such verbs are similar in every way to simple transitive verbs. Examples:

लड़का कुरसी ठीक करता है ।	*The boy fixes the chair.* (lit., *The boy makes the chair right.*)
नौकर कमरा साफ़ करता है ।	*The servant cleans the room.* (lit., *The servant makes the room clean.*)
हमारी माँ ने खाना तैयार किया ।	*Our mother prepared the food.* (lit., *Our mother made the food ready.*)
क्या दुकानदार दाम कम करेगा ।	*Will the shopkeeper reduce the price?* (lit., *Will the shopkeeper make the price less?*)

Nominal conjunct verbs: These consist of a noun followed by the verb करना. The noun element in such verbs not only helps to provide the meaning of the verb but also functions as the grammatical object of the verb करना. The object of the corresponding English sentence (whether a noun, pronoun, or infinitive) is always followed by a postposition (often का, की, or से). Examples:

मैं मदद करता हूँ ।	*I help.* (lit., *I do help.*)
मैं आपकी मदद करता हूँ ।	*I help you.* (lit., *I do your help.*)
हम शिक्षक का इन्तज़ार कर रहे हैं ।	*We are waiting for the teacher.* (lit., *We are doing the waiting of the teacher.*)
वे भारत जाने की कोशिश करेंगे ।	*They will try to go to India.* (lit., *They will make an attempt of going to India.*)
छात्र अपने दोस्त से बात कर रहा है ।	*The student is conversing (talking) with his friend.* (lit., *The student is making a conversation with his friend.*)

Note: There are some conjunct verbs that consist of a noun plus करना and function in all respects like simple transitive verbs; that is, the object of the sentence is either not followed by a postposition or is marked by को just as most transitive verbs are (see Section 24 on transitive verbs), e.g., शुरू करना *to begin,* काम करना *to work.* Example:

शिक्षक ने क्लास शुरू की ।	*The teacher began the class.*

Nominal conjunct verbs can be used in two types of constructions, where the subject of the sentence is always followed by a postposition and the verb agrees with the direct object: (1) sentences in perfective tenses with transitive verbs; (2) compulsion constructions. In these two types of constructions, with a nominal conjunct verb, the verb agrees with the noun element of the verb itself since the object is also followed by a postposition, which "blocks" the agreement.

Examples:

मैं आपकी मदद करता हूँ।	*I help you.*
मैंने आपकी मदद की।	*I helped you.*
मुझे आपकी मदद करनी चाहिये।	*I should help you.*
मैं अपने दोस्त का इन्तज़ार कर रहा हूँ।	*I am waiting for my friend.*
मैंने अपने दोस्त का इन्तज़ार किया।	*I waited for my friend.*
मुझे अपने दोस्त का इन्तज़ार करना चाहिये।	*I should wait for my friend.*
वह अपने घर की मरम्मत करेगा।	*He will repair his house.*
उसने अपने घर की मरम्मत की।	*He repaired his house.*
उसको अपने घर की मरम्मत करनी पड़ी।	*He had to repair his house.*
वह हिन्दी बोलने की कोशिश करता है।	*He tries to speak Hindi.*
उसने हिन्दी बोलने की कोशिश की।	*He tried to speak Hindi.*
उसको हिन्दी बोलने की कोशिश करनी चाहिये।	*He should try to speak Hindi.*

Note:

(1) All conjunct verbs with करना are transitive, or ने, verbs. They have their intransitive counterparts, in which होना is used in place of करना. These will be discussed in Section 38.

(2) In negative sentences, the negative particle नहीं generally comes after the non-verbal element and before करना. Examples:

उसने कल घर साफ़ नहीं किया।	*He did not clean the house yesterday.*
उन्होंने हमारी मदद नहीं की।	*They did not help us.*

Exercises

1. Substitution drill

I will clean the room.
मैं कमरा साफ़ करूँगा ।

close the door
return the books
finish the story
reduce the price
fix up my room
clean my house
prepare the sweets
begin the work

2. Transformation drill

He begins the work.
वह काम शुरू करता है ।

He should begin the work.
उसको काम शुरू करना चाहिये ।

मैं कमरा साफ़ करता हूँ ।
लड़का दरवाज़ा बन्द करता है ।
लड़की मेरी किताबें वापस करती है ।
पिता जी कहानी ख़त्म करते हैं ।
कपड़ेवाला साड़ी का दाम कम करता है ।
माँ खाना तैयार करती हैं ।
मैं अपना कमरा ठीक करता हूँ ।

3. Substitution drill

I repaired the table.
मैंने मेज़ की मरम्मत की ।

car
chair
watch
window

shoes
telephone
radio
door

4. Chain drill

Q: What (thing) did you repair?
आपने किस चीज़ की मरम्मत की ?

A: I repaired my car.
मैंने अपनी कार की मरम्मत की ।

5. Substitution drill

We should help everyone.
हमें सबकी मदद करनी चाहिये ।

him
our friends
our parents
ourselves
those children
Lisa
poor people
our family
them

6. Chain drill

Q: Whom do you help?
आप किसकी मदद करते हैं ?

A: I help my friends.
मैं अपने दोस्तों की मदद करता हूँ ।

Q: Whom should we help?
हमें किसकी मदद करनी चाहिये ?

A: We should help poor people.
हमें ग़रीब लोगों की मदद करनी चाहिये ।

7. Substitution drill

We waited for you.
हमने आपका इन्तज़ार किया ।

for our friends
for Christmas
for food
for the servant
for you (familiar form)
for your sister
for our teacher
for his letter

8. Chain drill

Q: For whom are you waiting?
आप किसका इन्तज़ार कर रहे हैं ?

A: I am waiting for my friend.
मैं अपने दोस्त का इन्तज़ार कर रहा हूँ ।

9. Substitution drill

He decided to go to India.
उसने भारत जाने का फ़ैसला किया ।

to sell his house
to study Urdu
to do a lot of work
to stay here

to write Hindi every day
to write a letter to the Governor
to send him money
to meet the President

10. <u>Substitution drill</u>

Ram tried to swim.
राम ने तैरने की कोशिश की ।

to finish the work
to sell the car
to read Urdu
to cook Indian food
to teach English
to speak fast
to learn the sitar
to speak French

11. <u>Transformation drill</u>

I will try to go to India.	I should try to go to India.
मैं भारत जाने की कोशिश करूँगी ।	मुझे भारत जाने की कोशिश करनी चाहिये ।

लड़का काम करने की कोशिश करेगा ।
छात्र हिन्दी बोलने की कोशिश करेंगे ।
हम उनकी मदद करने की कोशिश करेंगे ।
छात्र उर्दू लिखने की कोशिश करेंगे ।
मैं वहाँ आने की कोशिश करूँगी ।
वह काम ख़त्म करने की कोशिश करेगा ।
हम जल्दी बोलने की कोशिश करेंगे ।
हम ठीक समय पर आने की कोशिश करेंगे ।

12. Substitution drill

Practice speaking Hindi.
हिन्दी बोलने का अभ्यास करो ।
हिन्दी लिखने का
उर्दू पढ़ने का
उर्दू लिखने का
जल्दी बोलने का
ठीक लिखने का
जल्दी काम करने का
सितार बजाने का

13. Transformation drill

We were fixing the chairs.	We fixed the chairs.
हम कुरसियाँ ठीक कर रहे थे ।	हमने कुरसियाँ ठीक कीं ।
हम कमरा साफ़ कर रहे थे ।	
हम आपका इन्तज़ार कर रहे थे ।	
हम दोस्त की मदद कर रहे थे ।	
हम पढ़ने की कोशिश कर रहे थे ।	
हम उर्दू लिखने का अभ्यास कर रहे थे ।	
हम वहाँ जाने का फ़ैसला कर रहे थे ।	
हम कार की मरम्मत कर रहे थे ।	
हम काम ख़त्म कर रहे थे ।	
हम खाना तैयार कर रहे थे ।	

14. Transformation drill

I helped my friend.	I didn't help my friend.
मैंने अपने दोस्त की मदद की ।	मैंने अपने दोस्त की मदद नहीं की ।
हमने फ़्रैंच बोलने की कोशिश की ।	
उन्होंने नौ बजे क्लास शुरू की ।	

नौकर ने यह कमरा साफ़ किया ।
मेरे दोस्त ने कुछ किताबें वापस कीं ।
कपड़ेवाले ने साड़ी का दाम कम किया ।
उसने खिड़की बन्द की ।
मैंने अपनी कार की मरम्मत की ।
हमने पाँच बजे तक आपका इन्तज़ार किया ।

15. Oral questions

कौन मेरी मदद करेगा ?
आप किसकी मदद करेंगे ?
कौन हिन्दी बोलने की कोशिश करेगा ?
क्या तुम अपने दोस्त की मदद करने की कोशिश करोगे ?
आपने कल किसका इन्तज़ार किया ?
किसने इस खिड़की की मरम्मत की ?
आपने कब भारत जाने का फ़ैसला किया है ?
कौन हिन्दी बोलने का अभ्यास करते हैं ?
तुमने कल किससे बात की ?
तुम मेरी किताब कब वापस करोगे ?
तुम किसका इन्तज़ार कर रहे हो ?
किसने यह कमरा साफ़ किया ?
किसने भारत जाने का फ़ैसला किया ?
तुमने कब यह काम शुरू किया ?

16. Translation exercise

1. You should finish this work by five o'clock today.
2. Please try to come on time.
3. Who will help this old woman? I will help her.
4. What are you doing here? I am waiting for my friends.
5. Yesterday my husband repaired his (own) car.
6. He didn't return my books.

7. Rich people should help poor people.
8. The clothseller reduced the price of the sari for the foreigner.
9. Why didn't you wait for me after class?
10. Yesterday those students practiced writing Urdu.
11. They have decided to live in this house.
12. Hindi students should try to speak Hindi with each other every day.

32. THE EMPHATIC PARTICLES ही AND भी

Hindi frequently uses the particles ही and भी to emphasize a particular word or phrase in a sentence in addition to using other methods such as special intonation patterns (higher pitch, louder stress) or a change in word order. These emphatic particles immediately follow the word or phrase they emphasize.

भी: The particle भी generally can be translated as "too," "also" and in negative sentences as "even." It has an inclusive force, including the word or phrase that precedes it with some other entity or group. Examples:

मैं भी आज यह फ़िल्म देखूँगी ।
I too will see this film today (besides other people).
भारत में हमने ताजमहल भी देखा ।
In India, we saw the Taj Mahal also (in addition to seeing other things).
उस समय कमरे में एक भी छात्र नहीं था ।
There was not even one student in the room at that time.

Note: Hindi requires that भी follow immediately after the word or phrase it refers to, whereas in English the word "also" or "too" can occur elsewhere in the sentence.

ही: The particle ही has the general connotation of "just," "only." It has an exclusive force, excluding the word or phrase that precedes it from some other entity or group. Examples:

मैं आज यह किताब ही पढ़ूँगा ।	*Today I will read only this book (no other book).*
मेरे पास एक ही डॉलर था ।	*I had only one dollar (no more).*

मैंने उसको एक बार ही देखा है।	*I have seen him only once (only one time and no more).*

Sometimes ही is used simply to give special emphasis to the preceding word or phrase without any indication of exclusiveness. Examples:

आपका घर बहुत ही सुन्दर है।	*Your house is very beautiful.*
मैं जल्दी ही वापस आऊँगी।	*I will return very soon.*

Note:

(1) In a sentence ही can come between a noun or pronoun and the postposition following it, but भी cannot interrupt this sequence. Examples:

हम आपका ही काम कर रहे थे।	*We were doing only your work.*
हम आप ही का काम कर रहे थे।	*We were doing only your work.*
हम आपका भी काम कर रहे थे।	*We were doing your work too.*

(2) Emphatic particles, like postpositions, cannot occur in isolation. However, they should not be confused with postpositions. Postpositions follow nouns or pronouns and sometimes adverbs, while these emphatic particles can also follow adjectives and verbs. Unlike postpositions, they do not require the preceding word or phrase to take the oblique case.

(3) Various pronouns take special forms when followed by ही.

तुम	+	ही	=	तुम्हीं
यह	+	ही	=	यही
वह	+	ही	=	वही
इस	+	ही	=	इसी
उस	+	ही	=	उसी
इन	+	ही	=	इन्हीं
उन	+	ही	=	उन्हीं

With some adverbs ही may be written as a separate word or it may take a special form. When ही is written as a separate word, it has the connotation "only," but if it is joined with the adverb in a special form, it is used just for emphasis. Compare the following forms:

यहाँ	+	ही	= यहीं	*right here*	यहाँ ही	*only here*
वहाँ	+	ही	= वहीं	*right there*	वहाँ ही	*only there*
अब	+	ही	= अभी	*right now*	अब ही	*only now*
तब	+	ही	= तभी	*right then*	तब ही	*only then*

Exercises

1. Transformation drill
(Use the emphatic particle ही with the subject.)

Ram will cook the food.	Ram alone/Only Ram will cook the food.
राम खाना पकाएगा ।	राम ही खाना पकाएगा ।

वह लड़की जवाब देगी ।
मेरा भाई काम करेगा ।
ये छात्र उर्दू सीखेंगे ।
हमारे शिक्षक सवाल पूछेंगे ।
यह लड़की सुन्दर कविता लिखेगी ।
आपकी पत्नी कल वहाँ जाएगी ।
यह लड़का मेरी कार की मरम्मत करेगा ।
ये छात्र हिन्दी बोलने की कोशिश करेंगे ।
हमारे माता-पिता हमारी मदद करेंगे ।

2. Conversational response drill

I will see the film today.	We too will see the film today.
मैं आज फ़िल्म देखूँगी ।	हम भी आज फ़िल्म देखेंगे ।

मैं आज लाइब्रेरी जाऊँगी ।
मैं गाना गाऊँगी ।

मैं पार्टी में जाऊँगी ।
मैं नये जूते ख़रीदूँगी ।
मैं क्लास में हिन्दी बोलूँगी ।
मैं आज राम से मिलूँगी ।
मैं कल घर जाऊँगी ।
मैं शिक्षक से सवाल पूछूँगी ।
मैं दोस्त के साथ कॉफ़ी पिऊँगी ।

3. Transformation drill
(Add ही after the underlined words and make all necessary changes.)

We will give him the book.	We will give the book only to him.
हम उस को किताब देंगे ।	हम उसी को किताब देंगे ।

छात्र यहाँ पढ़ेंगे ।
वे लोग अब काम शुरू करेंगे ।
मैंने उन से सवाल पूछा ।
मैं यह सवाल नहीं समझता ।
हम वहाँ आप से मिलेंगे ।
मैं वह साड़ी चाहती हूँ ।
राम को यह किताब दीजिये ।
उस दिन मेरा भाई दिल्ली पहुँचा ।
इस से पूछिये ।
इन को दिल्ली जाना है ।
तब वह बोला ।
वह इस गाड़ी से बम्बई जाएगा ।
शिक्षक इन से सवाल पूछेंगे ।
आप यह काम ख़त्म कीजिये ।

4. Substitution drill

Only I work here.
मैं ही यहाँ काम करता हूँ ।
Only Ram
You too (polite form)

Only we
Only he
I too
Only you (familiar form)
His sister too
Only my brother
We too

5. Substitution drill

I will eat here.
मैं यहाँ खाऊँगा ।
right here
right now
those bananas too
only one banana
only in Delhi
two rotis too
right there
only three apples
there too
only this

6. Translation exercise

1. My parents eat only vegetarian food.
2. He will bring his two friends also to the party.
3. Right now they are working in the office.
4. Because I had to finish my essay, I slept only five hours last night.
5. Ram and Mohan also wanted to meet with him.
6. Please bring some sweets also with my tea.
7. She likes to study only in her (own) room.
8. Only he can help us.

9. Because of bad weather, only some students could come to class yesterday.
10. Please come again. Right now I am in a hurry.
11. We too were waiting just for them.
12. Tomorrow we will meet you right here.

33. THE CONJUNCTIVE PARTICIPLE (कर CONSTRUCTION)

If the same subject performs two actions one after another, the action that takes place before the second action can be expressed in Hindi by a conjunctive participle. These conjunctive participles are extremely common in Hindi and are often used to join two clauses together much like the English "and."

Formation: Conjunctive participles are formed by adding कर or के to the verb stem. Although कर and के can be used interchangeably, कर is used more in formal and written language while के is frequently used in spoken language. If the verb stem is कर itself, then the conjunctive participle can be formed only with के (कर कर is not possible).

Although conjunctive participles can be literally translated into English as "having --- ed," in Hindi they are used for a variety of English expressions. Examples:

यह सुनकर वह बोली ----।	*Having heard this, she said ---.*
उसने घर जाकर अपना काम किया ।	*He went home and did his work.* (lit., *Having gone home, he did his work.*)
मैं अख़बार पढ़कर दफ़्तर जाऊँगा ।	*After reading the newspaper, I will go to the office.*
आपसे मिलकर मुझे बड़ी ख़ुशी हुई ।	*I am very pleased to meet you.* (lit., *Having met you---.*)
उसकी आवाज़ सुनकर मैं बाहर गया ।	*When I heard his voice, I went outside.*
वह दिल्ली पहुँचकर आपको फ़ोन करेगा ।	*After reaching Delhi, he will call you.*
तेज़ी से दौड़कर उसने बस पकड़ी ।	*Running fast, he caught the bus.*

Note that the conjunctive participles in the following two examples are translated with adverbs in English.

संभलकर चलो ।	*Walk carefully.*
मेहरबानी करके (कृपा करके) खिड़की बन्द कीजिये ।	*Kindly close the window.*

Note:

(1) Since a conjunctive participle is used only when the same subject performs two actions, the subject is mentioned only once.

(2) Since the verb expressing the first action takes the conjunctive participle form, all the changes in number, gender, and tense agreement occur in the final verb. Also, it is the final verb that determines if the postposition ने is to be used with the subject in the perfective tenses. Examples:

उसने घर आकर अपना निबन्ध लिखा ।	*He came home and wrote his essay.*
वह काम ख़त्म करके बाज़ार गया ।	*He finished the work and went to the market.*

Exercises

1. Substitution drill

You ought to go to the office and do your work.
आपको दफ़्तर जाकर अपना काम करना चाहिये ।

कॉफ़ी पीकर
लाइब्रेरी जाकर
कहानी पढ़कर
दोस्त से मिलकर
घर जाकर
अख़बार पढ़कर

खाना खाकर
कुरसी पर बैठकर
यहाँ आकर

2. Substitution drill

I am very pleased to have met you.
मुझे आपसे मिलकर बड़ी ख़ुशी हुई ।
यहाँ आकर
यह किताब पढ़कर
ताज महल देखकर
यह फ़िल्म देखकर
दोस्त से मिलकर
यह समाचार पढ़कर
उस पार्टी में जाकर
हिन्दुस्तानी संगीत सुनकर

3. Substitution drill

He finished his work and went home.
वह अपना काम ख़त्म करके घर गया ।
दोस्त से बात करके
तुम्हारा खाना तैयार करके
दोस्त की मदद करके
गाड़ी की मरम्मत करके
अपनी मेज़ ठीक करके
दोस्त को फ़ोन करके
दरवाज़े बन्द करके
आपका इन्तज़ार करके

4. Substitution drill

After having eaten dinner, I will write him a letter.
मैं खाना खाकर उसको पत्र लिखूँगा ।

having met my friend
having played tennis
having seen the film
having finished this work
having read the newspaper
having returned from the office

5. Individual transformation drill

I will learn Hindi. I will go to India.
मैं हिन्दी सीखूँगा । मैं भारत जाऊँगा ।
After having learned Hindi, I will go to India.
मैं हिन्दी सीखकर भारत जाऊँगा ।

मेरी पत्नी घर आएगी । मेरी पत्नी खाना पकाएगी ।
आइये । मेरी मदद कीजिये ।
लड़का बैठा । लड़के ने किताब पढ़ी ।
हम कैम्पस जाएँगे । हम अपने दोस्तों से मिलेंगे ।
उसने दरवाज़ा खोला । वह अन्दर गया ।
लड़की बाज़ार गई । लड़की ने कुछ चीज़ें ख़रीदीं ।
यहाँ आइये । कुरसी पर बैठिये ।
वह घर पहुँचा । उसने बहन को बुलाया ।
मैं घर आई । मैंने अपना काम किया ।
मेरी बहन ने काम ख़त्म किया । मेरी बहन घर गई ।

6. Translation exercise
(Use conjunctive participles.)

1. You should go to Agra and see the Taj Mahal.
2. She sat and read the newspaper in the train.
3. She was very pleased to have met my parents.

4. They washed their hands and began to eat.
5. Having talked with his friends, he went home.
6. The farmer went and worked in the field.
7. The policeman ran and caught the thief.
8. We should go to the market and buy some sweets.
9. She came home and began to cook dinner.
10. After finishing their work, they will see a movie.

34. EXPRESSIONS WITH लगना

The intransitive verb लगना occurs in a variety of expressions and has different meanings in different contexts. The following are the most common usages of the verb लगना:

(1) The basic meaning of लगना is "to be attached to," "to be connected to," "to adhere to." Examples:

दीवारों पर फ़्रैंच तसवीरें लगी थीं।	*French paintings were hung on (attached to) the walls.*
आपके मुँह पर कुछ लगा है।	*Something is (stuck) on your face.*
खिड़कियों पर सफ़ेद परदे लगे हैं।	*White curtains are hung on the windows.*
लिफ़ाफ़े पर पचास पैसे के टिकट लगेंगे।	*Fifty paisa stamps will be put (attached) on the envelope.*

(2) Hindi frequently uses the verb लगना in indirect verb constructions to express physical feelings, sensations, and perceptions. In these constructions the verb लगना has the general connotation "to be affected by," "to be felt by." In such sentences, the subject of the corresponding English sentence (i.e., the person who feels or is affected by the physical sensation) becomes the indirect object followed by the postposition को and the noun representing the physical sensation or feeling functions as the subject, with which the verb agrees. Only a few nouns can be used in this type of construction. The most common are गरमी / गर्मी (F) *heat*, ठंड (F) *cold*, प्यास (F) *thirst*, भूख (F) *hunger*, धूप (F) *sunshine*, हवा (F) *air/wind*, चोट (F) *injury*, डर (M) *fear*. Examples:

मुझे प्यास लग रही है।	*I am feeling thirsty.* (i.e., *Thirst is affecting me.*)
हर दिन बारह बजे हमें भूख लगती है।	*Every day at 12 o'clock we get/feel hungry.*

आपको जाड़ों में यहाँ बहुत ठंड लगेगी।	*In winters you will feel very cold here.*
हमें भूख लगी है।	*We are hungry.* (i.e., *Hunger has affected us.*)
जंगल में मुझे डर लगा।	*I got frightened in the forest.*
बच्चों को अक्सर चोट लगती है।	*Children often get hurt/injured.*

(3) English sentences with expressions like "to seem," "to appear," can be translated into Hindi with the verb लगना in indirect verb constructions. In these sentences the noun or pronoun representing the person who perceives becomes the indirect object, followed by the postposition को. The person or thing about which the perception is made becomes the subject of the sentence, with which both the adjective and the verb agree.

The basic structure of such sentences is:

indirect object + को	subject	adjective	the verb लगना
उसको	हिन्दी	आसान	लगती है।
To him	*Hindi*	*easy*	*seems*

Examples:

उसको यह कहानी दिलचस्प लगी।
This story was interesting to him. (This story seemed/felt interesting to him.)
क्या आपको कल की पार्टी मज़ेदार लगी ?
Did you find (feel) yesterday's party fun? (Did yesterday's party appear enjoyable to you?)
मुझे हिन्दुस्तानी खाना अच्छा लगता है।
I like Indian food. (Indian food tastes/seems good to me.)
हमें आपका जाना बुरा लगा।
We didn't like your going. (Your going appeared/felt bad/ unpleasant to us.)
(मुझे) यह लगता है कि कल बारिश होगी।
It seems (to me) that it will rain tomorrow.

(4) In a special indirect verb construction the verb लगना also conveys the general meaning "to require," "to take." In this particular use the verb लगना expresses the amount of something (e.g., time, money, etc.) that is required to perform some activity. It agrees in number and gender with the word expressing the amount. The noun or pronoun representing the person by whom the amount is required becomes the indirect object, followed by the postposition को, and the activity for which the amount is required is indicated by the infinitive in oblique with the postposition में.

The basic structure of such sentences is:

indirect object + को	infinitive in oblique + में	amount	the verb लगना
उसको	खाना पकाने में	एक घंटा	लगा।
To him/her	*in cooking food*	*one hour*	*it took.*

Examples:

मुझे यूनिवर्सिटी जाने में आधा घंटा लगता है।
It takes me half an hour to go to the university.
भारत जाने में बहुत पैसा लगेगा।
It will take a lot of money to go to India.
ये रसगुल्ले बनाने में कितनी चीनी लगी ?
How much sugar did it take to make these rasgullas?

Exercises

1. Substitution drill

I'm feeling hungry. (lit., I am feeling hunger.)
मुझे भूख लग रही है।
प्यास
ठंड
गरमी

हवा
धूप
डर

2. Substitution drill

Ram has felt hunger. (i.e., Ram is hungry.)
राम को भूख लगी है ।
प्यास
गरमी
ठंड
डर
चोट

3. Chain drill

Q: Who is feeling cold?
किसको ठंड लग रही है ?

A: I am feeling cold.
मुझे ठंड लग रही है ।

4. Substitution drill

I like Indian food. (lit., Indian food tastes good to me.)
मुझे हिन्दुस्तानी खाना अच्छा लगता है ।
ये कपड़े
नये जूते
आपका घर
वह लड़की
हिन्दी पढ़ना
टेनिस खेलना
संगीत सुनना

5. Substitution drill

How do you like America? (lit., How does America feel to you?)
आपको अमरीका कैसा लगता है ?

हमारा देश
अपना देश
बर्कली
यहाँ का मौसम
हिन्दुस्तानी संगीत
हिन्दी पढ़ना
अमरीकन फ़िल्में
हिन्दुस्तानी मिठाइयाँ

6. Chain drill

Q: What do you like? (lit., What feels good to you?)
आपको क्या अच्छा लगता है ?

A: I like to see Hindi films. (lit., Seeing Hindi films feels good to me.)
मुझे हिन्दी की फ़िल्में देखना अच्छा लगता है ।

7. Transformation drill

Hindi seems easy to me.	Hindi seemed easy to me.
मुझे हिन्दी आसान लगती है ।	मुझे हिन्दी आसान लगी ।

मुझे यह किताब दिलचस्प लगती है ।
हमें संस्कृत मुश्किल लगती है ।
उसको भारतीय संगीत सुनना अच्छा लगता है ।
हमें आपका घर सुन्दर लगता है ।
मुझे वह छात्र होशियार लगता है ।
हमें ये बातें बुरी लगती हैं ।
उसको ठंडा मौसम अच्छा नहीं लगता ।
हमें मसालेवाला खाना मज़ेदार लगता है ।
मुझे उनकी बातें दिलचस्प लगती हैं ।

8. Substitution drill

How much time will it take you to read this book?
आपको यह किताब पढ़ने में कितना समय लगेगा ?

to cook dinner
to go to the university
to eat lunch
to clean the house
to write this letter
to read the newspaper

9. Substitution drill

It takes me ten minutes to go to the university.
मुझे यूनिवर्सिटी जाने में दस मिनट लगते हैं।

half an hour
two and a half hours
twenty minutes
one and a quarter hours
one and a half hours
a few minutes

10. Chain drill

Q: How much time does it take you to read the newspaper?
आपको अख़बार पढ़ने में कितना समय लगता है ?

A: Half an hour.
आधा घंटा।

11. Oral questions

आपको रोज़ दोपहर को कितने बजे भूख लगती है ?
तुम्हें क्या करना अच्छा लगता है ?

क्या तुम्हें उस कुरसी पर धूप लग रही है ?
आपको कौन-सा देश दिलचस्प लगता है ?
जब आपको डर लगता है, तब आप क्या करते हैं ?
आपको कैसा संगीत सबसे अच्छा लगता है ?
भारत जाने में कितना पैसा लगता है ?
उस दीवार पर क्या लगा है ?
आपको कल की पार्टी कैसी लगी ?
क्या आपको उस खिड़की के पास ठंड लग रही है ?
तुम्हें यह काम ख़त्म करने में कितना समय लगा ?
इस लिफ़ाफ़े पर कितने पैसे के टिकट लगेंगे ?
जब आपको प्यास लगती है, तब आप क्या करते हैं ?
तुम्हें कौन-सी भाषा सबसे सुन्दर लगती है ?

12. Translation exercise

1. The baby is hungry. Please give him some milk.
2. How much time does it take you to go home?
3. This Hindi film was (seemed) interesting to us.
4. A beautiful French painting was hung on (attached to) the wall.
5. The little girl got hurt yesterday.
6. How do you like our country?
7. It takes a lot of money to go to college.
8. You will feel very cold in Alaska.
9. We thought (felt) the food was too spicy.
10. Children often get scared at night.
11. It took me three hours to write this essay.
12. My sister likes to play the sitar.

35. THE SUBJUNCTIVE MOOD

Subjunctive forms in Hindi are identical to those of the future tense except that the suffix गा, गे, or गी is omitted. For example:

	Future forms		Subjunctive forms	
मैं	जाऊँगा,	पढ़ूँगा	जाऊँ,	पढ़ूँ
हम	जाएँगे,	पढ़ेंगे	जाएँ,	पढ़ें
आप	जाएँगे,	पढ़ेंगे	जाएँ,	पढ़ें
तुम	जाओगे,	पढ़ोगे	जाओ,	पढ़ो
तू	जाएगा,	पढ़ेगा	जाए,	पढ़े
यह	जाएगा,	पढ़ेगा	जाए,	पढ़े
वह	जाएगा,	पढ़ेगा	जाए,	पढ़े
ये	जाएँगे,	पढ़ेंगे	जाएँ,	पढ़ें
वे	जाएँगे,	पढ़ेंगे	जाएँ,	पढ़ें

Three verbs that have irregular future forms (होना, लेना, देना) also have irregular subjunctive forms:

	Future forms			Subjunctive forms		
	होना	लेना	देना	होना	लेना	देना
मैं	हूँगा (होऊँगा)	लूँगा	दूँगा	हूँ (होऊँ)	लूँ	दूँ
हम	होंगे	लेंगे	देंगे	हों	लें	दें
आप	होंगे	लेंगे	देंगे	हों	लें	दें
तुम	होगे	लोगे	दोगे	हो	लो	दो
तू	होगा	लेगा	देगा	हो	ले	दे

यह	होगा	लेगा	देगा	हो	ले	दे
वह	होगा	लेगा	देगा	हो	ले	दे
ये	होंगे	लेंगे	देंगे	हों	लें	दें
वे	होंगे	लेंगे	देंगे	हों	लें	दें

Note:

(1) The subjunctive form of a verb remains the same regardless of whether it refers to a masculine or a feminine subject.

(2) The negative particle used with the subjunctive is always न.

Subjunctive verb forms are used in a wide variety of constructions. In general, the subjunctive indicates desirability, possibility, probability, uncertainty, or a wish about some future action or event. It is best, however, to observe the specific constructions in which the subjunctive occurs and the meaning of each.

The subjunctive is used in two kinds of sentences: (A) simple sentences and (B) conditional sentences.

(A) Simple sentences: In simple sentences subjunctive verb forms are used to express several different meanings depending on the context. The most common are:

(1) In "should," "shall," or "may" questions: In such questions the subjunctive is used to ask for advice or permission.

अब हम कहाँ जाएँ ?	*Where shall we go now?*
इसके बारे में आपसे एक सवाल पूछूँ ?	*May I ask you a question about it?*
मैं अब घर जाऊँ ?	*May I go home now?*
हम आपकी मदद करें ?	*Should/Shall we help you?*
मैं आपके लिये चाय बनाऊँ ?	*Should/Shall I make tea for you?*

(2) In "let's" constructions: The subject हम is generally understood and the verb is in the plural. Very often such sentences are introduced with आओ or चलो.

आओ, बाहर चलकर खेलें।	*Come on, let's go out and play.*
चलो, आज एक फ़िल्म देखें।	*Let's see a film today.*
चलिये, अब कुछ काम करें।	*Let's do some work now.*

(3) As a request imperative: The subject आप is generally understood and the verb is always in the plural. This is the most polite form of request. It is almost like suggesting that someone do something rather than asking the person to do it.

(आप) कल हमारी पार्टी में आएँ।	*Please come to our party tomorrow.*
(आप) कुछ और चाय लें।	*Please have (take) some more tea.*
(आप) वहाँ न जाएँ।	*Please don't go there.*

(4) To express good wishes, congratulations and blessings: In phrases used in congratulating someone or in expressing good wishes or blessings the verb is always in the subjunctive.

जीते रहो।	*May you live long.*
सदा सुखी रहो।	*May you always be (stay) happy.*
जन्म-दिन मुबारक हो।	*Happy birthday.* (lit., *May (your) birthday be auspicious.*)
शादी पर बधाई हो।	*Congratulations on (your) wedding.*
तुम्हें सफलता मिले।	*May you have (get) success.*
आपके लिये नया साल शुभ हो।	*Happy New Year.* (lit., *May the New Year be auspicious for you.*)

(5) To indicate uncertainty: With adverbs such as शायद *perhaps*, the subjunctive form of the verb may be used to indicate greater uncertainty. Other forms, however, may also be used in such situations. Different verb forms convey different degrees of certainty. For example:

यह फ़िल्म शायद अच्छी हो ।
Maybe this film is good (but I really don't know).
यह फ़िल्म शायद अच्छी होगी ।
Maybe this film is (will be) good (at least I suppose it is).
यह फ़िल्म शायद अच्छी है ।
Probably this film is good (as a matter of fact, I am fairly sure it is).

(6) The subjunctive forms of होना may be added as auxiliaries to the habitual, progressive, and perfective forms of the main verb to form the subjunctive of each in order to indicate doubt or uncertainty in these tenses. The adverb शायद is generally used in such sentences.

शायद वह यहाँ पढ़ता हो ।	*Perhaps he studies here.*
शायद वह पढ़ रहा हो ।	*He may be studying.*
शायद वे बाज़ार गये हों ।	*They may/might have gone to the market.*
शायद उन्होंने कल यह फ़िल्म देखी हो ।	*They may/might have seen this film yesterday.*

(7) The subjunctive verb form is commonly used in subordinate clauses (कि clauses) after certain verbs or phrases to indicate that some future action or event is possible, desirable, necessary, or appropriate. For example:

मैं चाहता हूँ कि ----	*I want (that) ----*
(आपको) यह चाहिये कि ----	*It is necessary (for you) that ----*
(यह) ज़रूरी है कि ----	*It is important that ----*
(यह) संभव / मुमकिन है कि ----	*It is possible that ----*

Examples:

मैं चाहता हूँ कि आप भारत जाएँ ।	*I want you to go to India.*
आपको यह चाहिये कि आप हर रोज़ हिन्दी पढ़ें।	*It is necessary (for you) that you study Hindi every day.*

ज़रूरी है कि हम सब कल मिलें ।	*It is important that we all meet tomorrow.*
मुमकिन है कि वह पार्टी में न आए ।	*It is possible that he may not come to the party.*

(B) Conditional sentences: In conditional sentences, the "if" clause (conditional clause) generally precedes the "then" clause (principal clause). The "if" clause usually has the introductory अगर / यदि *if* in the beginning; the "then" clause always begins with the conjunction तो *then*.

Unlike in English, अगर in the "if" clause may be dropped, but तो in the "then" clause can never be dropped. Note that in English one can say either "If our team wins, then we'll celebrate" or "If our team wins, we'll celebrate." It is important to remember this distinction between the two languages.

Several verb forms are used in "if" and "then" clauses. In conditional sentences referring to the future, the most common combinations are:

"If" clause (conditional clause)	"Then" clause (principal clause)
Subjunctive	Subjunctive
Subjunctive	Future/Imperative
Future	Future/Imperative

Note: Here again the use of the indicative verb form implies that the speaker is certain about the realization of the statement while with the subjunctive verb form the speaker is less certain. Examples:

अगर मैं जयपुर जाऊँ, तो आपके लिए साड़ी ख़रीदूँ ?
If I go to Jaipur, shall I buy a sari for you?
अगर मैं दिल्ली जाऊँ, तो आपके परिवार से मिलूँगी ।
If I go to Delhi, I will meet your family.
अगर मौसम अच्छा होगा, तो हम गाँव चलेंगे ।
If the weather is (will be) good, we will go to the village.

अगर आप चाहें, तो मेरे साथ चलिये ।
If you wish, come with me.

Exercises

1. Substitution drill

Should (shall) I write the letter right now?
क्या मैं अभी पत्र लिखूँ ?

give money
go home
ask this question
talk with him
go to the market
bring a chair
eat a sweet
do this work
make (some) tea
buy a ticket

2. Transformation drill

We can write Urdu.	Should (shall) we write Urdu?
हम उर्दू लिख सकते हैं ।	हम उर्दू लिखें ?

मैं भारतीय खाना पका सकती हूँ ।
हम हिन्दी में बात कर सकते हैं ।
हम जल्दी चल सकते हैं ।
हम आपके साथ ओकलैण्ड जा सकते हैं ।
हम हर दिन आपसे यहाँ मिल सकते हैं ।
मैं शाम तक यह निबन्ध लिख सकता हूँ ।
मैं आपको अपनी कविता सुना सकती हूँ ।
हम यह हिन्दी की किताब पढ़ सकते हैं ।
मैं आपकी मदद कर सकता हूँ ।

3. Individual conversational response drill

Will he come today?	Yes, (perhaps) he may come today.
क्या वह आज आएगा ?	हाँ, शायद वह आज आए ।

क्या तुम कल फ़िल्म देखोगी ?
क्या वे लोग कल दिल्ली जाएँगे ?
क्या सीता वहाँ गाना गाएगी ?
क्या कल बारिश होगी ?
क्या तू कल अपना कमरा साफ़ करेगा ?
क्या वह लड़का कहानी सुनाएगा ?
क्या पैट्रोल का दाम बढ़ेगा ?
क्या आप आज लाइब्रेरी जाएँगे ?
क्या तुम आज अपनी बहन से मिलोगे ?
क्या तुम्हारा भाई कल आएगा ?
क्या ये छात्र अगले साल भारत जाएँगे ?

4. Transformation drill

You will not go there.	Please don't go there.
आप वहाँ नहीं जाएँगे ।	आप वहाँ न जाएँ ।

आप पैसे नहीं देंगे ।
आप यह फ़िल्म नहीं देखेंगे ।
आप इस कुरसी पर नहीं बैठेंगे ।
आप यह भारी मेज़ नहीं उठाएँगे ।
आप यह काम नहीं करेंगे ।
आप यह पानी नहीं पिएँगे ।
आप हमारे साथ चलेंगे ।
आप और चाय लेंगे ।
आप हमारे साथ खाना खाएँगे ।

5. Substitution drill

Come on, let's go home.
आओ / चलो, घर चलें ।
हिन्दी पढ़ें
अपना काम करें
मिठाइयाँ ख़रीदें
फ़िल्म देखें
राम से मिलें
पिता जी से कहानी सुनें
सीता से बात करें
चाय पिएँ
उसका गाना सुनें

6. Transformation drill

Perhaps he works here.	He may perhaps work here.
वह शायद यहाँ काम करता है ।	वह शायद यहाँ काम करता हो ।
आपके दोस्त शायद कल दिल्ली गये ।	
वे लड़के शायद बाहर खेल रहे हैं ।	
बच्चा शायद सो रहा है ।	
नौकर ने शायद कल कमरा साफ़ किया ।	
लड़की शायद लाइब्रेरी में पढ़ रही है ।	
छात्रों ने शायद कल यह कहानी पढ़ी ।	
वह लड़का शायद इस स्कूल में पढ़ता है ।	
उसकी बहन शायद कल बर्कली आई ।	
वह शायद दोस्त का इन्तज़ार कर रही है ।	

7. Individual conversational response drill

Where are my books?
मेरी किताबें कहाँ हैं ?

I don't know. They may (perhaps) be on the table.
(मुझे) मालूम नहीं । शायद मेज़ पर हों ।

ये छात्र कहाँ पढ़ते हैं ?
इस लड़की के साथ कौन है ?
यह बस कहाँ जाएगी ?
अगले साल आप कहाँ पढ़ेंगे ?
आपका दोस्त कल कहाँ जाएगा ?
अच्छी चाय कहाँ मिल सकेगी ?
आप कब यह फ़िल्म देखेंगे ?
ये छात्र कहाँ से हैं ?
ये लड़कियां कहाँ जा रही हैं ?
कौन कल खाना पकाएगा ?
अच्छा शाकाहारी खाना कहाँ मिलेगा ?

8. Substitution drill

I want you to go to India. (lit., I want that you should go to India.)
मैं चाहती हूँ कि आप भारत जाएँ ।

हम
वह छात्र
तुम
तुम्हारा भाई
मेरे माता-पिता
आप लोग
ये अमरीकन छात्र
मेरी बहन

9. Substitution drill

He wants you to come today. (lit., He wants that you should come today.)
वह चाहता है कि आप आज आएँ ।

meet his friend
go to India next year
learn Urdu

write a letter to the President
speak Hindi
sing a song
go to the party with him
work in this office

10. Chain drill

Q: What do you want?
आप क्या चाहते हैं ?

A: I want us to see this film today.
मैं चाहता हूँ कि हम आज यह फ़िल्म देखें ।

11. Substitution drill

If you (should) say so, (then) I will go there.
अगर आप कहें, तो मैं वहाँ जाऊँगा।
चाय बनाऊँगा
उसकी मदद करूँगा
उसके घर जाऊँगा
उसको बुलाऊँगा
यह काम करूँगा
दरवाज़ा बन्द करूँगा
यह कमरा साफ़ करूँगा
हिन्दुस्तानी खाना पकाऊँगा

12. Individual conversational response drill

Will you eat with me today?
क्या तुम आज मेरे साथ खाना खाओगे ?
If you (should) wish, (then) I will eat.
अगर तुम चाहो, तो खाऊँगा ।

क्या तुम आज मेरे साथ पार्टी में चलोगे ?
क्या तुम आज यह हिन्दी की फ़िल्म देखोगे ?
क्या तुम आज मेरी मदद करोगे ?
क्या तुम आज हिन्दुस्तानी खाना पकाओगे ?
क्या तुम आज मेरे भाई से मिलोगे ?
क्या तुम आज इस गाड़ी की मरम्मत करोगे ?
क्या तुम आज मेरे घर आओगे ?
क्या तुम आज यह काम करोगे ?

13. Translation exercise

1. Where are my papers? They might be on that table.
2. What shall I do? Shall I wait for them?
3. Next year I might live near the campus.
4. Please have (eat) dinner with us tonight.
5. He might also bring his friend to the party.
6. My parents may go to India next year.
7. Perhaps it may rain tomorrow.
8. She may be working in her office right now.
9. Let's drink some wine and (let's) dance.
10. I am feeling cold. Please close the window.
11. If you say so, I'll go with you.
12. If you want, I'll help you.
13. May I not sit on this big chair?
14. I am hungry. Let's eat now.
15. How many saris shall I buy?
16. His friends may have gone to Delhi yesterday.
17. She needs help. I want you to help her.
18. He wants the students to speak Hindi in the class.

36. THE SUFFIX वाला

वाला is a frequently used suffix in Hindi. It is particularly common in colloquial speech and can be added to a noun, adjective, adverb, or infinitive.

<u>Noun (in oblique form) + वाला:</u> When the suffix वाला is used with a noun, it conveys the general meaning that the person or thing is in some way associated with or characterized by that noun. Examples:

दूधवाली चाय	*tea with milk*
दिल्लीवाली गाड़ी	*the Delhi train* (i.e., *the train that goes to Delhi*)
पचास पैसेवाला टिकट	*a fifty paisa stamp*
चायवाला	*a tea vendor*
अख़बारवाला	*a newspaper man*
ताँगेवाला	*a tonga driver*
गाँववाला	*a villager*
लखनऊवाले	*Lucknow residents*
पंजाबवाला	*a Punjab resident*
उर्दूवाले	*Urdu speakers*
पैसेवाले	*people with money* (i.e., *rich people*)

मुझे दूधवाली चाय पसंद है ।
I like tea with milk.
दिल्लीवाली गाड़ी कब आएगी ।
When will the Delhi train arrive?
अख़बारवाला सात बजे आता है ।
The newspaper man comes at seven o'clock.
इस चायवाले के पास हमेशा गर्म चाय होती है ।
This tea vendor always has hot tea.

Note: As seen in the above examples, a noun + वाला phrase can function as an adjective or a noun and has different meanings in different contexts.

Adjective + वाला: Since the suffix वाला in itself has some adjectival force, its use with adjectives is often redundant. The only purpose an adjective + वाला phrase serves is to single out one particular person or thing in a group. Both the adjective and the suffix वाला agree with the noun referred to in number and gender. Examples:

वह लालवाली साड़ी दिखाइये ।
Please show (me) that red sari (i.e., *the red one*).
वे सस्तेवाले जूते मत ख़रीदो ।
Don't buy those cheap shoes (i.e., *the ones that are cheap*).
ये ताज़ीवाली मिठाइयाँ दीजिये ।
Please give (me) these fresh sweets (i.e., *the ones that are fresh*).

Adverb + वाला: When added to an adverb, the suffix वाला changes that adverb into an adjective which agrees with the noun modified in number and gender. Examples:

माँ अंदरवाले कमरे में हैं ।	*Mother is in the inside room (i.e., the room that is inside).*
ऊपरवाले कमरों में धूप है ।	*There is sunshine in the upstairs rooms.*
पासवाले घर में कौन रहता है ?	*Who lives in the nearby house?*
मुझे कलवाला अख़बार नहीं चाहिये ।	*I don't want/need yesterday's newspaper.*

Infinitive (in oblique) + वाला: The suffix वाला with a verb in oblique infinitive form can be used in one of the two following situations:

(1) To characterize a person as the doer of the action of the infinitive. In such sentences the suffix वाला functions like the agentive "-er" suffix in English.

Examples:

अख़बार बेचनेवाला आज नहीं आया ।	*The newspaper seller (i.e., the person who sells newspapers) didn't come today.*
हमारा घर साफ़ करनेवाली यहाँ रहती है ।	*Our housecleaner lives here.*
वह कपड़े बेचनेवाला अच्छी उर्दू बोलता है ।	*That clothseller speaks good Urdu.*

(2) To express that the action of the infinitive is about to take place. The basic structure of such sentences is:

subject	oblique infinitive + वाला	appropriate form of the verb होना *to be*

Examples:

हमारी बस आनेवाली है ।	*Our bus is about to come.*
मैं आपको फ़ोन करनेवाली ही थी ।	*I was just about to call you on the phone.*
जल्दी चलो, बारिश होनेवाली है ।	*Walk fast; it is going to/about to rain.*

Note: Often an English relative clause introduced by "who" or "which" can easily be translated into Hindi by using the oblique infinitive + वाला construction. Examples:

इस दुकान में काम करनेवाली औरत भारत से है ।
The woman who works in this shop is from India.
मद्रास में रहनेवाले लोग तामिल बोलते हैं।
The people who live in Madras speak Tamil.
नौ बजे आनेवाली गाड़ी आज लेट है ।
The train that comes at 9 o'clock is late today.

Exercises

1. Substitution drill

The clothseller will come tomorrow.
वह कपड़ेवाला कल आएगा ।

The shopkeeper
The shoe merchant
The tonga driver
The fruitseller
The bus conductor
The rickshaw driver
The tea vendor
The newspaper man

2. Substitution drill

Please show me this blue sari (i.e., this one which is blue).
मुझे यह नीलीवाली साड़ी दिखाइये ।

यह छोटीवाली किताब
यह बड़ावाला सन्तरा
वे महँगेवाले जूते
वे सस्तेवाले मोज़े
ये ताज़ीवाली मिठाइयाँ
वे सस्तीवाली सब्ज़ियाँ

3. Individual conversational response drill

Which sari should I buy, the yellow one or the red one?
कौन-सी साड़ी ख़रीदूँ, पीली या लाल ?

Please buy the red one.
लालवाली ख़रीदिये ।

कौन-सी कमीज़ दूँ, नीली या काली ?

कौन-से जूते पहनूँ, नये या पुराने ?
कौन-सी पेंसिल दूँ, छोटी या बड़ी ?
कौन-सा बकस उठाऊँ, हल्का या भारी ?
कौन-से फल ख़रीदूँ, कच्चे या पके ?
कौन-सी कुरसी लाऊँ, छोटी या बड़ी ?
कौन-से कपड़े ख़रीदूँ, महँगे या सस्ते ?
कौन-सी कापी दूँ, पीली या नीली ?
कौन-सी किताब पढ़ूँ, नई या पुरानी ?

4. Substitution drill

Come on, let's go into the inside room (the room that is inside).
चलो, अंदरवाले कमरे में चलें ।

बाहरवाले
नज़दीकवाले
नीचेवाले
ऊपरवाले
सामनेवाले
साथवाले
वहाँवाले
यहाँवाले

5. Substitution drill

You should read today's newspaper.
आपको आजवाला अख़बार पढ़ना चाहिये ।

कलवाला
परसोंवाला
यहाँवाला
पिछले महीनेवाला
कलकत्तेवाला
पिछले हफ़्तेवाला
दिल्लीवाला
न्यू यॉर्कवाला

6. Substitution drill

That boy is going to/about to go home.
वह लड़का घर जानेवाला है ।

going to/about to read this story
going to/about to finish his work
going to/about to open his shop
going to/about to come soon
going to/about to cook dinner
going to/about to meet his friends
going to/about to return home
going to/about to write a letter to the President

7. Transformation drill

He is going to Delhi. वह दिल्ली जा रहा है ।	He is going to/about to go to Delhi. वह दिल्ली जानेवाला है ।

मैं दरवाज़ा बन्द कर रही हूँ ।
वह पत्र लिख रही है ।
हम अपना काम ख़त्म कर रहे हैं ।
लड़के समाचारपत्र पढ़ रहे हैं ।
वह दुकान खोल रहा है ।
बारिश हो रही है ।
लड़की कहानी सुना रही है ।
हम लोग काम शुरू कर रहे हैं ।
मेरे माता-पिता कल आ रहे हैं ।
वह छात्र भारत जा रहा है ।

8. Chain drill

Q: When will your brother come to Berkeley?
आपका भाई कब बर्कली आएगा ?

A: He is going to come tomorrow.
कल आनेवाला है ।

9. Substitution drill

Please call the boy who works here.
यहाँ काम करनेवाले लड़के को बुलाइये ।
the woman who wears a sari
the man who wears a turban
the man who sells clothes
the children who play here
the student who learns Hindi
the man who smokes cigarettes
the men who work here
the girl who plays the sitar
the women who sell vegetables
the boy who lives in this blue house
the women who wash clothes

10. Translation exercise
(Use the वाला construction.)

1. I am going to (am about to) go to the university.
2. Please call the students who are learning Hindi.
3. The lower rooms are small, but the upstairs rooms are big.
4. Give me five fifteen-paisa stamps.
5. He is a resident of Delhi.
6. You shouldn't buy the shirts that are cheap.
7. The man in the white turban is writing a letter.
8. He is working in the adjoining room.
9. Our housecleaner will come tomorrow.
10. Ask the girl in the red sari; maybe she knows his address.
11. The newspaperman has not come yet.
12. I like my old shoes.
13. Do you know the student who lives in Oakland?
14. Walk fast. The film is going to (is about to) begin.
15. You should read the Delhi newspaper; it is better than the local newspaper.

37. INDEFINITE PRONOUNS AND ADJECTIVES

In Hindi the indefinites कोई and कुछ are used as both pronouns and adjectives and convey different meanings depending on the usage.

Indefinite pronouns: When used as a pronoun, कोई means "someone," "anyone," or "no one" (when used in a negative sentence) and is used to refer to a person, not to a thing. कोई as a pronoun always refers to a single person and therefore is never used in the plural. Examples:

वहाँ कोई काम कर रहा था ।	*Someone was working there.*
क्या कोई मेरी मदद करेगा ?	*Will someone/anyone help me?*
कोई उसके साथ नहीं गया ।	*No one went with him.*

The oblique of कोई is किसी. Examples:

किसी को बुलाइये ।	*Please call someone.*
किसी को जवाब मालूम नहीं था ।	*No one knew the answer.*

When used as a pronoun, कुछ means "something," "anything," or "nothing" (when used in a negative sentence). कुछ as a pronoun always refers to an indefinite amount of something in the singular. It is used for inanimate things only and therefore it is never used for people. कुछ does not have a special oblique form. Examples:

उसको इसके बारे में कुछ नहीं मालूम है ।	*He doesn't know anything about it.*
इस ग़रीब औरत के पास कुछ नहीं है ।	*This poor woman doesn't have anything.*
इसको कुछ दीजिये ।	*Please give her something.*
वहाँ कुछ नहीं हो रहा था ।	*Nothing was happening there.*

<u>Indefinite adjectives:</u> When used as indefinite adjectives, कोई and कुछ modify the following noun and mean "some" or "any" depending on their usage. कोई as an adjective may refer to a person or thing in singular only. In its adjectival use कोई may sometimes be used as an indefinite article similar to the English "a" or "an." The indefinite adjective कुछ, on the other hand, is used to refer to persons or things in the plural. For abstract things and bulk objects (non-countable objects) कुछ is used in the singular.

The following chart and examples will make this clear.

Type of noun	Singular	Plural
1. Person	कोई	कुछ
2. Countable object	कोई	कुछ
3. Bulk (non-countable) object	कुछ	--
4. Abstract thing	कुछ (or कोई)	--

Note:

(1) कोई is used only in the singular.

(2) In its adjectival use कुछ takes plural agreement, but when used with bulk objects and abstract things, it is treated as singular.

Examples:

1. कोई लड़की गा रही थी ।	*Some (a) girl was singing.*
क्या कोई छात्र कमरे में था ?	*Was there any (a) student in the room?*
वहाँ कोई औरत नहीं थी ।	*There was no (not one) woman there.*
कुछ लोग हमारे साथ आएँगे ।	*Some people will come with us.*
कुछ किसान खेतों में काम कर रहे हैं ।	*Some farmers are working in the fields.*

2. कोई किताब दीजिये ।	*Please give (me) some/any (a) book.*
हमारे पास कोई उर्दू की किताब नहीं है ।	*We don't have any (an) Urdu book(s).*
मेरे पास कुछ रेशमी साड़ियाँ हैं ।	*I have some silk saris.*
मैंने कुछ सन्तरे ख़रीदे ।	*I bought some oranges.*
3. इस ग़रीब आदमी को कुछ पैसा चाहिये ।	*This poor man needs some money.*
हम कुछ चाय पिएँगे ।	*We will drink some tea.*
मुझे कुछ ठंडा पानी दीजिये ।	*Please give me some cold water.*
4. मुझे आज कुछ काम है ।	*I have some work today.*
क्या कल तुम्हें कुछ फ़ुरसत होगी ।	*Will you have some free time tomorrow?*

Often in questions and negative statements either कोई or कुछ may be used with abstract nouns like काम or जल्दी. Examples:

क्या आज कोई (कुछ) काम है ?	*Is there any work today?*
मुझे कोई (कुछ) काम नहीं है ।	*I don't have any work.*
कोई (कुछ) जल्दी नहीं है ।	*There is no hurry.*

When used as an adjective, कोई changes to किसी in the oblique, but कुछ does not change. Examples:

वह किसी दुकान में काम करता है ।	*He works in some (a) shop.*
किसी छात्र से यह सवाल पूछो ।	*Ask some (any, a) student this question.*
मुझे कुछ दोस्तों से मिलना है ।	*I have to meet some friends.*

Note:

(1) The indefinites कोई and कुछ may also be used as adverbs modifying the following adjective. कुछ when used adverbially has the general connotation of "somewhat" or "a bit/a little." Adverbially, कोई is often used before a numeral meaning "about," "approximately." Examples:

वह कुछ उदास लगता है।	*He appears to be somewhat (a bit) sad.*
हमारे लिए उर्दू लिपि कुछ मुश्किल है।	*Urdu script is a little (somewhat) difficult for us.*
मीटिंग में कोई सौ लोग थे।	*There were about (approximately) a hundred people in the meeting.*

(2) The indefinites कोई and कुछ occur in several special phrases. Some common phrases are:

कोई और	-	*someone else; anyone else*
कुछ और	-	*something more; some more*
और कोई	-	*someone else; anyone else; some other; any other*
और कुछ	-	*something else*
कोई भी नहीं	-	*no one at all; no ___ at all*
कुछ भी नहीं	-	*nothing at all; no ___ at all*
कोई न कोई	-	*someone or other; some ___ or other*
कुछ न कुछ	-	*something or other; some ___ or other*
सब कुछ	-	*everything*
बहुत कुछ	-	*a great deal; quite a bit; a lot*

When these phrases are used as pronouns, they are treated as singular.

Exercises

1. Substitution drill

Someone is studying there.
वहाँ कोई पढ़ रहा है।

coming
sleeping
crying
laughing
singing

writing
dancing

2. Chain drill
(Answer with कोई as the subject.)

Q: What is going on there?
वहाँ क्या हो रहा है ?

A: Someone is singing there.
वहाँ कोई गा रहा है ।

3. Substitution drill

We should ask someone.
हमें किसी से पूछना चाहिये ।
converse with
help
meet
wait for
call
tell

4. Chain drill

A: You should help someone.
आपको किसी की मदद करनी चाहिये ।

B: Whom should I help?
किस की मदद करूँ ?

A: That old woman.
उस बूढ़ी औरत की ।

5. Individual conversational response drill
(Answer in the negative.)

Will that student sing?	No, no one will sing.
क्या वह छात्र गाएगा ?	नहीं, कोई नहीं गाएगा ।
क्या तुम्हारी बहन बाज़ार गई ?	
क्या तुम्हारा भाई यह काम करेगा ?	
क्या तुम सब लोग वहाँ जाओगे ?	
क्या वहाँ बहुत लोग थे ?	
क्या तुम मदद करोगे ?	
क्या आप इन्तज़ार करेंगे ?	
क्या तुम पूछोगे ?	
क्या तुम आज खेलोगे ?	

6. Substitution drill

We should read something.
हमें कुछ पढ़ना चाहिये ।

do
buy
bring
sing
eat
write

7. Substitution drill

He didn't say anything.
उसने कुछ नहीं कहा ।

tell
read
eat
drink
write

do
take
give

8. Translation exercise

1. Someone should ask the teacher this question.
2. Let's go home. Nothing will happen here now.
3. We want to ask you something.
4. Yesterday after class no one waited for me.
5. Please don't go in that room. Someone is sleeping there.
6. Tell me something about your family.
7. What did she give you? She didn't give me anything.
8. These days he is not doing anything.
9. She doesn't know anything about India.
10. He has nothing. Please give him something.

9. Substitution drill

Is there a (any) student in that room?
क्या उस कमरे में कोई छात्र है ?

teacher
book
foreigner
girl
table
chair
window
newspaper
boy
Indian woman
foreign student

10. <u>Conversational response drill</u>

You should ask some boy.	But there isn't any boy here.
आपको किसी लड़के से पूछना चाहिये ।	लेकिन, यहाँ तो कोई लड़का नहीं है ।
आपको किसी छात्र से बात करनी चाहिये ।	
आपको कोई अख़बार पढ़ना चाहिये ।	
आपको किसी कुरसी पर बैठना चाहिये ।	
आपको किसी बच्चे की मदद करनी चाहिये ।	
आपको किसी लड़की से मिलना चाहिये ।	
आपको किसी विदेशी से बात करनी चाहिये ।	

11. <u>Conversational response drill</u>

Which man shall I ask?	Ask any man.
मैं किस आदमी से पूछूँ ?	किसी आदमी से पूछिये ।
मैं किस कुरसी पर बैठूँ ?	
मैं किस किताब को पढ़ूँ ?	
मैं किस आदमी की मदद करूँ ?	
मैं किस कमरे में बैठूँ ?	
मैं किस लड़के को बुलाऊँ ?	
मैं किस छात्र से सवाल पूछूँ ?	

12. <u>Substitution drill</u>

There were some boys there.
वहाँ कुछ लड़के थे ।

students
women
children
money
wine
water
eggs
tea
work

13. Conversational response drill

Does he have some books?	No, he doesn't have any books.
क्या उसके पास कुछ किताबें हैं ?	नहीं, उसके पास कोई किताब नहीं है ।
क्या उसके पास कुछ पैसा है ?	
क्या उसके पास कुछ महँगी चीज़ें हैं ?	
क्या उसके पास कुछ चाय है ?	
क्या उसके पास कुछ शराब है ?	
क्या उसके पास कुछ पानी है ?	
क्या उसके पास कुछ साड़ियाँ हैं ?	
क्या उसके पास कुछ हिन्दी के रिकार्ड हैं ?	

14. Chain drill

Q: Do you have a (any) Hindi book?
क्या आपके पास कोई हिन्दी की किताब है ।

A: Yes, I have some Hindi books.
हाँ, मेरे पास कुछ हिन्दी की किताबें हैं ।

Q: Do you have some wine?
क्या आपके पास कुछ शराब है ?

A: Yes, I have some wine.
हाँ, मेरे पास कुछ शराब है ।

15. Translation exercise

1. My friend doesn't have any work these days.
2. I will buy some shirts from this store.
3. I need your help. Will you have some time tomorrow?
4. He gave me some Hindi books to read.
5. Do you have some Indian friends?
6. After class we should drink some tea.

7. I want to live in some Indian village.
8. Is there any good hotel in this city?
9. This summer I will go to some large city to work.
10. He wants to meet some Pakistani girl.
11. We bought some things for you from the store.
12. Ask any Hindi student this question.

38. INTRANSITIVE AND TRANSITIVE FORMS OF VERBS

As mentioned in Section 24, Hindi verbs are divided into two categories: intransitive and transitive. A transitive verb can take a direct object while an intransitive verb cannot. Generally a verb that is transitive in Hindi is also transitive in English, but the number of intransitive verbs in Hindi is much larger than in English.

In English often the same verb is used as intransitive and transitive. For example, note "to burn" and "to begin" in the following English sentences. In one sentence the verb is intransitive and in the other the same verb is transitive and has a direct object:

The house burned.	घर जला ।
He burned the house.	उसने घर जलाया ।
The play began.	नाटक शुरू हुआ ।
We began the play.	हमने नाटक शुरू किया ।

In Hindi, instead of using the same verb as intransitive and transitive, phonetically and semantically related pairs are used (such as जलना - जलाना, शुरू होना - शुरू करना in the above Hindi sentences). Such intransitive - transitive pairs are very common in Hindi.

<u>Formation of intransitive-transitive pairs:</u>

Hindi uses several patterns in forming these pairs. The following four patterns are the most common.

(1) Many transitive verbs are formed by adding आ to an intransitive verb stem.

Examples:

Intransitive verb		Transitive verb	
पकना	*to be cooked*	पकाना	*to cook*
बनना	*to be made, to be built*	बनाना	*to make, to build*
लगना	*to be installed/ attached/applied*	लगाना	*to install/attach/apply*
बचना	*to be saved*	बचाना	*to save*
पहुँचना	*to arrive/to reach*	पहुँचाना	*to take/bring somewhere*
उठना	*to rise, to get up*	उठाना	*to raise, to lift, to get (someone) up*
चलना	*to walk, to move, to be in motion*	चलाना	*to make someone walk, to drive, to put something in motion*

(2) In some cases, in addition to adding आ to an intransitive verb stem, if there is a long vowel in the preceding syllable, it is shortened or changed according to the following rules:

आ	becomes	अ
ई, ए, or ऐ	becomes	इ
ऊ or ओ	becomes	उ

Examples:

Intransitive verb		Transitive verb	
जागना	*to be awake*	जगाना	*to wake (someone) up*
भीगना	*to get wet*	भिगाना	*to make (something) wet*
लेटना	*to lie down*	लिटाना	*to lay someone/something (down)*
बैठना	*to sit*	बिठाना	*to seat (someone)*

घूमना	*to wander around, to tour*	घुमाना	*to show (someone) around*
सोना	*to sleep*	सुलाना	*to put (someone) to sleep*

Note that in the last example the consonant ल is also added.

(3) In contrast to the previous pattern some transitive verbs are formed by changing the initial or medial short vowels of the intransitive verb stems. Thus:

अ	becomes	आ
इ	becomes	ई or ए
उ	becomes	ऊ or ओ

Examples:

Intransitive verb		Transitive verb	
संभलना	*to be careful*	संभालना	*to exercise care for something/someone*
निकलना	*to come out, to go out*	निकालना	*to push out, to take out*
*बिकना	*to be sold*	बेचना	*to sell*
पिसना	*to be ground*	पीसना	*to grind*
रुकना	*to stop (intr.)*	रोकना	*to stop (tr.)*
खुलना	*to be opened*	खोलना	*to open*
*धुलना	*to be washed*	धोना	*to wash*
लुटना	*to be robbed*	लूटना	*to rob*

*Note the change of a consonant in the pairs.

(4) All the conjunct verbs that are formed by combining a noun or an adjective with करना use होना for their intransitive counterparts. Examples:

Intransitive verb		Transitive verb	
शुरू होना	*to begin (intr.)*	शुरू करना	*to begin (tr.)*
मरम्मत होना	*to be repaired*	मरम्मत करना	*to repair*

The patterns discussed above are the most common and useful patterns. There are a few other patterns that are less frequently used and more complicated.

Exercises

1. Transformation drill

A house is being built.
घर बन रहा है।
टैक्सी सड़क पर रुक रही है।
मोटर चल रही है।
पैसा बच रहा है।
सुन्दर साड़ियाँ बिक रही हैं।
खिड़की खुल रही है।
खाना पक रहा है।
किताबें बिक रही हैं।
कपड़े धुल रहे हैं।

That man is building a house.
वह आदमी घर बना रहा है।

2. Transformation drill

He is making beautiful toys.
वह सुन्दर खिलौने बना रहा है।
वह हिन्दी की किताबें बेच रहा है।
वह खिड़की खोल रहा है।
वह बस चला रहा है।
वह बहुत पैसा बचा रहा है।
वह भारतीय खाना पका रहा है।

Beautiful toys are being made.
सुन्दर खिलौने बन रहे हैं।

वह टैक्सी रोक रहा है ।
वह गंदे कपड़े धो रहा है ।
वह सुन्दर फूल बेच रहा है ।

3. <u>Transformation drill</u>
(Keep the same tense as in the original sentence.)

Those people sell books here.	Books are sold here.
वे लोग यहाँ किताबें बेचते हैं ।	यहाँ किताबें बिकती हैं ।

लड़की खिड़की खोलती है ।
यह आदमी गाड़ी चला रहा है ।
यह अमीर आदमी पैसा बचाता है ।
मेरे भाई ने कल कुरसियाँ बनाईं ।
मैं खाना पकाऊँगी ।
धोबी कपड़े धोता है ।
मैंने गाड़ी रोकी ।
हम लोग यहाँ अख़बार बेचेंगे ।
उसने दरवाज़ा खोला ।
वे लोग मकान बना रहे हैं ।
लड़का गाड़ी चलाएगा ।

4. <u>Transformation drill</u>

I opened the window.	The window (was) opened.
मैंने खिड़की खोली ।	खिड़की खुल गई ।

उसने गाड़ी रोकी ।
मेरी पत्नी ने मसालेवाला खाना पकाया ।
नौकर ने हमारा सामान निकाला ।
उसने कुछ पैसा बचाया ।
दुकानदार ने ताज़ी मिठाइयाँ बेचीं ।
धोबी ने हमारे कपड़े धोए ।
उसने यह बड़ा मकान बनाया ।

मैंने कल वे पुरानी चीज़ें बेचीं।
हमने यह सुन्दर मेज़ बनाई।
उसने कल क्या बेचा।

5. Transformation drill

(Use लड़का as the subject; change the intransitive verb to a transitive verb and compound it with देना.)

Beautiful toys were made. — The boy made beautiful toys.
सुन्दर खिलौने बन गये। — लड़के ने सुन्दर खिलौने बना दिये।
रिक्शा रुक गया।
हमारे सब कपड़े धुल गये।
कमरे का दरवाज़ा खुल गया।
वह पीली साड़ी बिक गई।
तसवीर दीवार पर लग गई।
हमारा खाना पक गया।
सब ताज़ी सब्ज़ियाँ बिक गईं।

6. Transformation drill

Beautiful flowers are sold in this shop. — What is sold in this shop?
इस दुकान में सुन्दर फूल बिकते हैं। — इस दुकान में क्या बिकता है ?
यहाँ हमारी बस रुकती है।
दस बजे तक यह खिड़की नहीं खुलती।
यहाँ महँगे कपड़े धुलते हैं।
इस शहर में सुन्दर खिलौने बनते हैं।
यहाँ हिन्दुस्तानी खाना पकता है।
इस दुकान में सुन्दर साड़ियाँ बिकती हैं।
यहाँ अच्छे और सस्ते कपड़े बनते हैं।

7. <u>Transformation drill</u>

Those people are making beautiful toys.	Who is making beautiful toys?
वे लोग सुन्दर खिलौने बना रहे हैं ।	कौन सुन्दर खिलौने बना रहा है ?

दुकानदार महँगी साड़ियाँ बेच रहा है ।
ड्राइवर मोटर रोकता है ।
हम गाड़ी से सामान निकाल रहे हैं ।
वह सुन्दर मेज़ बना रहा है ।
रिक्शेवाला रिक्शा चलाता है ।
धोबी ये कपड़े धोएगा ।
मेरी बहन खाना पकाएगी ।

8. <u>Chain drill</u>
(Ask a question using an intransitive verb with क्या or a transitive verb with कौन.)

Q: What is made here?
यहाँ क्या बनता है ?

A: Beautiful saris are made here.
यहाँ सुन्दर साड़ियाँ बनती हैं ।

Q: Who makes beautiful toys?
कौन सुन्दर खिलौने बनाता है ?

A: We make beautiful toys.
हम सुन्दर खिलौने बनाते हैं ।

9. <u>Transformation drill</u>

He is repairing the table.	The table is being repaired.
वह मेज़ की मरम्मत कर रहा है ।	मेज़ की मरम्मत हो रही है ।

लड़का दोस्त का इन्तज़ार कर रहा है ।
हम काम शुरू कर रहे हैं ।

वह खिड़की बन्द कर रहा है ।
मैं खाना तैयार कर रही हूँ ।
वे लोग काम ख़त्म कर रहे हैं ।
लड़की घर साफ़ कर रही है ।
वह बच्चों की मदद कर रही है ।
हम हिन्दी बोलने की कोशिश कर रहे हैं ।

10. Transformation drill

(Add any appropriate subject and change the verb from intransitive to transitive.)

The chair was repaired.	I repaired the chair.
कुरसी की मरम्मत हुई ।	मैंने कुरसी की मरम्मत की ।
दोस्त का इन्तज़ार हुआ ।	
दरवाज़ा बन्द हुआ ।	
क्लास शुरू हुई ।	
खाना तैयार हुआ ।	
बूढ़ी औरत की मदद हुई ।	
कमरा साफ़ हुआ ।	
कहानी ख़त्म हुई ।	
हिन्दी बोलने की कोशिश हुई ।	

11. Oral questions

ताज़ी सब्ज़ियाँ कहाँ बिकती हैं ?
बस कौन चलाता है ?
यह क्लास कब शुरू होती है ?
आप किसका इन्तज़ार कर रहे हैं ?
आपका घर कौन साफ़ करता है ?
यह रेलगाड़ी कहाँ रुकती है ?
क्या इस रेस्ट्रान्ट में अच्छा हिन्दुस्तानी खाना पकता है ?
टिकट-घर की खिड़की कब खुलेगी ?
सुन्दर साड़ियाँ कहाँ बनती हैं ?
ये कपड़े कब धुलेंगे ?

यह कमरा कब साफ़ हुआ ?
कौन ग़रीब लोगों की मदद करेगा ?
यहाँ किसका इन्तज़ार हो रहा है ?
इन सड़कों की मरम्मत कब होगी ?
कल फ़िल्म कितने बजे ख़त्म हुई ?

12. Translation exercise

(Translate the following sentences into Hindi. Then rewrite them with a transitive verb and an appropriate subject.)

1. The car stopped in front of my house.
2. The play began at seven o'clock in the evening.
3. A new house is being built on that street.
4. Expensive clothes are washed here.
5. Beautiful silk clothes are made in this city.
6. Books in (of) many languages are sold in this bookstore.
7. Every day our class ends at ten o'clock in the morning.
8. Good Indian food is cooked here.
9. This chair was being repaired yesterday.
10. The poor people were helped.

39. VERB STEM + चुकना CONSTRUCTION

The auxiliary verb चुकना is frequently used after a verb stem to indicate completion of the action described by the verb stem. It is generally translated as "to finish doing (something)." In English the adverb "already" easily conveys the actual sense of चुकना in this construction. Examples:

क्या आप खाना खा चुके हैं ?	*Have you finished eating?/Have you already eaten?*
बच्चे घर जा चुके हैं ।	*The children have already gone home.*

The main verb in this construction always remains in stem form, and all the changes in person, number, and gender agreement occur only in the auxiliary verb चुकना. Except for the progressive tenses, this construction is found in all tenses; but because it is used mainly to convey the completion of an action, it is most commonly found in the perfective tenses. The verb चुकना is an intransitive verb; therefore the ने construction is never used in the perfective tenses, even when the stem of the main verb is transitive.Examples:

मैंने खाना खाया ।	*I ate dinner.*
मैं खाना खा चुका ।	*I already ate dinner.*

क्या आपने ताज महल देखा है ?	*Have you seen the Taj Mahal?*
क्या आप ताज महल देख चुके हैं ?	*Have you already seen the Taj Mahal?*

हम रोज़ शाम को सात बजे तक खाना खा चुकते हैं ।
Every day we finish eating dinner by 7 p.m.
मैं कल तक यह निबन्ध लिख चुकूँगी ।
I will finish writing this essay by tomorrow.

Exercises

1. Transformation drill

He is reading the book. He has already read the book.
वह किताब पढ़ रहा है। वह किताब पढ़ चुका है।
मेरे बच्चे खेल रहे हैं।
हम अपना काम कर रहे हैं।
मैं खाना खा रहा हूँ।
मेरे पिता जी अख़बार पढ़ रहे हैं।
हमारी माँ खाना पका रही हैं।
मैं बच्चों को कहानी सुना रही हूँ।
कृष्ण बाँसुरी बजा रहा है।
वह दफ़्तर जा रहा है।

2. Conversational response drill

Did you eat? Yes, I already ate.
क्या तुमने खाना खाया ? हाँ, मैं खाना खा चुका।
क्या तुमने यह किताब पढ़ी ?
क्या तुमने माँ को पत्र लिखा ?
क्या तुमने यह कहानी पढ़ी ?
क्या तुम आज मन्दिर गये ?
क्या तुमने आगरे का ताज महल देखा ?
क्या तुमने आज नमाज़ पढ़ी ?
क्या तुमने चाय पी ?
क्या तुमने वह फ़िल्म देखी ?

3. Substitution drill

When will he finish reading this book?
वह कब तक यह किताब पढ़ चुकेगा ?

doing this work
writing this letter

cooking dinner
repairing the car
writing the essay
reading this story

4. Substitution drill

When I arrived there, (by then) he had already gone to school.
जब मैं वहाँ पहुँचा, तब तक वह स्कूल जा चुका था ।
सो
खाना खा
काम ख़त्म कर
आराम कर
किताब पढ़
नमाज़ पढ़
भाषण दे
कॉफ़ी पी
बच्चों को कहानी सुना
नहा

5. Substitution drill

He came when we had already finished the work.
जब हम काम कर चुके थे, तब वह आया ।
read the newspaper
eaten dinner
read this story
rested
written the letter
listened to the music
drunk tea
finished our work
gone home

6. Translation exercise

1. We have already seen this Hindi film.
2. When I came into the class, the students had already read the story.
3. I will finish writing my essay by tomorrow.
4. She had already washed all her clothes.
5. Maybe he has already gone home.
6. The children have already done all their school work. Now they can play.
7. He has already seen all the famous temples of India.
8. Every day by six o'clock she finishes cooking dinner.
9. When we arrived at the train station, (by then) the train had already left (gone).
10. Come on, let's eat now. But I have already eaten.

40. OBLIQUE INFINITIVE + लगना CONSTRUCTION

The intransitive verb लगना when preceded by the oblique infinitive of the main verb means "to begin the action described by the oblique infinitive." The main verb in this construction always takes the oblique infinitive form, and all the changes in person, number, and gender agreement occur only with लगना. Since लगना is an intransitive verb, the ने construction is never used in the perfective tenses even when the main verb is transitive.

Although the oblique infinitive + लगना construction occurs in present, past, and future tenses, it is most frequent in the perfective tenses; it is never used in progressive tenses. Examples:

पत्र पढ़कर लड़की रोने लगी ।
Upon reading the letter, the girl began to cry.
छात्र भारत के बारे में सवाल पूछने लगे ।
The students began to ask questions about India.
रोज़ पाँच बजे वह खाना पकाने लगती है।
Every day she begins to cook dinner at five o'clock.
यह सुनकर आप हँसने लगेंगे ।
Upon hearing this, you will start laughing.

Exercises

1. Transformation drill

He studies Hindi.	He began to study Hindi.
वह हिन्दी पढ़ता है ।	वह हिन्दी पढ़ने लगा ।
हमारा दोस्त गाना गाता है ।	
मेरी बहन कहानी सुनाती है ।	

मेरी बच्ची हँसती है ।
हम अपना काम करते हैं ।
बच्चे पार्क में खेलते हैं ।
हम संगीत सुनते हैं ।
बच्चा दूध पीता है ।
वे लोग सुन्दर खिलौने बनाते हैं ।

2. Substitution drill

Upon hearing this, she began to cry.
यह सुनकर वह रोने लगी ।

began to laugh
began to work
began to write the letter
began to cook dinner
began to go
began to play
began to read the newspaper

3. Transformation drill

He began to work.	He began to work.
उसने काम करना शुरू किया ।	वह काम करने लगा ।

उसने गाना शुरू किया ।
उसने यूनिवर्सिटी में पढ़ना शुरू किया ।
उसने खाना खाना शुरू किया ।
उसने टेलीविज़न देखना शुरू किया ।
उसने हिन्दी पढ़ना शुरू किया ।
उसने कहानी सुनाना शुरू किया ।
उसने रोज़ टेनिस खेलना शुरू किया ।
उसने रोज़ लाइब्रेरी जाना शुरू किया ।
उसने सितार बजाना शुरू किया ।
उसने भारतीय संगीत सीखना शुरू किया ।

4. Substitution drill

After arriving home, she will begin to work.
घर पहुँचकर वह काम करने लगेगी ।

to study Hindi
to play with friends
to drink tea
to converse with her friends
to clean the house
to cook dinner
to read a book
to listen to the radio

5. Translation exercise

1. After coming home, the children began to play.
2. Upon reading her friend's letter, she began to cry.
3. They began to study about India.
4. Today the weather is good, but tomorrow it will begin to rain again.
5. After dinner they will begin to dance.
6. He began to sing with his friends.
7. Having gone home, he began to repair his car.
8. Every day after dinner he starts to watch television.
9. It begins to rain here in November.
10. Tomorrow we will begin to read a Hindi story.

41. THE PRESUMPTIVE MOOD

Presumptive forms indicate presumption or supposition on the part of the speaker about some action, state, or event. The speaker assumes that the statement is very likely to be true but is not completely certain about it.

Formation: In addition to expressing the future of "to be," the future forms of the verb होना are used to express presumption.

	Masculine forms	Feminine forms
मैं	हूँगा (होऊँगा)	हूँगी (होऊँगी)
हम	होंगे	होंगी
आप	होंगे	होंगी
तुम	होगे	होगी
तू	होगा	होगी
यह	होगा	होगी
वह	होगा	होगी
ये	होंगे	होंगी
वे	होंगे	होंगी

Examples:

उसके माता-पिता आजकल दिल्ली में होंगे ।
His parents must be (are probably) in Delhi these days.
वह लड़की भारत से होगी ।
That girl must be (is probably) from India.
ये अमरीकन लोग अमीर होंगे ।
These Americans must be (are probably) rich.

इन छात्रों को आजकल बहुत काम होगा ।
These students must have (probably have) a lot of work these days.
उन लोगों के पास बहुत पैसा होगा ।
Those people must have (probably have) a lot of money.
उसको जवाब मालूम होगा ।
He must know (probably knows) the answer.

Note:

(1) In the English translations above "must" is frequently used to indicate probability or presumption. This "must" should be distinguished from the "must" used in English to express obligation (e.g., I must work now).

(2) Since the presumptive forms and the future forms of the verb होना *to be* are the same, the exact meaning of sentences using these forms depends on the context.

In order to express presumption or supposition in different tenses, the appropriate future forms of the verb होना are used as the auxiliary verb with the habitual, progressive, or perfective forms of the main verb. Examples:

वह अमीर आदमी इस बड़े घर में रहता होगा ।
That rich man must live (probably lives) in this big house.
ये लोग बंगाली बोलते होंगे ।
These people probably speak Bengali.
आजकल वह बहुत मेहनत कर रहा होगा ।
These days he must be working (is probably working) very hard.
वह इस समय दूरदर्शन देख रहा होगा ।
He must be (is probably) watching television at this time.
वह कल बम्बई नहीं गया होगा ।
He probably did not go to Bombay yesterday.
आपने यह गाना सुना होगा ।
You must have (probably have) heard this song.

तुमने भारत में ताजमहल देखा होगा।
You must have (probably have) seen the Taj Mahal in India.

Note: The subject of a transitive verb in the presumptive perfect tense is marked by the postposition ने (as it is in other perfective tenses), and the verb agrees with the object.

Exercises

1. Substitution drill

Ram must be (is probably) at home right now.
राम अभी घर में होगा।
क्लास में
अपने कमरे में
वहाँ
पार्टी में
दोस्त के घर में
यूनिवर्सिटी में

2. Substitution drill

That boy must be (is probably) from India.
वह लड़का भारत से होगा।
वह लड़की
वे छात्र
ये लोग
वे लड़कियाँ
आपका दोस्त
उसके माता-पिता
ये औरतें

3. Substitution drill

That boy must be (is probably) an Indian.
वह लड़का हिन्दुस्तानी होगा ।

अच्छा छात्र
पाकिस्तान से
बर्कली का रहनेवाला
बहुत होशियार
अमीर
उसका दोस्त
विदेशी
हिन्दी का छात्र
बंगाल से

4. Substitution drill

Those students must study (probably study) at this university.
वे छात्र इस यूनिवर्सिटी में पढ़ते होंगे ।

हिन्दी सीखते
इस बड़े घर में रहते
रोज़ यूनिवर्सिटी आते
यहाँ काम करते
रात को देर तक पढ़ते
यहाँ खेलते
अँग्रेज़ी बोलते
रोज़ लाइब्रेरी जाते

5. Substitution drill

Your brother must be working (is probably working) at this time.
आपका भाई इस समय काम कर रहा होगा ।

खाना खा
हिन्दी पढ़
खाना पका

घर जा
सो
दफ़्तर में काम कर
समाचारपत्र पढ़
हमारा इन्तज़ार कर
दफ़्तर से लौट
दोस्तों के साथ खेल
दूरदर्शन देख

6. <u>Transformation drill</u>

The girl is speaking English.
लड़की अँग्रेज़ी बोल रही है ।
The girl must be speaking (is probably speaking) English.
लड़की अँग्रेज़ी बोल रही होगी ।

वे लोग काम कर रहे हैं ।
लड़का किताबें पढ़ रहा है ।
लड़के गाना गा रहे हैं ।
राम बाज़ार जा रहा है ।
शीला दोस्त का इन्तज़ार कर रही है ।
वह भारत के बारे में बता रहा है ।
वे छात्र हिन्दी पढ़ रहे हैं ।
वे लड़कियाँ पार्टी में जा रही हैं ।

7. <u>Transformation drill</u>

Those people went to the party yesterday.
वे लोग कल पार्टी में गये ।
Those people must have gone (probably went) to the party yesterday.
वे लोग कल पार्टी में गये होंगे ।

उसने कल हमारा इन्तज़ार किया ।
उन छात्रों ने कल हिन्दी की फ़िल्म देखी ।

मेरी माँ ने कल हिन्दुस्तानी खाना पकाया ।
वह् कल अपने दोस्तों से मिला ।
मेरी बहन कल शिकागो पहुँची ।
उसने कल दोस्त की मदद की ।
शिक्षक ने कल भारत के बारे में बताया ।
उसने कल काम ख़त्म नहीं किया ।
वे छात्र कल लाइब्रेरी नहीं गये ।

8. <u>Substitution drill</u>

You must have (probably have) seen this film.
आपने यह् फ़िल्म देखी होगी ।

heard his lecture
bought some saris
heard this news
met the President
read today's newspaper
eaten Indian food
seen the Taj Mahal
learned Urdu
heard Indian music

9. <u>Substitution drill</u>

He must have (probably has) a lot of money.
उसके पास बहुत पैसा होगा ।

many Hindi books
some Hindi records
my book
an expensive car
our address
your photograph
some money
nothing

10. <u>Individual conversational response drill</u>
(Answer the following questions using the presumptive.)

Where is Ram?	He must be (is probably) at home.
राम कहाँ है ?	घर में होगा ।

ये लड़कियाँ कहाँ से हैं ?
वे छात्र क्या कर रहे हैं ?
यह लड़का कहाँ जा रहा है ?
किसने यह कविता लिखी ?
उन्होंने कल क्या पढ़ा ?
यह लड़की कहाँ काम करती है ?
वे छात्र कहाँ पढ़ते हैं ?
मेरी किताब किसके पास है ?
वह कब बर्कली पहुँचा ?
ये लड़कियाँ कहाँ रहती हैं ?
उसने कब यह काम ख़त्म किया ?
ये लोग कौन-सी भाषा बोल रहे हैं ?
बर्कली में कितने लोग रहते हैं ?
ये लोग किसका इन्तज़ार कर रहे हैं ?

11. <u>Translation exercise</u>

1. In Delhi, these foreigners must have stayed at (in) the Ashoka hotel.
2. You must have my address. Do you need my telephone number also?
3. You must have heard his lecture. How was it?
4. Where is John? He must be working in the office right now.
5. She must have gone home to help her mother.
6. You must have met his sister in New York.
7. He speaks good Hindi. He must have lived in India.
8. They must have thought about it.
9. Those students must be studying in the library.
10. They must have read a lot of books about India.
11. These women have a lot of nice clothes. They must be rich.
12. She is in your class. You must know her name.

42. RELATIVE-CORRELATIVE CONSTRUCTIONS

Relative-correlative constructions are used to join two sentences that share a common noun, pronoun, adjective, or adverb. Notice how the two English sentences are joined together in the following examples.

"I gave you the book." "You should read the book."
"You should read the book (that/which) I gave you."

"The students are studying Hindi." "The students want to go to India."
"The students who are studying Hindi want to go to India."

Thus the common element in the first sentence is "the book" and in the second sentence "the students."

In English, as seen in the above examples, relative clauses are introduced by words such as "who," "which," etc. that are also used as interrogatives. These relative pronouns are often omitted in English, as in the first example above. In Hindi, however, relative pronouns are never dropped, and there is a clear distinction between relatives and interrogatives. Hindi has a separate set of relatives, which are used in introducing relative clauses but not for asking questions. Interrogatives are used only in questions and not in introducing relative clauses.

The following chart shows some of the parallel sets of pronouns, adjectives, and adverbs found in Hindi. Each set has four forms: (1) "near" (proximate forms), (2) "far" (non-proximate forms), (3) interrogative forms, and (4) relative forms.

Near (proximate)	Far (non-proximate)	Interrogative	Relative
यह / ये *this/these*	वह / वे *that/those*	कौन / क्या *who/what(?)*	जो *who/that/which*
यहाँ *here*	वहाँ *there*	कहाँ *where(?)*	जहाँ *where*
इधर *in this direction*	उधर *in that direction*	किधर *in which direction(?)*	जिधर *in which direction*
इतना *this much*	उतना *that much*	कितना *how much(?)*	जितना *as much*
इतने *this many*	उतने *that many*	कितने *how many(?)*	जितने *as many*
ऐसा *like this/such*	वैसा *like that*	कैसा *like what(?), of what kind(?)*	जैसा *such as, of which kind*
ऐसे *this manner*	वैसे *that manner*	कैसे *how(?), in what manner(?)*	जैसे *like, as, in which manner*
अब *now*	तब / तो *then*	कब *when(?)*	जब *when*

As shown in the above chart, all the interrogatives begin with the consonant क while the relatives begin with ज. The relatives in Hindi are paired with correlatives, which are the corresponding "far" (non-proximate) forms.

The basic pattern of relative-correlative sentences:

In the commonly preferred pattern of relative-correlative constructions in Hindi, a relative clause precedes the main clause. A relative clause always contains a relative word (pronoun, adjective, or adverb) and the main clause is usually introduced with its corresponding correlative. Thus the standard pattern is:

relative word | relative clause || correlative word | main clause

Relative-correlative pairs

जो (pronoun or adjective)	जो (जिस, जिन)	*the one who/which*	वह / वे (उस, उन)	*he, she, that, they*
	जो भी	*whoever, whichever, whatever*	वही (वह+ही)	*only he/she/that*
जब (adverb of time)	जब	*when*	तब / तो	*then*
	जब भी	*whenever*	तभी (तब+ही)	*right then*
जहाँ (adverb of place)	जहाँ	*where*	वहाँ	*there*
	जहाँ भी	*wherever*	वहीं (वहाँ+ही)	*right there*
जिधर (adverb of direction)	जिधर	*in which direction*	उधर	*in that direction*
	जिधर भी	*in whichever direction*	उधर ही	*in that very direction*
जितना (adjective)	जितना	*as much as*	उतना	*that much*
	जितना भी	*however much*	उतना ही	*just/only that much*
जितने (adjective)	जितने	as many as	उतने	*that many*
	जितने भी	however many	उतने ही	*just/only that many*

जैसा	जैसा	*of what kind*	वैसा	*of that kind*
(adjective)	जैसा भी	*whatever kind*	वैसा ही	*just that kind*
जैसे	जैसे	*which manner*	वैसे	*that manner*
(adverb of manner)	जैसे भी	*whatever manner*	वैसे ही	*that very manner*

Note:

(1) Although the relative clause usually precedes the main clause, the clause order is reversible, and word order within a clause can also be changed for emphasis. Sometimes, as in English, the relative clause may also come in the middle of the main clause. Examples:

जो निबन्ध आपने लिखा, वह बहुत अच्छा है। — *The essay (that) you wrote is very good.*

वह निबन्ध बहुत अच्छा है, जो आपने लिखा।
वह निबन्ध, जो आपने लिखा, बहुत अच्छा है।

Notice that no matter what word order one chooses, the common element (i.e., the primary person or thing that is being discussed in both clauses) occurs towards the beginning of the sentence.

(2) The oblique singular and plural forms of जो are जिस and जिन respectively.

(3) When relative words are followed by भी, they convey the English meaning "-ever." Examples:

जब भी	=	*whenever*
जहाँ भी	=	*wherever*

(4) It is not unusual for a correlative to be followed by the emphatic particle ही, which in such instances is roughly equivalent to the English "the same" or "the very." Example:

जो भी आप कहेंगे, वही मैं करूँगी ।
I will do whatever you say.
(lit., *Whatever you will say, that [the same/that very thing] I will do.*)

Examples of relative - correlative pairs:

जो लड़का इस घर में रहता है, वह् मेरा दोस्त है ।
The boy who lives in this house is my friend.
(lit., *Which boy lives in this house, he is my friend.*)

जिस आदमी ने यह् किताब लिखी है, वह् भारत से है ।
The man who wrote this book is from India.

वे लोग आज यहाँ नहीं हैं, जिनसे आप कल मिले थे ।
Those people whom you met yesterday are not here today.

जब वह् घर आई, तब / तो उसने यह् समाचार सुना ।
When she came home, (then) she heard this news.

जब भी आप आना चाहें, तब / तो हमें फ़ोन कीजिये ।
Please call us (on the phone) whenever you want to come.

जहाँ आपकी दुकान है, वहाँ हमेशा बहुत भीड़ होती है ।
There is always a big crowd where your shop is.

जिधर हम जा रहे हैं, उधर कुछ पुरानी इमारतें हैं ।
There are some old buildings (in the direction) where we are going.

जितना पैसा तुम चाहते हो, उतना मैं नहीं दे सकती ।
I can't give as much money as you want.

जितने लोग इस शहर में हैं, उतने बर्कली में नहीं हैं ।
There aren't as many people in Berkeley as there are in this city.

जैसा काम तुम्हें पसन्द है, वैसा ही तुम्हें करना चाहिये ।
You should do the kind of work you like.
(lit., *The kind of work you like, that kind [of work] you should do.)*

जैसे आप अँग्रेज़ी बोलते हैं, वैसे ही हम बोलने की कोशिश करेंगे ।
We will try to speak English in the same way as you do.

Exercises

1. Transformation drill

The girl is cooking food. The girl is my sister.
लड़की खाना पका रही है । लड़की मेरी बहन है ।
The girl who is cooking food is my sister.
जो लड़की खाना पका रही है, वह मेरी बहन है ।

छात्र इस क्लास में पढ़ते हैं । छात्र अच्छी हिन्दी बोलते हैं ।
आदमी सितार बजा रहा है । आदमी मेरा दोस्त है ।
लड़का यहाँ काम कर रहा है । लड़के का नाम राम है ।
बच्चे यहाँ खेल रहे हैं । बच्चों को बुलाओ ।
मेज़ इस कमरे में है । मेज़ पर अपनी किताबें रखो ।
कुरसी पर लड़का बैठा है । कुरसी मेरी है ।
लोग हिन्दी बोलते हैं । लोगों से बात कीजिये ।
लड़के किताबें पढ़ रहे हैं । किताबें लाइब्रेरी की हैं ।

2. Substitution drill

Yesterday I met the boy who lives in Delhi.
कल मैं उस लड़के से मिला, जो दिल्ली में रहता है ।

who works in this shop
who is your friend
who is your friend's son
who studies Hindi
who studies with you

whose name is Ram
whose parents live in India
whose brother works here
who plays the sitar
who lives in this village

3. Substitution drill

I'll also go where you go. (lit., Where you will go, (there) I will also go.)
जहाँ आप जाएँगे, वहाँ मैं भी जाऊँगा ।

eat
study
buy books
play
learn Hindi
drink coffee
stay
work

4. Substitution drill

Let's go where there are beautiful trees. (lit., Let's go there where there are beautiful trees.)
जिधर सुन्दर पेड़ हैं, उधर चलें ।

बड़ी मस्जिद
ताज महल
लाल क़िला
पुराने मन्दिर
मशहूर इमारतें
पुराना बाज़ार
आपका घर
सुन्दर फूल

5. Substitution drill

I do as much work as you do. (lit., As much work as you do, that much I also do.)

जितना काम आप करते हैं, उतना मैं भी करता हूँ।

books as you will buy
films as you have seen
books as you have read
years as you will study Hindi
friends as you have
miles as you can walk
bananas as you can eat
money as you want

6. Transformation drill

He came home. I went to school.
वह घर आया। मैं स्कूल गया।
When he came home, I went to school.
जब वह घर आया, तब / तो मैं स्कूल गया।

शिक्षक कमरे में आये। हम चुप हो गये।
मैं पढ़ रहा था। मैंने शोर सुना।
उसने राम को देखा। राम खेल रहा था।
मैं घर आऊँगी। मैं आपको फ़ोन करूँगी।
हमने आपको बुलाया। आप कहाँ थे ?
वह दफ़्तर पहुँचा। उसने यह समाचार सुना।
तुम यहाँ नहीं थे। वह तुमसे मिलने आया।
मैं भारत जाऊँगी। मैं हिन्दी बोलूँगी।
वह गैसोलीन ख़रीदने गया। उसको बहुत इन्तज़ार करना पड़ा।

7. Substitution drill

I will do just the kind of work you want. (lit., Such work as you want, just that kind (of work) I will do.)
जैसा काम आप चाहते हैं, वैसा ही (काम) मैं करूँगा ।

book	give
food	cook
story	tell
song	sing
cloth	show
things	give
house	show
letter	write

8. Substitution drill

I'll try just as you do. (lit., As you try, just like that I will try.)
जैसे आप कोशिश करते हैं, वैसे ही मैं (कोशिश) करूँगी ।

speak Hindi
do this work
play the sitar
earn money
cook food
work hard
fix the car
teach English

9. Individual conversational response drill

Which sari shall I buy?	Buy whichever one you like. (lit., Whichever (one) you like, just that one you buy.)
मैं कौन-सी साड़ी ख़रीदूँ ?	जो भी तुम्हें पसन्द हो, वही ख़रीदो ।

हम कब आपके घर आएँ ?
मैं आप के लिये कैसा खाना पकाऊँ ?

हम कहाँ काम करें ?
मैं सितार कैसे बजाऊँ ?
हम किधर घूमने चलें ?
आपकी बहन अगले साल कहाँ पढ़ेगी ?
मैं उसको कितना पैसा दूँ ?
ये बच्चे कहाँ खेल सकते हैं ?
मैं किस छात्र से सवाल पूछूँ ?
हम कितने लेख पढ़ें ?
मैं कब आपको फ़ोन करूँ ?

10. Translation exercise

1. The boy who read this book yesterday is a good student.
2. I will play with the little girl who is crying.
3. Americans do not speak English the way the British do.
4. Women can (also) fix cars just as men do.
5. I don't have as much money as you do.
6. There aren't as many students at Stanford as there are at Berkeley.
7. Don't bring the table on which I have put my things.
8. I will do whatever you (will) say.
9. Whenever someone needs help, we should help him.
10. We shouldn't go into that room when the baby is sleeping there.
11. She wants to meet the man who wrote this book.
12. I will go right when you (will) go.
13. Whenever she goes to India, she speaks only Hindi.
14. I don't have the kinds of books that you like.
15. The children were not at home when mother came.
16. There are beautiful trees where we live.

APPENDIX I

Pronouns

Direct	Oblique	Forms with को	Forms with का, के, and की	With ने
मैं	मुझ	मुझको / मुझे	मेरा, मेरे, मेरी	मैंने
हम	हम	हमको / हमें	हमारा, हमारे, हमारी	हमने
आप	आप	आपको	आपका, आपके, आपकी	आपने
तुम	तुम	तुमको / तुम्हें	तुम्हारा, तुम्हारे, तुम्हारी	तुमने
तू	तुझ	तुझको / तुझे	तेरा, तेरे, तेरी	तूने
यह	इस	इसको / इसे	इसका, इसके, इसकी	इसने
वह	उस	उसको / उसे	उसका, उसके, उसकी	उसने
ये	इन	इनको / इन्हें	इनका, इनके, इनकी	इन्होंने
वे	उन	उनको / उन्हें	उनका, उनके, उनकी	उन्होंने
क्या (sg.)	किस	किसको / किसे	किसका, किसके, किसकी	--
कौन (sg.)	किस	किसको / किसे	किसका, किसके, किसकी	किसने
क्या (pl.)	किन	किनको / किन्हें	किनका, किनके, किनकी	--
कौन (pl.)	किन	किनको / किन्हें	किनका, किनके, किनकी	किन्होंने
कोई	किसी	किसी को	किसी का, किसी के, किसी की	किसी ने
कुछ	कुछ	कुछ को	कुछ का, कुछ के, कुछ की	कुछ ने
जो (sg.)	जिस	जिसको / जिसे	जिसका, जिसके, जिसकी	जिसने
जो (pl.)	जिन	जिनको / जिन्हें	जिनका, जिनके, जिनकी	जिन्होंने

APPENDIX II

Cardinal numbers

० शून्य				
१ एक	११ ग्यारह्	२१ इक्कीस	३१ इकत्तीस	४१ इकतालीस
२ दो	१२ बारह्	२२ बाईस	३२ बत्तीस	४२ बयालीस
३ तीन	१३ तेरह्	२३ तेईस	३३ तैंतीस	४३ तैंतालीस
४ चार	१४ चौदह्	२४ चौबीस	३४ चौंतीस	४४ चवालीस
५ पाँच	१५ पंद्रह्	२५ पच्चीस	३५ पैंतीस	४५ पैंतालीस
६ छह्, छः	१६ सोलह्	२६ छब्बीस	३६ छत्तीस	४६ छियालीस
७ सात	१७ सत्रह्	२७ सत्ताईस	३७ सैंतीस	४७ सैंतालीस
८ आठ	१८ अठारह्	२८ अट्ठाईस	३८ अड़तीस	४८ अड़तालीस
९ नौ	१९ उन्नीस	२९ उनतीस	३९ उनतालीस	४९ उनचास
१० दस	२० बीस	३० तीस	४० चालीस	५० पचास

५१ इक्यावन	६१ इकसठ	७१ इकहत्तर	८१ इक्यासी	९१ इक्यानवे
५२ बावन	६२ बासठ	७२ बहत्तर	८२ बयासी	९२ बानवे
५३ तिरपन	६३ तिरसठ	७३ तिहत्तर	८३ तिरासी	९३ तिरानवे
५४ चौवन	६४ चौंसठ	७४ चौहत्तर	८४ चौरासी	९४ चौरानवे
५५ पचपन	६५ पैंसठ	७५ पचहत्तर	८५ पचासी	९५ पचानवे
५६ छप्पन	६६ छियासठ	७६ छिहत्तर	८६ छियासी	९६ छियानवे
५७ सत्तावन	६७ सड़सठ	७७ सतहत्तर	८७ सत्तासी	९७ सत्तानवे
५८ अट्ठावन	६८ अड़सठ	७८ अठहत्तर	८८ अट्ठासी	९८ अट्ठानवे
५९ उनसठ	६९ उनहत्तर	७९ उन्यासी	८९ नवासी	९९ निन्यानवे
६० साठ	७० सत्तर	८० अस्सी	९० नब्बे, नव्वे	१०० सौ

१०००	एक हज़ार
१००,०००	एक लाख
१०,०००,०००	एक करोड़

Above one hundred, Hindi follows the English pattern but the conjunction "and" is never used in Hindi as it sometimes is in colloquial English, e.g., १२३ एक सौ तेईस, ५४२ पाँच सौ बयालीस, २३२१ दो हज़ार तीन सौ इक्कीस.

Ordinal numbers

पहला
दूसरा
तीसरा
चौथा
पाँचवाँ
छठा
सातवाँ
आठवाँ
नवाँ / नौवाँ
दसवाँ
ग्यारहवाँ / ग्यारवाँ
बारहवाँ / बारवाँ
... and so on.

Note:

(1) Ordinals function like adjectives and agree with the following noun in number and gender.

(2) Ordinal numbers from 1 through 4 and 6 are irregular. For the rest the suffix वाँ, वें, or वीं is used. If a number ends in ह (as in ग्यारह), ह may be dropped before adding वाँ, वें, or वीं, e.g., ग्यारवीं or ग्यारहवीं.

(3) When dates are given, the ordinal number is used for the first only. (Here too a cardinal number can be used, e.g., एक मई or पहली मई are both possible.) For the rest, the cardinals are used, e.g., पाँच मई, पन्द्रह जून.

GLOSSARY
Hindi - English

ABBREVIATIONS

M	masculine noun
F	feminine noun
PN	proper noun
sg	singular
pl	plural
Tr	transitive verb
Intr	intransitive verb
Tr (non-ने)	transitive verb that does not use the ने construction in perfective tenses
Ind. Intr	indirect intransitive verb

NOUNS

अँग्रेज़ M	Britisher, Englishman
अँग्रेज़ी F	English (language)
अख़बार M	newspaper
अण्डा / अंडा M	egg
अध्यापक M	teacher
अभ्यास M	practice
अमरीका PN(M)	America
अमरीकन M/F	American
अलास्का PN(M)	Alaska
अशोका होटल PN(M)	Ashoka Hotel
आँख F	eye
आग F	fire
आगरा PN(M)	Agra
आदमी M	man, human being
आना M	anna (one-sixteenth of a rupee)
आम M	mango
आराम M	rest (relaxation)
इतवार M	Sunday
इतिहास M	history
इन्तज़ार / इंतज़ार M	waiting, wait
इमारत F	building
उपन्यास M	novel

उर्दू F	Urdu
एथेन्स PN(M)	Athens
ऐफ़िल टावर PN(M)	Eiffel Tower
ऐम्पायर स्टेट बिल्डिंग PN(F)	Empire State Building
ओकलैण्ड / ओकलैंड PN(M)	Oakland
औरत F	woman
कपड़ा M	cloth; clothing
कपड़ेवाला M	clothseller
कमरा M	room
क़मीज़ / कमीज़ F	shirt
कलकत्ता PN(M)	Calcutta
क़लम / कलम M/F	pen
कराची PN(M)	Karachi
कविता F	poem; poetry
कहानी F	story
क़ागज़ / कागज़ M	paper
कानपुर PN(M)	Kanpur
कापी F	notebook
कॉफ़ी F	coffee
काम M	work
कार F	car
कारण M	cause, reason
किताब F	book
क़िला M	fort
किलोग्राम M	kilogram
किलोमीटर M	kilometer
किसान M	farmer
क़ीमत F	price
कुरसी / कुर्सी F	chair
कृष्ण PN(M)	Krishna
केला M	banana
कैम्पस M	campus
कैलिफ़ोर्निया PN(M)	California
कोशिश F	attempt
क्रिसमस PN(M)	Christmas
क्लास M/F	class
ख़बर F	news
खाना M	food
खिड़की F	window
खिलौना M	toy
ख़ुशी F	happiness
खेत M	field
गज़ M	yard (measurement)
गड़बड़ F	confusion; mess, disorder; unrest
गरमी / गर्मी F	heat; summer
गवर्नर M	governor
गाँव M	village
गाड़ी F	vehicle; car; train
गाना M	song
गाहक M/F	customer
गीत M	song, lyric, poem
गुजरात PN(M)	Gujarat
गुरुवार M	Thursday
गुसलख़ाना M	bathroom
गैसोलीन F	gasoline
गोश्त M	meat
ग्रीस PN(M)	Greece
घटना F	incident, event
घड़ी F	watch; clock
घण्टा / घंटा M	hour
घर M	home, residence, house
घास F	grass
चप्पल F	sandal
चाकू M	knife

चाचा M — uncle (father's brother)
चाय F — tea
चावल M — rice
चिट्ठी F — letter
चिड़िया F — bird
चीज़ F — thing
चोट F — injury
चोर M — thief
छात्र M/F — student
छात्रा F — student (F)
छुट्टी / छुट्टी F — vacation
जंगल M — forest, jungle
जन्म-दिन M — birthday
ज़मीन F — land, ground
जयपुर PN(M) — Jaipur
ज़रूरत F — necessity, need
जल्दी F — haste, hurry
जवाब M — answer
जाड़ा M — cold; winter
जॉन PN(M) — John
जानवर M — animal
जापान PN(M) — Japan
जीवन M — life
जुकाम M — cold (sickness)
जूता M — shoe
जूतेवाला M — shoeseller
जेन PN(F) — Jane
झाड़ू F — broom
झूठ M — falsehood, lie
झोला M — bag, shoulder bag
टिकट M/F — ticket; stamp
टिकट घर M — ticket office, booking office
टेनिस M — tennis
टेलीग्राफ़ ऐवन्यू PN(M) — Telegraph Avenue
टेलीफ़ोन M — telephone
टेलीविज़न M — television
टैक्सी F — taxi
टोपी F — hat, cap
ठण्ड / ठंड F — cold, coldness
डर M — fear
डाक F — mail
डाकू M — dacoit
डॉलर M — dollar
डेविड PN(M) — David
ड्राइवर M — driver
तबला M — tabla (a kind of Indian drum)
तमाशा M — show, spectacle; entertainment
तराजू F — (weighing) balance, scales
तसवीर F — picture, portrait, photograph
ताँगा M — tonga
ताँगेवाला M — tonga driver
ताज महल PN(M) — Taj Mahal
तामिल F — Tamil
तारीख़ F — date
थैला M — bag
दफ़्तर M — office
दरवाज़ा M — door
दादा M — grandfather
दाम M — price
दाल F — lentils, pulses
दिन M — day
दिनांक M — date
दिल्ली PN(F) — Delhi
दीवार F — wall
दुकान F — shop

दुकानदार M	shopkeeper	पानी M	water
दुख M	sadness, unhappiness	पार्क M	park
		पार्टी F	party
दुनिया F	world	पिता M	father
दूध M	milk	पियानो M	piano
दूरदर्शन M	television	पीटर PN(M)	Peter
देर F	delay	पीतल M/F	brass
देवता M	god	पुलिसवाला M	policeman
देश M	country	पुस्तकालय M	library
दोपहर F	afternoon; noon	पेड़ M	tree
दोस्त M/F	friend	पेन्सिल / पेंसिल F	pencil
धूप F	sunshine	पेरिस PN(M)	Paris
धोबी M	washerman	पैट्रोल M	petrol, gasoline
नदी F	river	पैसा M	money
नमाज़ F	namaz (Muslim prayer)	पौंड / पौण्ड M	pound
		प्याला M	cup
नाटक M	play	प्यास F	thirst
नाम M	name	प्रदेश M	state; region; territory
निबन्ध / निबंध M	essay	प्रेसीडेण्ट / प्रेसीडेंट M	president
नौकर M	servant; employee	फ़र्श M	floor
न्यू यॉर्क PN(M)	New York	फल M	fruit
पगड़ी F	turban	फलवाला M	fruitseller
पतझड़ M	autumn, fall	फ़िल्म F	film
पता M	address; information	फुटबॉल F	football
पति M	husband	फुरसत / फुर्सत F	leisure, free time
पत्नी F	wife	फूल M	flower
पत्र M	letter	फ़ैसला M	decision
पपीता M	papaya	फ़्रेंच F	French (language)
परदा / पर्दा M	curtain	फ़ोन M	telephone
परिवार M	family	बंगाल PN(M)	Bengal
परीक्षा F	examination	बंगाली F	Bengali (language)
पलंग M	bed	बकस M	box
पहाड़ M	mountain	बग़ीचा / बगीचा M	garden
पाकिस्तान PN(M)	Pakistan	बच्चा M	child, baby

बच्ची F child, baby
बधाई F congratulations
बनारस PN(M) Banaras
बम्बई / बंबई PN(F) Bombay
बरतन / बर्तन M (cooking) vessel
बरसात F rainy season; rain
बर्कली PN(M) Berkeley
बस F bus
बहन / बहिन F sister
बहू F bride
बाँसुरी F flute
बाग़ M garden
बाज़ार M bazaar, market place
बात F thing; matter; fact; what is said
बाप M father
बार F time(s)
बारिश F rain
बाल M hair
बीमारी F illness; disease
बुख़ार M fever
बुढ़िया F old woman
बुधवार M Wednesday
बृहस्पतिवार M Thursday
बेटा M son
बेटी F daughter
बेर M ber (a fruit)
बैंगकाक PN(M) Bangkok
भाई M brother
भारत PN(M) India
भालू M bear
भाषण M speech
भाषा F language
भीड़ F crowd
भूख F hunger
मंगलवार M Tuesday
मकान M house
मज़दूर M worker, laborer
मदद F help
मद्रास / मदरास PN(M) Madras
मन्दिर / मंदिर M Hindu temple
मरम्मत F repair
मरीज़ M patient, sick person
मसाला M spice(s)
मस्जिद F mosque
महीना M month
माँ F mother
माँ-बाप M pl parents
मांउट ऐवरेस्ट PN(M) Mount Everest
मामा M uncle (mother's brother)
माता F mother
माता-पिता M pl parents
मार्था PN(F) Martha
मिठाई F sweet(s)
मिनट M minute
मीटिंग F meeting
मील M mile
मुँह M face; mouth
मुरग़ा / मुर्ग़ा M rooster; chicken
मुरग़ी / मुर्ग़ी F hen; chicken
मेज़ F table
मेम साहब F lady
मेहनत F hard work
मोची M cobbler
मोज़ा M sock, stocking
मोटर F motor; car
मोहन PN(M) Mohan

मौसम M weather; season
यूनिवर्सिटी F university
रविवार M Sunday
रविशंकर PN(M) Ravi Shankar
रसगुल्ला M rasgulla (an Indian sweet)
राजा M king
रात F night
राम PN(M) Ram
राष्ट्रपति M/F president
रिकार्ड M record
रिक्शा M/F rickshaw
रिक्शेवाला M rickshaw driver
रुपया M rupee; money
रेडियो M radio
रेलगाड़ी F train
रेशम M silk
रेस्ट्रान्ट M restaurant
रोज़ M day
रोटी F roti (a flat round bread), bread
रोम PN(M) Rome
लखनऊ PN(M) Lucknow
लड़का M boy; son
लड़की F girl; daughter
लस्सी F lassi (a cold beverage)
लाइब्रेरी F library
लाल क़िला PN(M) the Red Fort (in New Delhi)
लिपि F script
लिफ़ाफ़ा M envelope
लीसा PN(F) Lisa
लेख M article

लोग M pl people
वक़्त M time
वजह F reason, cause
वसन्त / वसंत M spring
वाइट हाउस PN(M) White House
वाक्य M sentence
विज्ञान M science
विदेश M foreign country
विदेशी M/F foreigner
विद्यार्थी M/F student
विश्वविद्यालय M university
विषय M subject
शक्ति F power
शतरंज F chess
शनिवार M Saturday
शराब F wine, liquor
शर्मा जी PN(M) Sharma ji
शहर M city
शादी F marriage
शाम F evening
शाहजहाँ PN(M) Shah Jahan
शिकागो PN(M) Chicago
शिक्षक M/F teacher
शीला PN(F) Sheila
शुक्रवार M Friday
शुरू M beginning
शैरन PN(F) Sharon
शोर M noise
श्री लंका PN(M) Sri Lanka
संगीत M music
संस्कृत F Sanskrit
सच M truth
सड़क F street
सन्तरा / संतरा M orange
सप्ताह M week

सफलता F	success	सैली PN(F)	Sally
सब्ज़ी F	vegetable	सोमवार M	Monday
सभ्यता F	civilization; decency	स्कूल M	school
समय M	time	स्टीव PN(M)	Steve
समाचार M	news	स्टैनफ़र्ड PN(M)	Stanford
समाचार पत्र M	newspaper	हंगामा M	uproar, commotion
सवाल M	question	हड़ताल F	strike
सवेरा / सबेरा M	morning	हफ़्ता M	week
सहेली F	female friend (of another female)	हवा F	air; wind
		हाथ M	hand
साड़ी F	sari	हिन्दी / हिंदी F	Hindi
सामान M	baggage; material; things	हिन्दुस्तान / हिंदुस्तान PN(M)	India
साल M	year	हिन्दुस्तानी / हिंदुस्तानी M/F	Indian
साहब M	gentleman		
सिगरेट F	cigarette	हिन्दू / हिंदू M/F	Hindu
सितार M	sitar	हिमालय PN(M)	the Himalayas
सीता PN(F)	Sita	होटल M	hotel
सुबह F	morning	होनोलूलू PN(M)	Honolulu
सेब M	apple	हौलैंड / हौलैण्ड PN(M)	Holland
सैन फ़्रैन्सिस्को PN(M)	San Francisco		

PRONOUNS

आप	you (polite)	तुम	you (familiar)
आपको	(to) you (polite)	तुम लोग	you (pl), you people
आप लोग	you (pl), you people	तुम्हें	(to) you (familiar)
इनको / इन्हें	(to) them	तू	you (intimate)
इसको / इसे	(to) him/her	मुझे	(to) me
उनको / उन्हें	(to) them	मैं	I
उसको / उसे	(to) him/her	यह	he/she/it
किनको / किन्हें	(to) whom (pl)	यही	he/she/it (emphatic)
किसको / किसे	(to) whom (sg)	ये	they
किसी को	(to) someone,	ये लोग	these people
	(to) anyone	वह	he/she/it
कुछ	something, anything	वही	he/she/it (emphatic)
कुछ नहीं	nothing	वे	they
कोई	someone, anyone	वे लोग	those people
कोई नहीं	no one	सब	all
कौन	who	सब कुछ	everything
क्या	what	सब लोग	everyone (pl)
जिनको / जिन्हें	(to) whom (pl)	सभी	all (emphatic)
जिसको / जिसे	(to) whom (sg)	हम	we
जो	who, which	हम लोग	we people
तुझे	(to) you (intimate)	हमें	(to) us

ADJECTIVES

अगला	next
अच्छा	good
अपना	one's own
अमरीकन	American
अमरीकी	American
अमीर	rich
आधा	half
आपका	your, yours (polite)
आसान	easy
इतना	this much
इतने	this many
इनका	their
इसका	his, her/hers, its
उतना	that much
उतने	that many
उदास	sad
उनका	their
उसका	his, her/hers, its
ऊँचा	high
एक	one, a
ऐसा	of this kind/type
और	other, additional, more, else
कच्चा	unripe, raw
कम	little, few; less
काफ़ी	enough; much, many
काला	black; dark
कितना	how much
कितने	how many
किनका	whose (pl)
किसका	whose (sg)
किसी का	someone's
कुछ	some, a few

कैसा	how; of what kind/type
कोई	some, any
कौन-सा	which
ख़त्म	finished
ख़राब	bad; spoiled; defective
गन्दा / गंदा	dirty
गरम / गर्म	hot; warm
ग़लत	wrong, incorrect
ग़रीब	poor
गुजराती	Gujarati, of Gujarat
चार	four
चुप	silent, quiet
चौड़ा	wide (inanimate objects only)
चौथा	fourth
छोटा	small; short; young
जयपुरी	of Jaipur
ज़रूरी	necessary, important
जितना	as much as
जितने	as many as
जिनका	whose (pl)
जिसका	whose (sg)
जैसा	like, similar to
जो	which, that
ज़्यादा	more, many; too much, too many
ठण्डा / ठंडा	cold, cool
ठीक	right, correct
डेढ़	one and a half
ढाई	two and a half
ताज़ा	fresh
तीन	three

तीसरा	third
तुम्हारा	your, yours (familiar)
तेरा	your, yours (intimate)
तैयार	ready, prepared
थोड़ा	a little, some, few
दिलचस्प	interesting
दुखी	sad
दूसरा	second; other
दो	two
नया	new
नीला	blue
पक्का / पका	ripe
पतला	thin; narrow
पहला	first
पंजाबी	of Punjab
पाँच	five
पाकिस्तानी	of Pakistan
पिछला	last, previous
पीला	yellow
पुराना	old (inanimate nouns only)
पौन	three quarters
पौने...	...minus one quarter
प्यासा	thirsty
बंगाली	Bengali, of Bengal
बड़ा	big, large; elder
बढ़िया	excellent, of good quality
बनारसी	of Banaras
बन्द / बंद	closed; stopped
बहुत	much, many
बाक़ी	remaining, left over
बासी	stale
बीमार	ill, sick
बुरा	bad
बूढ़ा	old, aged (people only)
भारतीय	Indian, of India
भारी	heavy
भूखा	hungry
मज़ेदार	enjoyable; delicious
मद्रासी / मदरासी	of Madras
मशहूर	famous
महँगा	expensive
मीठा	sweet
मुबारक	auspicious
मुमकिन	possible
मुश्किल	difficult
मेरा	my, mine
मोटा	fat; thick
यह	this
ये	these
रेशमी	silken, made of silk
लम्बा / लंबा	long; tall
लाल	red
वह	that
वापस	returned, given back
विदेशी	foreign
वे	those
वैसा	of that kind/type
शाकाहारी	vegetarian
शुभ	auspicious
सफ़ेद	white
संभव/ सम्भव	possible
सब	all
सवा	one and a quarter
सस्ता	cheap, inexpensive
साढ़े...	...plus one half
साफ़	clean

सारा	whole, entire	हर	each, every
सिर्फ़	only	हरा	green
सुखी	happy	हलका / हल्का	light (in weight or color)
सुंदर / सुन्दर	beautiful		
सौ	one hundred	हिन्दुस्तानी / हिंदुस्तानी	Indian, of India
हमारा	our, ours	होशियार	smart, clever

POSTPOSITIONS

का / के / की	possessive postposition: of, belonging to, related to
की तरफ़	towards
की वजह से	because of
के अन्दर / के अंदर	in, inside
के आगे	in front of, ahead of
के ऊपर	on, upon, above, over, on top of
के कारण	because of
के नज़दीक	close to, near
के नीचे	under, beneath, below
के / से पहले	before
के पास	near; in the possession of
के पीछे	behind, in back of
के बाद	after
के बारे में	about, relating to
के बाहर	outside of
के लिए / के लिये	for
के साथ	with, along with, together with
के सामने	in front of, opposite
को	to
तक	by (a certain time), until, up to
ने	past tense agent marker
पर	on, at, upon
में	in, into, among
से	from; with; by means of; comparative postposition: than; since
से दूर	far from

VERBS

(का) अभ्यास करना Tr	to practice
आना Intr	to come
(को) आना Ind. Intr	to know
आराम करना Tr	to rest
(का) इन्तज़ार / इंतज़ार करना Tr	to wait (for)
(का) इन्तज़ार / इंतज़ार होना Intr	to be waited (for)
उठना Intr	to rise, to get up
उठाना Tr	to lift, to pick up
उड़ना Intr	to fly
उतरना Intr	to go down, to get off
ऊबना Intr	to become bored
कम करना Tr	to reduce, to make less
कमाना Tr	to earn
करना Tr	to do; to make
कहना Tr	to say, to state
काम करना Tr	to work
कूदना Intr	to jump
(की) कोशिश करना Tr	to try
(की) कोशिश होना Intr	to be tried
खड़ा होना Intr	to stand
ख़त्म करना Tr	to finish, to end
ख़त्म होना Intr	to be finished, to be ended
ख़राब होना Intr	to become bad, to go bad
ख़रीदना Tr	to buy
खाना Tr	to eat
खिलना Intr	to bloom, to blossom
खिलाना Tr	to make someone play; to feed
खुलना Intr	to be opened
(को) ख़ुशी होना Ind. Intr	to be happy
खेलना Tr/Tr (non-ने)	to play
खोलना Tr	to open
गाना Tr	to sing
गिरना Intr	to fall
घुमाना Tr	to show (someone) around

घूमना Intr	to wander, to tour around, to take a walk
चढ़ना Intr	to climb, to go up
चलना Intr	to move; to walk
चलाना Tr	to cause to move, to drive
चाहना Tr	to want, to wish, to desire
(को) चाहिये Ind. Intr	to need, to want
चुकना Intr/Tr (non-ने)	to be finished; to have already done (something)
चुप होना Intr	to be quiet, to be silent
छूना Tr	to touch
जगना / जागना Intr	to wake up
जगाना Tr	to wake up, to arouse
जलना Intr	to burn
जलाना Tr	to burn
जल्दी करना Tr	to hurry
जानना Tr	to know
जाना Intr	to go
जीना Intr	to live, to be alive
झूठ बोलना Tr	to tell a lie
टूटना Intr	to be broken
टेलीफ़ोन / फ़ोन करना Tr	to phone
ठीक करना Tr	to fix, to make right
ठीक होना Intr	to be fixed, to be all right
डरना Intr	to fear, to be afraid
तैयार करना Tr	to prepare, to make ready
तैयार होना Intr	to be ready
तैरना Intr	to swim
थकना Intr	to be tired
दिखाना Tr	to show
(को) दुख होना Ind. Intr	to be sad, to feel sad
देखना Tr	to look, to see
देना Tr	to give
दौड़ना Intr	to run
धुलना Intr	to be washed
धोना Tr	to wash
नमाज़ पढ़ना Tr	to perform namaz (Muslim prayer)
नहाना Intr	to bathe

नाचना Intr	to dance
निकलना Intr	to come out, to emerge
निकालना Tr	to take out; to remove
पकड़ना Tr	to catch, to hold, to grasp
पकना Intr	to be cooked; to ripen
पकाना Tr	to cook
पड़ना Intr	to fall; to lie (down)
पढ़ना Tr	to read; to study
पढ़ाना Tr	to teach
(को) पता होना Ind. Intr	to know
(को) पसन्द / पसंद होना Ind. Intr	to like
पहनना Tr	to wear, to put on
पहुँचना Intr	to arrive
पहुँचाना Tr	to take something or someone somewhere, to cause to reach
पाना Tr/Tr (non-ने)	to get, to obtain; to be able to
पिसना Intr	to be ground
पीना Tr	to drink
पीसना Tr	to grind
पूछना Tr	to ask
फटना Intr	to be torn, to burst
(का) फ़ैसला करना Tr	to decide
बचना Intr	to be saved; to remain (unused)
बचाना Tr	to save; to retain
बजना Intr	to ring; to strike (said of time); to be played (said of an instrument)
बजाना Tr	to play (an instrument)
बढ़ना Intr	to increase, to advance
बताना Tr	to tell
बनना Intr	to be made
बनाना Tr	to make
बन्द / बंद करना Tr	to close; to end
बन्द / बंद होना Intr	to be closed; to be ended
बात करना Tr	to talk, to converse
बारिश होना Intr	to rain
बिकना Intr	to be sold

बिठाना Tr	to seat (someone)
बुलाना Tr	to call
बेचना Tr	to sell
बैठना Intr	to sit
बोलना Tr/Tr (non-ने)	to speak
भागना Intr	to run, to flee
भिगाना Tr	to make wet
भीगना Intr	to get wet
भूलना Tr (non-ने)	to forget
भेजना Tr	to send
(की) मदद करना Tr	to help
(की) मदद होना Intr	to be helped
मरना Intr	to die
(की) मरम्मत करना Tr	to repair
(की) मरम्मत होना Intr	to be repaired
मारना Tr	to hit; to beat; to kill
(को) मालूम होना Ind. Intr	to know
(को) मिलना Ind. Intr	to get, to obtain
(से) मिलना Tr (non-ने)	to meet (with)
मुस्कुराना / मुसकराना Intr	to smile
मेहनत करना Tr	to work hard
(को) याद आना Ind. Intr	to remember
रखना Tr	to put, to place, to keep
रहना Intr	to live, to stay; to remain
रुकना Intr	to stop; to stay
रोकना Tr	to stop
रोना Intr	to cry
(को) लगना Ind. Intr	to feel (something); to seem; to be spent (time, money, etc.); to cost
(से / पर) लगना Intr	to be attached / connected to
लगना Intr/Tr (non-ने)	to begin (to do something)
लगाना Tr	to apply; to attach; to place
लड़ना Tr/Tr (non-ने)	to fight, to quarrel
लाना Tr (non-ने)	to bring
लिखना Tr	to write
लिटाना Tr	to lay down

लुटना Intr	to be robbed
लूटना Tr	to rob
लेटना Intr	to lie down
लेना Tr	to take
ले आना Tr (non-ने)	to bring
ले चलना Tr (non-ने)	to take along
ले जाना Tr (non-ने)	to take away
लौटना Intr	to return
वापस आना Intr	to come back
वापस करना Tr	to give back
वापस जाना Intr	to go back
शुरू करना Tr	to start, to begin
शुरू होना Intr	to be started, to begin
संभलना Intr	to be careful, to be cautious
संभालना Tr	to exercise care for someone or something
सकना Intr/Tr (non-ने)	to be able to
सच बोलना Tr	to tell the truth
समझना Tr/Tr (non-ने)	to understand
सड़ना Intr	to rot
साफ़ करना Tr	to clean
साफ़ होना Intr	to be cleaned
सिगरेट पीना Tr	to smoke a cigarette
सीखना Tr	to learn
सीना Tr	to sew
सुनना Tr	to hear, to listen
सुनाना Tr	to tell, to recount, to recite
सुलाना Tr	to put to sleep
सूखना Intr	to dry up
सोचना Tr	to think
सोना Intr	to sleep
हँसना Intr	to laugh
होना Intr	to be; to become; to happen, to take place

ADVERBS

अक्सर	often
अन्दर / अंदर	inside
अब	now
अभी	right now, just now
आगे	ahead, in front; in the future
आज	today
आजकल	nowadays, these days
इधर	here, this way, in this direction
उधर	there, that way, in that direction
ऊपर	above
ऐसे	in this way
कब	when
कभी	sometime, ever
कभी नहीं	never
क़रीब	approximately; near
कल	tomorrow; yesterday
कहाँ	where
कहीं	somewhere, anywhere
काफ़ी	quite
किधर	where, in which direction
कैसे	how, in what way
क्यों	why
जब	when
ज़रूर	certainly
जल्दी (से)	quickly
जहाँ	where
जिधर	in which direction
जैसे	as, like
ज़्यादा	very (much), too (much)
तब	then, at that time
तभी	just then, just at that time
दिन में	during the day
दिन भर	all day
दूर	far
देर से	late
दोपहर को	at noon; in the afternoon
धीरे	slowly
नज़दीक	near, close
नीचे	below
परसों	the day after tomorrow; the day before yesterday
पहले	at first; first of all; previously
पास	near, nearby
पीछे	behind, in back
फिर	again; afterwards; then
फिर भी	nevertheless, still
...बजे (पर)	at ...o'clock
बहुत	very, very much; too
बाद में	afterwards, later
बाहर	outside
यहाँ	here
यहीं	right here, at this very place

रात को	at night	सदा	always
रात में	during the night	सवेरे / सबेरे	in the morning
रोज़	daily, every day	साथ	together, side by side
लगभग	approximately	सामने	in front, opposite
वहाँ	there	सिर्फ़	only, merely
वहीं	right there, at that very place	सुबह को	in the morning
		हमेशा	always
वैसे	thus, in that way	हर दिन	every day
शाम को	in the evening	हर रोज़	every day
शायद	perhaps, maybe		

CONJUNCTIONS

अगर	if	तो	then
इसलिए / इसलिये	therefore	यदि	if
और	and	या	or
कि	that	लेकिन	but
क्योंकि	because		

PARTICLES

न	negative particle: not
नहीं	negative particle: not
भी	emphatic particle: also, too
मत	negative particle
ही	emphatic particle: only, just

About the Author

USHA R. JAIN is Senior Lecturer in Hindi in the Department of South and Southeast Asian Studies, University of California at Berkeley.

ISBN 0-944613-25-X | $35.00